Gender, Authenticity and Leadership

Gender, Authenticity and Leadership

Thinking with Arendt

Rita A. Gardiner
The University of Western Ontario, Canada

palgrave
macmillan

First published 2015 by
PALGRAVE MACMILLAN

Palgrave Macmillan in the UK is an imprint of Macmillan Publishers Limited,
registered in England, company number 785998, of Houndsmills,
Basingstoke, Hampshire, RG21 6XS

Palgrave Macmillan in the US is a division of St Martin's Press LLC,
175 Fifth Avenue, New York, NY 10010.

Palgrave is the global academic imprint of the above companies and has
companies and representatives throughout the world.

Palgrave® and Macmillan® are registered trademarks in the United States,
the United Kingdom, Europe and other countries

ISBN 978-1-349-49875-8   ISBN 978-1-137-46045-5 (eBook)
DOI 10.1057/9781137460455

This book is printed on paper suitable for recycling and made from fully
managed and sustained forest sources. Logging, pulping and manufacturing
processes are expected to conform to the environmental regulations of the
country of origin.

A catalogue record for this book is available from the British Library.

A catalog record for this book is available from the Library of Congress.

To my family and friends, past, present and future

Contents

List of Figures and Table

Figures

Table

Acknowledgements

I wish to express my heartfelt thanks to Helen A. Fielding, who introduced me to Hannah Arendt's work some years ago. It was definitely not love at first sight but, in time, Arendt became an intellectual friend to me, an interlocutor who I sometimes find exasperating, at others times, intellectually engaging, but whose company is never dull. I would also like to thank two of the friendliest writing critics one could hope to meet, Jennifer Chisholm and Katy Fulfer. My writing buddies have read my first efforts with a kindness that has not always been warranted, but for which I am sincerely grateful. I also want to express my thanks to Anne Kinsella and Chris Roulston for their input on earlier versions of these chapters. Finally, I express my love and gratitude to my partner-in-dialogue for many years, my dear husband, Michael.

1
Introduction

The common and the ordinary must remain our primary concern, the daily food of our thought – if only because it is from them that the uncommon and the extraordinary emerge.[1]

Hannah Arendt

Several years ago I attended a fundraising event at which some women in the community were receiving awards for their work. The women honored came from different walks of life. Each gave a passionate speech that included thanking friends and colleagues for their part in the honoree's success. However, the last speaker took a different route. In her speech she said 'I'm an authentic leader.' My immediate, visceral response was: 'Isn't that for others to judge?' Little did I realize that my first encounter with the concept of authentic leadership would lead to this book, in which I consider the interconnections among gender, leadership and authenticity.

In what follows, I examine the conceptual underpinnings of a management theory called authentic leadership to discover why it has paid so little attention to gender. In much of the scholarly literature on authentic leadership to date, I argue that there is a failure to interrogate the complexities surrounding the concept of authenticity, especially as it relates to situated, gendered embodiment. For instance, a critical interrogation reveals an underlying presupposition that authenticity means the same thing to everyone, and manifests itself identically. I disagree with this viewpoint, as well as highlight the pitfalls that arise from scholars' assumption that a quality-like 'authenticity' is measurable.

1

Rather than encouraging a genuine approach to leadership, I suggest that authentic leadership may tell us more about social conformity than it teaches us about authenticity. Conversely, thinking with Hannah Arendt can help to uncover inherent difficulties with the discourse of authentic leadership. Her insights provide a richer lens through which to consider the ways in which gender, authenticity and leadership intersect. Following Arendt, I contend that each individual, because of her life experiences, has a unique way of perceiving the world that is both relational and embodied. I seek to demonstrate how an Arendtian analysis can deepen our comprehension of authentic leadership by showing how our embodied actions are mediated by our relationships, as well as the social environment.[2] For example, our way of being is constantly impinged upon by social factors, some of which we remain unaware. Nevertheless, this background knowledge has an effect, not only upon the way that we perceive the world, but with respect to how we interpret the actions of others. In short, context matters. But context is often overlooked in authentic leadership scholarship, which means that differences fade into the background.

Furthermore, thinking with Arendt reveals some hidden assumptions behind dominant themes within the discourse of authentic leadership. For instance, underlying this discourse is an assumption, sometimes explicit, on other occasions implicit, that authentic leadership will result in individual success, as well as better organizational outcomes. Yet insofar as all action is contingent, we cannot predict leadership success ahead of time. Moreover, I find myself puzzled by claims that authentic leaders can effect positive change merely by virtue of their charisma. Not only does this reinforce the belief that charisma is necessarily good for leaders, it ignores the damage that 'larger than life' personalities can cause to organizations and the people they lead.

A secondary research aim is to understand why, at this particular historical juncture, the theory of authentic leadership has emerged. Specifically, why do today's leaders need a theoretical justification to teach them how to act authentically? Is a desire for authentic leadership an antidote to an ever-increasing bureaucratic existence that serves to distance people from one another, or is it an attempt to make leaders more accountable for their actions? For instance, in exploring the literature I was surprised at how leadership scholars linked the concept of authenticity with ideas of greater efficiency (Chan, 2005). Although I recognize that it is important for a leader to be effective, there are times when the demands for leadership efficiency may serve to obscure larger questions of ethics. Perhaps this is not so surprising in a world in which people's actions are measured on short-term outcomes. Yet the present-mindedness that seems to permeate many organizations is precisely why a desire for efficiency may override questions of ethics. I will return to the topic of efficiency versus ethics throughout the book, as I believe the privileging of the former at the expense of the latter is one of the foremost societal challenges we face.

For Arendt (1958), the modern drive to organizational efficiency has severe drawbacks, not least of which is that, in Western society, we have become 'a society of jobholders' (p. 40). In Arendtian terms, theories such as authentic leadership have a tendency to obscure 'the who' of the individual over 'the what' of the role. As such, a common occurrence in modernity, according to Arendt, is to focus on what a person does, and care more about their social status as opposed to who they are as an individual. This focus on social status, in other words, leads to a lack of recognition of individual difference.

One reason for this lack of attention to difference may be because many scholars who write on authentic leadership lean toward positivist forms of inquiry and behavioral explanations. Arendt was resistant to behavioral explanations, because she argued these explanations focus on the most insidious trends in modern society, namely, social conformity, and the ensuing suppression of individual uniqueness. In organizational terms, Arendt (1958) views bureaucracy as potentially the most tyrannical form of leadership, since it is based on what she called 'the rule of nobody' (p. 40). This nameless, faceless form of organizational rulership serves to suppress the plurality of human expression in favour of social conformism.

The dominant paradigm in authentic leadership scholarship privileges a leader's self-knowledge. As a consequence, it can lead to a kind of 'disembodied narcissism' in leaders, because a focus on self may be at the expense of an awareness of situational context. Sometimes, it seems as if authentic leaders possess 'God-like qualities' (Wilson, 2013, p. 56). Yet while some men and women may consider themselves to be 'authentic leaders', believing in one's inherent authentic superiority is a problem. No-one is authentic, or for that matter inauthentic, in all contexts. What is more, in regarding themselves as authentic, some leaders may have a view of themselves that is profoundly out of touch with lived experience. Because life is messy and rarely conforms to one's desires, we must guard against this type of disembodied narcissism, which places personal desires above communal well-being.

Although a leader's vision is often touted as fundamental to success, I want to question this assertion by contending that it is a leader's values, communicated and shared with others that matters most. It is these shared values, rather than personal vision, that help to ensure that leaders do not act in a manner that is unethical. In our exploration of authentic leadership, we will consider how it is ethical action, rather than authentic intent, that is fundamental to an authentic engagement with others. This kind of authentic engagement requires a relational approach to leadership. It also requires us to consider how structural inequities, cultural contexts and gender socialization affect our understanding of what constitutes authentic leadership. These are some of the issues I am concerned with in this book.

I have organized the chapters as follows. In Chapter 2, I provide a review of authentic leadership, and outline some of the problems I see with this discourse. I argue that this theory has, for the most part, overlooked the ways in which ideas about authenticity are influenced by patterns of gender socialization. I also seek to understand why the theory of authentic leadership has emerged at this time. As such, we need to ask the question: why is it scholars now believe leaders need a theoretical justification to teach them how to act authentically?

In the section on leadership training, I contend that training programs designed to increase a person's authenticity serve to reinforce normative ideas of what constitutes a good leader. Rather than developing genuine leaders, this training may result, paradoxically, in increasing social conformity. This conformity works in two ways. First, there is an adherence to external conformism, that is, the laws we obey as a member of society. Second, there is internal conformism, and the manner in which we modify our behaviour to fit what we perceive is in keeping with others. This can lead, in a Foucauldian sense, to the attenuation of difference, and the ongoing formation of docile bodies (Foucault, 1995). On the one hand, the disciplining of difference encourages homogeneity; on the other, it reinforces a social hierarchy. Additionally, there is often an assumption that by displaying particular behaviors a leader is being authentic. However, this ignores how leaders may be merely complying with what they think is expected of them and, thus, are being hypocritical. As a result, leadership training that purports to teach authenticity may not be conducive to genuine action.

After situating authentic leadership studies within the broader context of leadership scholarship, I turn to the work of Arendt, and demonstrate how an Arendtian analysis offers insights into some conceptual gaps within the current theory of authentic leadership. Yet while Arendt has much to tell us about the importance of creating environments where dialogue and debate flourish, she has little to say about gender and leadership. Therefore, in Chapter 3, I augment her ideas about leadership with insights from current scholarship on the topic of gender and leadership. One central argument I put forward is that the concept of intersectionality, so popular in feminist theorizing, is underutilized in leadership studies. Alongside gender and questions of authenticity, I suggest that we must consider how different identity characteristics can have a bearing upon how leaders are perceived. Thus, it is integral to comprehend how gender, together with other social factors such as race and class, influence societal perceptions of what constitutes authenticity in leadership.

To understand the ways in which gender may influence our ideas about authentic leadership, it is necessary to consider how material conditions affect how we think about leaders. By considering the workplace in relation to gender socialization, I show how ideas about leadership are influenced by normative ways of thinking about gender roles. As such, normative ways of thinking about leadership will have an effect on our notions of authentic leadership. Simply put, women leaders are often regarded as out of place in the gender hierarchy. This displacement may encourage them to feel a lack of spatial belonging, which may be one reason why so many women do not regard themselves as leaders. This lack of fit may also be the reason why some women resort to hierarchical ways of leading. In trying to live up to some ideal leadership standard, the danger is that some people become so caught up in their desire for success that they forget to distinguish between their role as leader and themselves as individuals. While assimilation may appear to be a strategic route to the top, it merely perpetuates structural inequality, and does little to explain authenticity.

In Chapter 4, I show how theories of the present are influenced by gendered perspectives of the past. Here, I illustrate the ways in which the concept of authenticity has been shaped by bourgeois ideas about gendered identity. Specifically, I trace the antecedents of authenticity back to the Age of Enlightenment, since this was when modern ideas surrounding authenticity were initially formulated (Taylor, 1991). In regards to the formation of the liberal subject, I show how authenticity is linked to gendered ideas about virtue. Gendered notions of what constitutes virtuous action placed limitations on women's ability to perceive themselves, and be seen as, leaders within the public realm. As a result, Enlightenment notions of virtue serve to constrain women's autonomy and, hence, limit their ideas about their own possibilities.

By understanding authenticity through the lens of the past, we may open up new avenues of inquiry that shed light on the connections among gender, authenticity and leadership in ways that complement current scholarship. For example, I suggest this historical diminishment of women's potential ability to lead may still bear an influence on societal views regarding leadership. Consequently, a lingering trace of gender prejudice toward women leaders may be embedded within the cultural imagination.

In Chapter 5, I consider the concept of authenticity through the lens of existential, hermeneutic phenomenology as this philosophical tradition has gone the furthest to develop an account of the authentic self. Considering authentic leadership through the lens of existential hermeneutic phenomenology provides us with a greater depth of understanding human existence that can enrich current scholarship. In particular, I explore Martin Heidegger's theory of authenticity, as elucidated in his magnum opus, *Being and Time*. His notion of authenticity is sometimes referenced by leadership scholars, but rarely in depth (Algera and Lips-Wiersma, 2012).

One of my primary purposes in this chapter is to rethink Heidegger's concept of authenticity in light of Arendt's diverse insights into the complex webs of relationships and interwoven narratives that affect our comprehension of what it means to be authentic. I argue that her account of what it means to be unique enriches Heidegger's definition of authenticity because of her emphasis on the relational quality of human existence. While Heidegger sees authenticity as emerging from silent resolution, for Arendt (1958), uniqueness lies in speech and action. She maintains that it is our unique ability to bring something new into the world that is central to understanding human existence. According to Arendt, it is through our actions that we insert ourselves into the world (p. 176). Metaphorically, each act is akin to a second birth, because it brings something novel into existence. Her emphasis on natality stands in contrast to Heidegger's belief that it is by coming to terms with death that we realize our potential for authenticity.

Furthermore, an Arendtian analysis can help illuminate some hidden consequences that arise from leadership that is self-oriented. Put simply, a focus on the self can lead to a disconnection from the world of others. This disconnection can prove harmful as leaders may begin to view others instrumentally, as no more than a means to an end. By looking at extreme examples, such as totalitarianism, we will see how issues such as personal responsibility and judgement may be negatively affected by a focus on a leader's vision.

Thinking with Arendt also reveals how leadership requires not only an internal sense of purpose, but also a genuine responsiveness towards others. Such a responsive orientation necessitates a willingness to think from different perspectives. To enhance my own understanding of the different perspectives regarding gender, authenticity and leadership, I conducted a qualitative phenomenological investigation in which I interviewed ten senior women leaders in the university sector. My guiding question was: how do senior women leaders describe their experiences of authenticity, or lack thereof, in the university work-place? Emerging from these women leaders' accounts is a plethora of ethical tensions regarding the conflicts between personal principles and institutional priorities.

In Chapter 6, I discuss the methodology I adopted for this study, which is rooted in hermeneutic, existential phenomenology. Arendt quoted in Hill (1979) adopted the term 'thinking without a banister' to describe her methodological approach. Thinking without a banister refers to how we try and think from the position of another so as to enhance our understanding. However, Arendt was reluctant to discuss her methodology in detail. Therefore, I briefly consider two major thinkers in the phenomenological tradition, specifically, Edmund Husserl and Martin Heidegger, and show how their different perspectives influence current discussions in qualitative phenomenology. I also explore how feminist theory can help provide a deeper understanding of some methodological concerns.

In the qualitative component of this inquiry, I focussed on the experiences of senior women leaders because there is a lack of attention paid to how gender socialization influenced ideas about what constitutes authenticity in leadership (Sinclair, 2013). The reason why I chose the higher education sector is because of my background knowledge, having worked for more than 20 years in university administration, and as a member of various leadership teams. This situated knowledge is important from a phenomenological perspective, as it allows me to consider these participants' understanding of women's leadership alongside my own lived experiences. Interviewing these women leaders brought to light how other intersections of identity, such as class and race, have a bearing on our understanding of authentic leadership.

In Chapters 7 and 8, I turn to the narrative and thematic accounts gleaned from these women leaders so as to obtain a richer understanding of the ways in which gender, authenticity and leadership interconnect. In retelling these personal narratives, I seek to enrich our knowledge of what constitutes authentic leadership through their descriptions of concrete, lived experience. Moreover, as a humanities scholar, I am intrigued by how narrative accounts can serve to broaden our comprehension of the place of authenticity in leadership, precisely because of the richness and diversity of lived experience. While I recognize that what is remembered is not necessarily what occurred, nevertheless, these accounts open up fresh ways of thinking about authenticity as it relates to gender and leadership.

In Chapter 8, I consider five themes that arose from these interviews. The first theme I discuss concerns conflicts that arise when institutional objectives are at odds with personal convictions. The second theme relates to the connection between leadership, care and relationships. Gender and embodiment constitutes the third theme, intersectional identity constitutes the fourth theme, and anxiety represents the final theme. Then, I consider outlying themes that have phenomenological importance. Finally, I bring together the different strands of the discussion to consider how these women's descriptive accounts shed light on the diverse ways in which gender, authenticity and leadership interconnect.

What emerges from these research findings is a different way of thinking about the place of authenticity in leadership. Not only do these women leaders offer insights into ethical dilemmas in regards to the institutional workings of power and privilege, they also demonstrate how gender affects their ability to navigate institutional barriers. Their narratives illustrate how gender differences reinforce hierarchies in subtle and, sometimes, not so subtle ways. Thus, a focus on situated, gendered embodiment brings to light new ways of thinking about authenticity and leadership. In particular, we will see leadership described as a relational enterprise, founded upon mutual respect and trust. Viewing authentic leadership through a relational lens allows us to see previously hidden aspects of this phenomenon. For example, a common pattern to emerge across the interviews was the importance of building strong relationships through a sense of care. Indeed, caring was perceived as integral to many research participants' understanding of the place of authenticity in leadership. Research findings suggest, therefore, that it is the self in relation that is fundamental to comprehending what it might mean to lead authentically (Eagly, 2005).

When we broaden our definition of what constitutes authentic leadership so as to account for the myriad ways in which we live and lead, we discover how people without positional authority can change their communities in profound ways. Thus, leadership is not dependent upon a person's organizational position, but rather on how people's actions demonstrate how much they care for the world. This more expansive context, together with Arendt's insights, opens up new avenues of thinking about the interconnections among gender, authenticity and leadership.

In the concluding chapter, I show how, over the course of writing this book, my thinking about the interconnections among gender, authenticity and leadership has shifted dramatically. A comment one research participant said has stayed with me. This woman maintained that we need to challenge the notion that leadership is dependent upon a particular institutional position. Women lead in all walks of life; the problem is that much of this leadership goes unnoticed, or is ignored. Her words reminded me of what I had always known, but had forgotten.

I perceive a correspondence between the extraordinary, everyday actions that these women leaders described to me, and Arendt's insistence that power is generated whenever a group of committed individuals are willing to work together to fight against perceived injustices. From an Arendtian perspective, such spontaneous acts demonstrate how individuals work alongside their communities to try and improve others' lives. However, these everyday acts by women in their communities are rarely described as leadership. Thus, conventional ways of thinking about leadership may be at the expense of a deeper understanding of how people lead in the world.

At the beginning of this project, my intention was to focus on leadership within an institutional setting. What became apparent, however, is that leadership within the context of an institution is not how these women described their understanding of what it meant to be an authentic leader. Rather, they spoke of leadership as situational, and considered it from a much wider, societal lens than I had initially anticipated. Hence, what emerges from their descriptive accounts is that it is not sufficient to concentrate on how women lead in institutions. Rather, we need to describe how people lead in a diversity of situations. By considering what it means to lead beyond the confines of the work environment, we gain insights into how a focus on gender can redefine our understanding of the role of authenticity in leadership. Although I am not implying that these accounts are indicative of women's leadership *per se*, I am suggesting that the patterns that emerge from these narratives, alongside a consideration of Arendt's work, serve to enrich our understanding of the ways in which gender, authenticity and leadership interconnect.

2
Authentic Leadership

In this chapter, I consider the main tenets of authentic leadership scholarship, and bring them into conversation with the work of Hannah Arendt. In examining current scholarship, I suggest there is a tendency to privilege a leader's self-knowledge. Such an approach may serve to suppress a plurality of perspectives and, in turn, work against the creation of a meaningful environment. Conversely, thinking with Arendt complements existing scholarship because it alerts us to the need to consider equality and difference. Specifically, her concept of uniqueness, understood as a person's particular qualities and social location, together with her notion of plurality, or how we exist in a world of others, can deepen our understanding of how notions of authenticity informs leadership. The manner in which we see ourselves is always related to who we are in specific contexts. It is through action and speech that each individual reveals herself to others (Arendt, 1958, pp. 181–188). This individual unveiling is always related to a person's cultural and socio-historical place in the world.

I argue that the discourse of authentic leadership tells us more about social conformity and gender socialization than it teaches us about authenticity. Social conformity is a problem for leadership because it may suppress uniqueness in favour of uniformity. In Arendtian terms, in trying to live up to some homogeneous standard, leaders may, sometimes unwittingly, other times deliberately, perpetuate a particular style of leadership that is in conflict with their inimitable identity. As such, a person's unique qualities may be obscured by their social role as leader. Social conformism is counterproductive to authenticity because it is premised on fitting in, rather than allowing a person's distinctive self to shine forth.

I begin by outlining the main themes put forward by scholars of authentic leadership. Next, I consider some criticisms and alternative perspectives, and then situate this discourse within the wider context of leadership studies. Following this, I consider leadership programming as it relates to authenticity, especially the ways in which such training may reinforce Anglo-American models of leading. Then I turn to Arendt to see what insights she may provide. Finally, I gather together these divergent strands to see what emerges regarding the interconnections among gender, authenticity and leadership.

Authentic leadership: An overview

The concept of authentic leadership gained popularity in 2003 with the publication of Bill George's book *Authentic Leadership: Rediscovering the Secrets to Creating Lasting Value*. Due to the myriad ethical scandals within the corporate sector, he argued that the concept of leadership needs to be completely rethought. What was required to fix the ethical gap are leaders who are morally responsible, have a deep sense of purpose and stay true to core values. These qualities, George contended, enable leaders to establish the relationships necessary to build a strong organization, and help them lead with conviction and self-discipline.

Around the same time George published this business bestseller, the construct known as authentic leadership was gaining traction within the academic community. According to Peter Northouse (2013), there are three different approaches to authentic leadership. The first approach, outlined by Boas Shamir and Galit Eilam (2005), maintains that authentic leaders are original since they choose not to copy others. From this perspective, it is the insights gained from each leader's life story that enables them to obtain the necessary self-knowledge to lead in an authentic way. The second approach to authentic leadership is represented by Alice Eagly (2005), who focuses on the effects of gender on the relationships between leader and follower. But by far the dominant scholarly approach is the developmental perspective identified by Bruce Avolio, in collaboration with various colleagues.

From this dominant perspective, authentic leadership has four main dimensions, namely, i) self-awareness, ii) balanced information processing, iii) relational transparency and iv) internalized moral perspective (Gardner and Avolio, 2005). First, self-awareness enables authentic leaders to understand their strengths and weaknesses, and be cognizant of the effect they have on others. Second, balanced information processing improves a leader's decision-making process, because it allows them to analyse data objectively. Third, relational transparency refers to a leader's trustworthiness and demonstration of appropriate emotional response. The fourth dimension of authentic leadership consists of a leader's internalized moral perspective, which means they are guided by inner values, rather than societal pressures. In sum, authentic leaders are perceived as being genuine in their self-presentation, so that there is no 'fake' self on display. Not only are these leaders always honest, they display the correct emotion for the right situation.

It is argued that a leader's self-understanding enables them to be consistent in their dealings with others (Avolio and Mhatre, 2011). Through this heightened self-awareness, authentic leaders are able to foster strong relationships by role-modeling positive behaviour. A leader's optimistic attitude allows them to develop a positive work environment. Hence, authentic leaders not only improve overall morale, but also increase employee effectiveness. Put simply, authenticity can be good for the bottom line. In addition, authentic leaders are perceived as better able to achieve institutional goals because of their transparent dealings with others (Avolio and Mhatre, 2011). Together with their ability to be unbiased, authentic leaders are perceived as leading in accordance with their values, and remaining steadfast to their principles, irrespective of context.

Scholars maintain that authentic leaders exhibit four psychological components. These components are confidence, hope, optimism and resilience (Avolio and Gardner, 2005). *Confidence* ensures that a leader has the self-belief necessary to accomplish tasks successfully. *Hope* enables leaders to inspire others through their willpower. *Optimism* ensures that these leaders can maintain a positive outlook, while *resilience* allows them to recover from adversity. It is further argued that an authentic leader's positive behaviour encourages a sense of institutional belonging amongst employees, which leads to higher levels of hope and trust among members of an organization.

For many scholars, authentic leadership is intrinsically connected to positive thinking. As an example, Gardner *et al.* (2011) maintain the core components of authentic leadership are self-awareness, positive self-regulation, positive self-development and a positive moral perspective (p. 1123). Here we note that the word 'positive' is repeated three times to underscore the value of having an optimistic outlook, no matter what the circumstance. Another benefit of an authentic leader's positive thinking is that it helps them to distinguish between adaptive and maladaptive self-reflection (Avolio *et al.*, 2009). Adaptive self-reflection means that a leader is aware of, and can critically assess their beliefs and behaviours in a constructive manner. Conversely, maladaptive self-reflection is destructive, since too much rumination may generate negative emotions such as self-doubt or anxiety. It is only through what these authors describe as positive developmental interventions that leaders are able to make the right decision (Avolio *et al.*, 2009, p. 42). This suggests that it is possible for leaders to take up the right amount of self-reflection. However, the distinction between maladaptive and adaptive self-reflection may have more to do with conforming to dominant paradigms about what constitutes good leadership than being connected, in any deeper way, with authenticity.

From concept to practice

Although past research in authentic leadership aimed at building a conceptual framework, Bruce Avolio and Keith Mhatre (2011) argue there are now measurable tools and reliable techniques to test for authenticity in leadership. One such measurement tool is a survey instrument known as the ALQ (Authentic Leadership Questionnaire), initially developed by Avolio and colleagues in The Gallup Institute at The University of Nebraska. Through extensive empirical testing, Avolio and Mhatre claim there is positive proof that the four dimensions to authentic leadership – self-awareness, balanced processing, relational transparency and internalized moral perspective – are verifiable. Thus, empirical data from various research studies serve to demonstrate the previous conceptual claims about authentic leadership.

Other scholars look to medical science for insights into authentic leadership. For example, Paul McDonald (2009) argues that recent breakthroughs in neuroscience offer additional techniques to gauge authenticity in leaders. Indeed, he claims that neuroscience can provide scientific evidence to back up the four major components of authentic leadership outlined earlier. For instance, McDonald contends that self-awareness has an internal aspect informed by introspection, as well as an external element influenced by social factors. In addition, he argues neuroscience reveals that the brain treats information in different ways depending upon whether we are told something by someone we know well, as opposed to a stranger. This knowledge, states McDonald, sheds light on how self-awareness works within a social context.

Neuroscience research can also offer insight into the second dimension of authentic leadership, that is, balanced information processing. According to McDonald, the brain processes soft and hard data in the same way. As a consequence, the brain perceives rewards, such as financial incentives or enhanced reputation, in an equivalent manner. He suggests this may be the reason why some people are willing to forego financial compensation for a better job title.

The third dimension of authentic leadership – relational transparency – can also be informed by neuroscience research. It appears that particular facial elements create a negative response in a region of the brain known as the amygdale, which affects how we judge people. What this means, according to McDonald, is that we judge some people as more trustworthy than others based on their appearance. Those whom we find non-threatening are more likely to obtain a positive appraisal, especially when we perceive them as similar to ourselves.

The final dimension of authentic leadership is internalized moral perspective. McDonald states that neuroscience shows us that leaders who focus on negative experiences are less able to engage in self-regulation, which seems to reinforce Avolio *et al.*'s (2009) claim about adaptive versus maladaptive thinking. Such negative thinking adversely affects the ability to access the prefrontal regions of the brain responsible for self-focused thinking, and may cloud a leader's ability to make balanced decisions.

In addition, McDonald argues that neuroimagining techniques can offer insight into how we make ethical decisions. Apparently, each person has their own neuroimagining signature that operates independently from cognitive decision-making. In practical terms, this means that ethical decisions are spontaneous, rather than rule-bound. This implies that ethical decision-making occurs in the moment, rather than as a result of reasoned deliberation. Such spontaneity is relevant to how Arendt (1958) understands human action. She argued that it is through words and deeds that each of us brings forward something new into the world. Yet no matter how much we may desire to control our self presentation, we are unable to do so, because we cannot predict with certainty how our actions will be taken up by others. Such uncertainty is an intrinsic component of human existence. As a consequence, we cannot know for sure whether what we perceive as ethical action will always be regarded as such by others.

Ethics and efficiency

Leadership scholars also connect a leader's authenticity with the potential for greater efficiency (Chan, 2005; Avolio *et al.*, 2005). While it is laudable that these scholars are concerned about ethical behaviour in leaders, I do not believe that ethical dilemmas will be solved through a focus on efficiency. Indeed, current explanations of authentic leadership veer toward an instrumental way of perceiving relationships because of this connection between ethics and efficiency. This instrumental way of thinking begins with the hypothesis that authentic leadership rests upon a particular set of characteristics. From these characteristics, scholars build survey instruments to gain empirical evidence to confirm their thesis. But all this does is to reaffirm their original hypothesis. What this body of evidence does is to produce a particular way of thinking about authenticity that may obscure anything that does not fit neatly within the established framework. But life does not work as smoothly as our conceptual frameworks might wish; leadership is a messy business and we must recognize this reality. Moreover, leaders who do not conform to this matrix may be perceived as inauthentic when they may actually be the converse. We must be careful to ensure that our theoretical conceptualizations are rich enough to account for the everyday practices of leaders, both good and bad. This conflation of efficiency and ethics leads to a narrow way of thinking about the place of authenticity in leadership.

Such an instrumental approach to the theory and practice of authentic leadership brings to mind Heidegger's (1977, pp. 283–319) notion of *Gestell*, or enframing. He argues that a serious problem in modernity derives from how we perceive things through a scientific worldview that privileges calculation and efficiency above all else. This mode of thinking tries to establish in advance how we encounter the world. This tendency can be observed through the emphasis on measurement, efficiency and quantification in much of the scholarship. This instrumental way of thinking can have damaging consequences, not least because it fails to comprehend the depth and breadth of human existence.

Rather than offering us insight into what it might mean to lead authentically, I suggest that dominant approaches to authentic leadership may lead to a rigidity of thinking and a covering over of individual difference. So while some scholars argue there are four dimensions to authentic leadership, as in, self-awareness, balanced information processing, relational transparency and internalized moral perspective, focussing exclusively on these four dimensions leads to a prescriptive way of thinking about leadership that obscures the multiplicity of lived experience.

Furthermore, as Joanne Ciulla (2008) points out, there is often confusion in leadership accounts between description and prescription, which can lead to false assumptions being drawn. For instance, there is a conflation in the scholarly literature between leaders who are ethically motivated and those leaders who are effective at exercising leadership, which Ciulla refers to as the 'Hitler problem' (p. 59). As a result, a leader can appear to be efficient without in any way being ethical. Therefore, it is critical to acknowledge that efficient leadership does not automatically lead to ethical action. Moreover, efficiency understood by the language of performance measurement and outcomes-based thinking serves to ignore contingency in favour of scientific explanations that privilege consistency. This predilection for measurable results in authentic leadership scholarship encourages a belief that truth is obtainable from data without fully acknowledging that leadership is always context-dependent. To understand how that leadership operates in diverse contexts, we need to move beyond explanations that confuse description with prescription.

Authentic leadership emerged from earlier research into looking at how transformational leaders create organizational change (Avolio, 2013). For example, Bass and Steidlmeir (1999) argue that leaders need to be both authentic and transformational, and avoid acting in a false manner, which they defined as 'pseudo-transformational' (p. 181). Thus, it is important that leadership is grounded in an ethical worldview so as to guard against unbridled self-interest. But, increasingly, the way that we judge a leader's success is through profit-based measurements. Whenever we focus on financial success as the primary measurement, it may be to the long-term detriment of a leader's personal integrity, and the institution's well-being.

In the preceding discussion, I have pointed to problems that may ensue when we perceive authentic leadership in a narrowly defined manner. Until recently, much of the published work on authentic leadership was based either on conceptual ideas or quantitative research. For instance, the majority of publications on authentic leadership published up to 2010 were conceptual pieces, most of which reflect a positivist orientation (Gardner et al., 2011). On top of that, three-quarters of the published articles on authentic leadership were written by North American scholars in management or business studies. In reviewing these studies, Gardner et al. argue there is too much reliance on survey measurements. They say it is time for new research that elicits thick narratives and explores ethical issues in greater depth, a central argument of the present study. Next, I want to consider some alternative perspectives, as well as criticisms, of mainstream approaches to authentic leadership.

Alternative viewpoints

In their exploration of authentic leadership, Shamir and Eilam (2005) see a connection with the Aristotelian concept of *eudaimonia*. This concept refers to a person's well-being through self-actualization. As a consequence, they maintain that 'when people are eudaimonically motivated, they are fully engaged both in their own self-actualization and in using their virtues, talents and skills for the greater good' (p. 397). From this perspective, it seems that authentic leaders base their actions on their values and commitments, and show integrity in their dealings with others. Shamir and Eilam also note that authentic leaders have a high level of self-resolution, which helps them act in concert with their beliefs. One constant is that 'the authentic leader is motivated by internal commitment' (p. 398). This suggests that an authentic leader must act out of personal conviction to encourage others to share her vision. Similarly, Lester Levy and Mark Bentley (2007) argue that authentic leaders need to be true to themselves and act upon their beliefs for the common good.

What these definitions fail to acknowledge is that truth, like authenticity, is a contestable concept. Such an approach to the study of leadership does not account adequately for the myriad ways in which institutional bias and social prejudice adversely affect who gains access to leadership roles. Moreover, there are many times when a leader's convictions may have been genuine, but have led to disastrous results. Here we would do well to remember Arendt's (1958) claim that it is not whether leaders are good that matters; rather, it is whether their leadership is good for the world. In fact, we need to ask ourselves: would a world populated by authentic leaders necessarily be a better one? I will return to this question. For now, I wish to discuss why context is so important to understanding the merits, or lack thereof, of the place of authenticity in leadership.

In thinking about the place of authenticity in leadership, we need to take into account how we come to understand the world. For example, as a result of the myriad experiences that make up our life, each of us has a particular, situated perspective. This unique perspective will influence our comprehension of what constitutes authenticity in leadership. Our understanding will also be influenced by the situational context. Indeed, context is critical to understanding the role of authenticity in leadership. But Alice Eagly (2005) maintains that many leadership scholars ignore the differences that exist within communities, especially as it relates to social identity. In her view, how we perceive leaders will be influenced by our unique way of thinking about the world that is, in turn, influenced by a vast array of social factors.

For example, tensions may arise when a woman leader displays a lack of stereotypical feminine behaviour by being perceived as overly aggressive or autocratic. Because of her gender, a woman leader may be castigated for actions that from a male leader may appear as 'normal' leadership behaviour. But it is not only gender that needs to be taken into consideration. Depending upon the particular situation, different axes of identity can be foregrounded. In some instances, a leader might be discriminated against because of gender while, in another situation, a leader may experience discrimination because of race or sexual orientation. In considering what it might mean to lead authentically, an array of intersectional factors must be considered.

So, as we see, context matters. But context is often missing from discussions into what constitutes authenticity in leadership. What is similarly lacking is any discussion of the body. The reason why embodiment is ignored by most authentic leadership scholars, according to Donna Ladkin and Steve Taylor (2010), is due to the focus on the leader's 'true' self. Yet within a work environment, it is not a person's inner thoughts that matter since it is through their speech and action that leaders are judged. Although Francis Yammarino *et al.* (2008) contend that authentic leaders enhance overall workplace effectiveness, because a leader's honest approach will be received positively by others, Ladkin and Taylor (2005) express reservations. They argue that one issue rarely addressed is how a leader may act in what she regards as an authentic manner, but still not be perceived as such by others. For example, one of the main roles of a leader, state Ladkin and Taylor, is to embody 'the identity story of the group' (p. 70). In conveying the institutional narrative, a leader needs to establish a rapport with her audience. Whenever leaders are unable to convey the institutional story in a meaningful way, they will be unlikely to persuade others to share in their vision and effect change, something deemed critical to leadership success. Thus we see how contextual factors are important when considering not only how a leader can express herself in what she regards as an authentic manner, but also how others take up this leader's authenticity. Put simply, it does not matter how authentic a leader may view herself, what is important is how a community perceives the leader's actions to be in keeping with collective values.

Hence, there is a tension between how leaders view themselves, and how others perceive their actions. This is one reason why authenticity does not arise out of awareness of inner values, but in a relational manner (Sparrowe, 2005). The emphasis on a leader's inner self serves to overshadow the importance of the role that others play. By viewing authentic leaders as constant with personal beliefs, this abstracts them from their situational context, and ignores how past history may be of relevance to present events. Moreover, being authentic, according to Raymond Sparrowe (2005), does not necessarily mean a person will be moral. I think we can take this insight further, since to suggest that authentic leadership is inherently moral is to suggest that we will all perceive a person's actions in the same way.

Underpinning some authentic leadership scholarship is a religious or spiritual perspective. For instance, Karin Klenke (2007) argues that spirituality is at the heart of authentic leadership. This spiritual dimension enables employees to gain meaning as they search for something transcendent to augment the paucity of their lives. But there may be problems with an emphasis on spirituality in the workplace. For instance, if we see spirituality as essential to authentic leadership, what happens to those employees who are agnostic or atheist? Although spirituality may be beneficial for some, it may negatively affect those who do not conform to a particular belief system. Indeed, Ciulla (2000) criticizes modern management for emphasizing individual facets at the expense of creating a just workplace. Management should be careful to resist any practices that border on psychological exploitation. What is required of employers is to offer each worker a respectful environment and a living wage.

While spirituality may offer some workers a positive dimension, this is not the case for all, and cannot be at the expense of decent pay and working conditions. Sinclair (2007) cautions that a spiritual approach may not be conducive to workers' spiritual enlightenment as it may mask structural inequities. Sometimes, it may be adopted by unscrupulous leaders to coerce others into doing their will. Indeed, the current leadership craze regarding authenticity is, in Sinclair's view, a response to the growing anxiety that we are losing our identity in the workplace. Indeed, she finds the discourse of authentic leadership troubling because the norms by which authenticity is judged have deep social, economic and political causes, many of which are not acknowledged.

Other scholars suggest that leadership studies should be rooted in the human sciences, not least because when we study issues like authenticity, we are really looking at ourselves (Ciulla, 2008, p. 393). The problem is that, ever since the Age of Enlightenment, scientific discourse has been afforded greater cultural caché than the humanities.

Nonetheless, Ciulla maintains that it is stories that offer us insight into human experience in ways that scientific theories cannot, a contention reaffirmed recently by Gosling and Villiers (2013). Thus, we need a diversity of narratives alongside scientific inquiry to help us understand concepts such as authentic leadership. These manifold narratives can enrich the field of authentic leadership because they may offer us deeper understanding regarding lived experience.

As an example, when we think about what authentic leadership might mean, each of us will have different ideas, informed by the stories we read, the movies we watch and our experiences in the workplace and beyond. Hence, what characterizes authenticity in leadership changes over time and place, because each community has different values that are firmly embedded in social relations (Marturano, 2008). Certain traits have entrenched meaning within a particular community, rather than just being rooted in a person's psychology. Furthermore, Marturano claims that it is not so much that individual leaders possess charisma, but that others regard them as magnetic. The problem, however, is that it is easy to become swept away by the rhetorical genius of charismatic leaders. Given that authentic leadership emerges out of a discourse that sees leaders as transformational partly due to their charismatic personalities, we need to interrogate the positive and negative aspects of charisma (Ladkin, 2006; Avolio, 2013).

Such larger than life personas may prove detrimental to an organization, according to Amanda Sinclair (2007), since their belief in themselves may override alternate viewpoints. From her work with leadership teams, she has observed a common tendency exhibited by senior managers toward dependency and obedience. This manifests itself as believing that the leader is the only person who can solve a particular predicament. As a result, leaders start to perceive themselves as omniscient. Too much emphasis on a leader's capabilities may mask others' insecurities, and result in an abrogation of personal responsibility. Ignoring the effects of these power relationships is a mistake, asserts Sinclair, since it does not help us understand how leaders may, at times, feel powerless to act while, in other circumstances, gain too much influence over others. As such, mainstream accounts of authentic leadership fail to account for questions of power and inequality.

I have surveyed some alternative approaches as well as criticisms of authentic leadership so as to provide a richer, conceptual framework. Now I want to turn to what is often regarded as a fundamental component of authentic leadership; that is, vision.

Vision

The purpose of vision, according to James Kouzes and Barry Posner (2007), is to offer leaders a blueprint that serves as their guiding light for the future. These authors suggest that good leaders have a mental image of what success looks like even before they embark on a project, similar to the way that an engineer might envisage a prototype. This mental clarity enables a leader to move forward provided they can enlist others to help them achieve their goals. Yet such a planned approach to leadership may not always be sufficient. As unexpected problems occur, reverting to a blueprint may be of little use in times of crisis. Furthermore, this way of thinking about vision is based on the illusion that leaders are able to control future events, because they are able to plan everything in advance. However no leader, no matter how visionary, can plan for every eventuality. Thus, every leadership vision has to be open to contingency.

Others scholars perceive vision as an integral component of authentic leadership because of its instructive capacity. For example, R. W. Terry (1993) contends that a truly visionary leader teaches others, providing insight so that people understand. For others to become motivated, a leader must be able to effectively convey the importance of this vision to the organization as a whole. Yet not all leadership visions are positive for organizations. Indeed, if a person's vision is disconnected from an ethical worldview, a leader's visionary approach may prove counterproductive. Moreover, too much confidence in a particular vision may encourage a leader to behave in self-indulgent ways. This is one reason why Terry Price (2003) argues that an undue focus on a leader's authentic vision may actually promote unethical leadership (p. 80). In thinking about vision in relation to leadership, therefore, we must bear in mind that not every leader engages in an ethical way of behaving. Indeed, some leaders may use vision as a proprietary tactic so as to obtain short-term gains that benefit themselves over and above what is good for the organization in the long term. It is conceivable that a leader's vision may be authentic in the sense of being motivated by personal design, but not in terms of fostering the common good. A strong leadership vision, no matter how authentic it may be, does not necessarily correspond to ethical action or intent.

Authentic visions do not necessarily have ethical intent. This is one reason why focussing on a leader's authenticity, or lack thereof, is insufficient for understanding who will behave in an ethical manner within any given context. In thinking about the connection between authenticity and ethics, some leadership scholars suggest that ethical decision-making depends on the leader's willingness, not only to listen to their conscience, but also to act in concert with those values.

In his discussion of the place of authenticity in leadership, Chris Branson (2010) argues that ethical decisions are based on the interplay between rational, objective knowledge and subjective, interpretive knowledge. The problem, he contends, is that moral integrity can be compromised by our selfish desires. (Indeed, there are numerous examples whereby leaders have sacrificed long-term sustainability for short-term profits.) But, how does a leader make sure they are acting ethically? According to Branson, it is by ensuring that the pure voice of the moral self is attended to above 'the confusion and chatter that fills our minds' (p. 5). Yet the purity of a person's moral self is, to my mind, a dubious claim that does little to help leaders decide what is and what is not ethical action. In fact, this focus on the leader's inner voice may serve to negate the fact that this confusion and chatter might actually be the dialogue and debate that Arendt (1958) perceives as crucial to the development of a meaningful environment.

What is at stake here is to comprehend when it is important for leaders to assert their values, and when it is necessary to listen to others. I'm not suggesting that this is an either/or position for leaders. However, I am contending that ethical decision-making is a complex affair for which no leadership rubric, no matter whether virtue- or empirically-based, is fully equipped to deal with the diverse challenges a leader may face. Thus authenticity is not a fact but an ideal that may prove useful inspiration for some leaders yet cannot be seen as an absolute. Rather than dealing in abstractions which can lead to a kind of disembodied narcissism in leaders, we need to deal with concrete examples.

For instance, an ongoing challenge that any leader faces is to judge at what point it is appropriate to go with one's gut feelings, and when it is necessary to listen to alternative views. Such judgement will depend on many factors. One such consideration is the clash that may occur between a leader's personal desires and organizational responsibilities. For example, it is only when leaders face an ethical dilemma, according to Milorad Novicevic *et al.* (2006), that questions of authenticity become relevant in the workplace. In differentiating between personal and organizational responsibility, these authors claim that executives experience tension whenever their personal values collide with organizational expectations. In stressful situations, therefore, it is important for leaders to hold on to their self-esteem, rather than be swayed by others, as moral decision-making may be affected adversely by 'group think'. One effect of this moral disintegration, contend Novicevic *et al.*, is that executives refuse to accept personal responsibility for the organization's ethical failures. Leaving most decisions to the leader can have negative implications in that others refuse to accept their own culpability when things go awry.

Yet it is often argued that the primary role of a leader is to solve organizational dilemmas. But what is an appropriate strategy for a leader to adopt at times of crisis? One possible approach, according to Donna Ladkin (2006), is for leaders to engage with Heidegger's notion of dwelling with an issue, rather than acting immediately. When there is no easy solution, she contends that dwelling with a difficult dilemma can help leaders solve particularly intransigent issues because it enables them to see potential solutions, not just from their own perspective, but also from the viewpoint of others. This way of orienting oneself to the world requires leaders to adopt an open disposition. Such openness to the other is one way of showing care. Thus, Ladkin argues that dwelling can offer new, creative solutions that allow a leader to stay with their own values while, at the same time, being willing to enter into a deep relationship with others.

In practical terms, such openness requires the leader to be present-minded rather than future-oriented, and to be willing to create an environment for thinking issues through, rather than determining the right vision ahead of time. From this perspective it is not so much that a leader's vision is paramount but how they are willing to engage with others in promoting action that is good for the organization at large. This requires leaders to suspend their positional power (Ladkin, 2006). A suspension of power requires courage and humility on the leader's part, as well as a willingness to entertain divergent views. Furthermore, acting ethically means offering a person or a problem our meaningful attention. This requires us to step back from our own concerns so as to be fully open to the particular situation at hand. When we are open to experience, we allow things to come into appearance that otherwise may go unnoticed. In short, we become more receptive, because we are willing to see a problem from different perspectives.

In their haste to put forward a new theory, leadership scholars fail to comprehend fully the ontological roots of authenticity (Algera and Lips-Wiersma, 2012). It is a mistake to look for methods and techniques before dwelling on the fundamental question of what it means to be authentically human. Moreover, if authentic leadership becomes no more than a management technique, it may exacerbate unethical action, rather than solve ethical problems and institutional dilemmas. Thus it is a mistake to value leaders in terms of short-term individual success at the expense of the promotion of ethical relationships and work environments.

To sum up, I have explored the main arguments made by proponents of authentic leadership, as well as considered alternative perspectives and critiques. What is missing from current leadership accounts is a deeper understanding of the connections between authentic leadership and a particular way of viewing the world (Heil, 2010). Before turning to see what insights we can glean from Arendt, I want to situate authentic leadership within the broader domain of leadership studies.

Leadership perspectives

One particularly influential scholar was James MacGregor Burns who, in 1978, published a book entitled *Leadership*, widely regarded as a foundational text in this genre. In this book, he differentiates between two types of leadership. The first type, transactional leadership, illustrates how leaders act in an instrumental manner to achieve their goals. The second type, transformational leadership, refers to those leaders who exhibit charisma, and are able to effect organizational change by virtue of their powerful personalities. This change may not always be beneficial, since charismatic leaders sometimes wreak havoc on organizations, especially when a leader is overly narcissistic. Moreover, as we saw previously, a leader's excessive adherence to a particular vision may work to the detriment of the organization as a whole, a point we will return to in Chapter 4 by looking at Heidegger's ill-fated leadership of a university during the Nazi era.

To understand the way leadership works, Burns maintains that one must first comprehend the essence of power and realize that, ideally, leadership is formed in relationship, and connected to purpose. The problem in the modern workplace is that bureaucratic structures may work to the detriment of ethical leadership, because stability is prized over spontaneity. This desire for stability ensures bureaucracies take on a culture of mediocrity that permeates the organization, and functions to obstruct challenges to the status quo (Burns, 1978). Thus, whether a person's actions are virtuous or not matters less than if she complies with a particular mode of behaving.

Although subordinates may perceive bureaucratic authority as legitimate, they may also fight against its constraints, sometimes consciously, sometimes unconsciously, because it fails to offer them a space whereby they are able to be the best they can be. Spontaneity is also constrained by the focus on outcome-based measurements. People lose hope when the workplace is no more than an environment of conforming to policies that they may find unsatisfactory or even unethical. Thus, Burns shows us how bureaucratic conformity can be detrimental, and serve to suppress individual uniqueness, as well as dialogue and dissent. As we will see later, his views are similar to Arendt's critique of bureaucracy.

A different approach to the topic of leading was advanced by Peter Greenleaf (2002[1977]) with his concept of 'servant leadership'. Greenleaf's approach proved popular with people who desired a more communitarian approach to leading, as well as with those looking for a spiritual dimension in leadership. He contended that concern with the well-being of a community was being erased by the desire for profit. This lack of care was evident within many organizational structures, and he tried to understand why that might be the case. One problem Greenleaf identified was that, in the modern workplace, there is an overemphasis on the leader at the expense of the management or organizational team. But the abrogation of power to one individual can have negative consequences, especially in regard to ethical decision-making. Servant leadership was Greenleaf's attempt to put ethical action at the heart of leadership by demonstrating how important it was for leaders to see themselves as serving their institutions, rather than themselves.

A negative trend Greenleaf perceives in the modern workplace is that talented individuals with conceptual skills are sidelined in favour of those who are more operationally-minded. Yet he maintains that conceptual thinkers are an essential component of any management team, not least because these are the people who ask the most difficult questions. But rather than questioning why a decision was being made, there is increasing pressure on leaders to act quickly and efficiently. The problem is that without the input of those who are willing to question a leader's decision, a management team may become complacent and, as a consequence, fail in its duty to serve its community responsibly. A lack of dialogue and debate within the management team may be an early indication of an unhealthy organization. In the long term, this refusal to challenge a leader's authority will be a detriment to the organization, because whenever a management team fails to question the leader's actions, it can lead to group think.

In his discussion of universities, Greenleaf notes that it is not sufficient for conceptual thinkers to be part of the faculty; they must also be part of the senior leadership team. Without the influence of conceptual thinkers, he argues that a university can quickly turn into an uncaring institution, and lose sight of its deeper purpose. Larger questions are overtaken by economic imperatives. One such imperative is the unquestioned belief that growth is good. Anyone who has the temerity to reject this model will quickly find themselves out of place, and possibly out of a job.

Yet when someone chooses to voice their dissent, they are regarded as disloyal, rather than seen as upholding personal values. According to Keith Grint (2005), those who dare to question are often replaced by yes people who turn into irresponsible followers, precisely because they refuse to tell leaders they are making a bad decision for fear of reprisal. What leadership needs most, he states, are constructive dissenters who recognize that leaders are not omniscient beings. In Grint's opinion, we need to abandon Plato's question: 'Who should rule us?', and focus instead on Popper's question: 'How can we stop our rulers ruining us?' (p. 40), a sentiment with which Arendt would likely have found common cause.

I have provided this overview of leadership scholarship so as to situate authentic leadership within a broader context. One issue that emerges is that too much control in the hands of the leader can lead to ethical problems. Furthermore, it appears that bureaucratic structures are placing too much emphasis on a leader's effectiveness, which may prove detrimental to ethical action. Indeed, it would seem that too much belief in a leader's capabilities can sometimes result in a lack of responsibility on the part of others. Moreover, too much belief in a leader's capabilities can result in a lack of responsibility on the part of others.

In the following section, I want to examine how various scholars perceive the benefits and drawbacks of leadership training, as it relates to questions of authenticity. It will be shown that while leadership scholars perceive authentic leadership as good for organizations, this is not always the case. What is more, an Anglo-American bias in leadership training may result in cultural differences being ignored.

Leadership training

Some scholars suggest that just as business schools can teach students management skills so, too, can leadership programs train people to be leaders (Kouzes and Pozner, 2007). To master the art of leadership, these authors assert, one must first develop 'the instrument of leadership', that is, the self (p. 344). Other scholars maintain that leadership programs can teach people to be authentic. For example, Adrian Chan (2005) contends that when leaders add authenticity to their leadership skill-set, it serves as a 'leadership multiplier', which can improve individual and organizational success. But this presupposes that a person's ability to know herself is a straightforward process, and that it is possible to train a person to become an authentic leader. I see two problems with this type of thinking. First, it is difficult to comprehend how such leadership training could be evaluated. Would program evaluation consist of the completion of a questionnaire where a leader ranked her level of authenticity before and after completion of a training course? Or would program success be judged on the perceptions of others prior to and after a leader's makeover? Second, what complicates the idea of leadership programming, as it pertains to authenticity, is that training someone to perform in a particular way would seem to run counter to a person expressing her personal views. Hence, I question the idea that authenticity can be learned through the right training. If authenticity is perceived as an individual attribute, it seems paradoxical to train leaders to be authentic. In fact, training people to perform leadership authentically would seem to curtail individuality and increase conformity to a particular framework of thinking. On the one hand, it is difficult to see how something as deeply personal as an individual's authenticity could be obtained from specific training. On the other, if such a quality can be taught, then it suggests that Western notions of individuality are a myth.

Cecily Cooper, Terry Scandura and Chester Schriesheim (2005) argue that it is pointless to develop authentic leadership programs until there is agreement as to what the construct means. They further contend that it is unlikely that an adult's ethical behaviour can be changed, since a person's moral outlook has already been formed through social and cultural processes. Bill George (2003) concurs, arguing that leadership training often consists of lists of characteristics that leaders are supposed to emulate. But conforming to another's ideal of authentic leadership will not enable a person to develop their strengths, nor help them lead in a genuine manner. Rather, such training merely encourages people to construct what they presume to be a socially acceptable leadership image.

Such image-making, according to George, is at the heart of the contemporary crisis of leadership. He connects the current leadership crisis with the narcissistic cult of personality that is endemic, not only in the corporate sector, but also in other arenas. Because leaders of Fortune 500 companies are perceived as possessing knowledge, wealth and prestige, it is not so surprising that in our status-conscious world others may want to emulate these successful leaders. If someone wishes to adopt the methods of a successful leader, perhaps they will be more effective. However, it is unclear as to how adopting another person's style of leadership can be, in any meaningful way, authentic. Rather, it is important to recognize that authenticity is not an attribute that can be generalized and, at the same time, remain unique to an individual.

Although some scholars maintain that they can develop leadership training programs that allow leaders to express themselves in an individual way, this is disputed by a Swiss study (Endrissat *et al.*, 2007). Here, 26 managers were asked their opinions about leadership training. These managers expressed hostility toward the leadership training they had taken part in, not least because they argued that this training encouraged them to act in a particular way, which they regarded as inauthentic. Leadership training, far from allowing leaders to discover their own style, made them feel like phonies. So while some leadership scholars see authentic leadership training as a way for people to express their individuality, this is not borne out by this particular study. On the contrary, leadership programming is perceived as encouraging people to conform to a particular ideal of what an authentic leader should be. From their research findings, these scholars conclude that leadership programming needs to be much less formulaic, especially if it is to have relevance across cultures.

A significant problem with leadership training is that it adheres to the belief that it is possible to 'track down the truth about leadership and train [people] in it' (Sinclair, 2013, p. 13). Yet such training not only obscures individual difference, but also masks socio-cultural differences. Indeed, Jill Blackmore (2009) argues that most leadership training is designed according to Anglo-American models that do not necessarily mesh well with other cultural environments. Because different cultures operate out of different ideological frameworks, she suggests that people think about leadership in divergent ways. When local customs and contexts are ignored, this may result in leadership programs failing to respect cultural diversity. Moreover, there is an implicit assumption, states Jacquie Ford (2006), that leadership is necessary to an organization's well-being. This emphasis on leadership may evoke a sense of helplessness on the part of employees, who become convinced that leaders are essential for their organization to flourish. Why this is problematic is because it can result in an unwillingness on the part of others to take responsibility for their own actions.

In examining some of the strengths and weaknesses of leadership training, we see how ideas about authenticity are influenced by Western ideas. But teaching leaders to follow a Western model may not translate well across cultures. Thus, leadership programming must consider cultural contexts, as well as social and historical factors, if it is to be relevant in different communities. Now I want to consider what insights thinking with Arendt can offer.

Thinking with Arendt

Earlier we examined how the dominant motif in authentic leadership is comprised of four dimensions, that is, self-awareness, balanced information processing, relational transparency and internalized moral perspective. In what follows, I demonstrate why this way of conceptualizing leadership is problematic from an Arendtian perspective. I begin by critiquing the scholarly focus on a leader's self-knowledge.

For Arendt (1958), self-knowledge as the basis for understanding is a deeply flawed notion. The widespread belief in inner depth is, in her opinion, a fallacy. Thus, a person can never know herself in the manner that proponents of authentic leadership suggest since, according to Arendt, the person who appears clearly to others remains partially hidden from the actor herself. It is because we can never know fully who we are that we cannot base a theory of leadership on the self. Rather than self-knowledge, she maintains that it is through action and speech that people demonstrate who they are, and reveal actively their unique personal identities (p. 179).

Arendt insists that we fail to comprehend who someone is because we place too much emphasis on their social role. For example, it is commonplace in Western society that, when introduced to a new person, a standard question is: what do you do? People are often judged, consciously or unconsciously, on their response, since certain professions are regarded more highly than others. But someone's profession fails to alert us to a person's uniqueness. Rather, '[w]ho somebody is or was we can know only by knowing the story of which he is himself the hero ... everything else we know of him, including the work he may have produced and left behind, tells us only what he is or was' (p. 186). Thus we need to be careful not to conflate what a person does with who they are. Otherwise, we risk losing that which is integral to that person, namely, their unique style of being.

In Arendt's view, a person's unique identity is always to be understood as both relational and embodied because each time we act and speak we do so within an already existent web of human relationships. Yet how we perceive ourselves is different to how we appear to others, since we can never see ourselves from the outside. Arendt (1971) contends that we do not appear to the world in the guise of an inner self; rather, we appear before others through self-display. Although we may try to manage our self-presentation, there will always be aspects that escape our control.

Furthermore, Arendt contests the surface/depth idea of subjectivity by stating our common conviction that what is inside ourselves, our 'inner life,' is more relevant to what we 'are' than what appears on the outside is an illusion (p. 30). In the world of appearances, that is the world we share with others, we show ourselves through our actions. In the world of the mind, that is the world of the self, we reveal ourselves through the medium of thought. Simply put, it is through action that we disclose ourselves to others, while it is through reflection that we reveal ourselves to ourselves.

Self-knowledge, as we understand it, is a concept unknown to the Greeks, since it derives from a Christian worldview. Arendt (1958) contrasts the modern understanding of self with that of ancient Greece, and notes how the Greeks used the term *daimon* to refer to something that was intrinsic to a particular individual, not a fleeting quality like happiness. This distinctive identity is not indicative of a person's talents or shortcomings, because character traits tell us what a person is good, or bad, at doing. By contrast, the *daimon* relates to who a person is, that is, their essence. For the Greeks, a person's essence could only be articulated after their death, at which point it is the role of the storyteller to recount a person's life.

In relation to leadership, Arendt argues that too much emphasis on self-knowledge contradicts the contingent nature of action. She maintains that a leader should not be judged on her achievements, the outcome of which can never be known in advance, but rather on her initiative, since it is impossible to plan for all eventualities because of action's unpredictability. Such unexpectedness, although intrinsic to human existence, contravenes the rules and regulations a society puts in place to ensure law and order.

Arendt traces the desire for law and order back to Plato who, she contends, disliked the vagaries of action. He regarded men as mere puppets on a stage, controlled by the invisible hand of fate, and preferred *poeisis* (making) to *praxis* (action) because the former had a predictable outcome (p. 185). It was because Plato wanted to give human affairs solidity that he argued that action, because of its capricious nature, should be separated from thought. Arendt maintains that Plato's disillusionment with political life, as a result of the trial and subsequent execution of Socrates, was to have major repercussions on ways of thinking about leadership. The paradox is that Plato's separation of thought and action went against Socratic teaching and was to have damaging consequences for ideas about leadership. Instead of the collective equality of the citizens of the *polis*, the new criterion for ruling was based upon a separation between the leader and the led. In Arendt's words,

> The supreme criterion of fitness for ruling others is, in Plato and in the aristocratic tradition of the West, the capacity to rule one's self. Just as the philosopher-king commands the city, the soul commands the body and reason commands the passion (p. 224).

In laying a political foundation based on law, Plato argued that action, because of its unpredictability, must be separated from thought. Over time, knowledge became linked to commanding others, whereas action is connected with obedience and the execution of orders. With this decisive split between beginning and ruling, Arendt maintains that Plato's ideas led the way for a conception of ruling that was anathema to human freedom, because plurality was denied in favour of sovereignty. Plurality, for Arendt (1958, p. 8), represents the fact that although each of us is human, and therefore similar, we are also distinct, since 'nobody is ever the same as anyone else who ever lived, lives or will live'. But a Platonic notion of leadership favours hierarchy. As a result, the notion of the leader as *primus inter pares*, that is first among equals, is dislodged in favour of the superiority of one master.

Arendt also criticizes how Plato conceived of this new kind of public leadership as akin to that of the head of the household. In ancient Greece, the head of the household had similarities to modern ideas about tyrants, since male citizens had total power over all who lived within their household. Arendt contends that basing a theory of leadership on the master/slave relationship of the household ensures that communal action is usurped in favour of a supreme hierarchy between the head of the household and everyone else. This form of leadership as mastery undermines the role of action in leadership, because the leader is seen as the person who initiates action, which others carry out in line with his commands. The separation between the one who envisions something and those who carry out the task ushered in a hierarchical understanding of rulership that served to debase an authentic understanding of human freedom. In effect, the separation between thinking and action led to the rule of the few over the many, and the fallacy of the strong man who is deemed to be all-powerful because he acts alone (Arendt, 1958, p. 40).

Yet the notion of the strong, isolated leader is a myth, states Arendt, as it is only through working together that action can be accomplished. She notes how the Greek word *archein* originally meant to begin something, as well as to lead, whereas the Latin equivalent was *agere*, which means to lead by setting something in motion (Arendt, 1958, p. 177). Subsequent linguistic changes result in the importance of working collectively becoming forgotten. Now, a leader is seen as someone who begins an action, which others execute on his behalf. This disconnection between the leader and others is potentially dangerous, since a leader's isolation from others may create an atmosphere of fear and suspicion.

In contradistinction, Arendt perceives of the Greek *polis* as an example of an authentic realm of freedom because it was the place where citizens came together as equals to share their views and make decisions on public affairs. A willingness to appear before others was perceived as critical to freedom. It required courage to devote oneself to public life because it meant a willingness to share your views with others. Conversely, a life lived at home was not regarded as a good life, because it meant that a man was not taking an active part in the *polis*. In fact, Arendt tells us that privacy originally meant deprivation. Thus, being outside the public realm – the fate of most men and all women in Ancient Greece – meant that a person was not considered fully human. Although the *polis* was the realm of freedom for male citizens, for the majority of people, that is, women, slaves, as well as working-men, this arena of liberty was closed. To use a modern analogy, one could say that the originating realm of Western freedom was like an elite men's club, since it was only male citizens with property and birthright who were allowed to take part in political affairs.

For the Greeks, the word 'public' had two distinct meanings. The first meaning related to being seen and heard. In this sense, public refers to how an individual appears, and interacts with others. The second definition of public is world, which represents the sum of human activity (Betz Hull, 2002). Sometimes, Arendt refers to this second meaning of public as *inter-est*, meaning the space that resides between us. A good example would be a table that we sit around to share ideas. This in-between space constitutes the place of human interaction. Additionally, she argues that to show oneself in public was essential to the Greek understanding of action. What constituted excellence in action was limited to deeds conducted in the public arena.

The political sphere was equated with the highest form of existence, since this was the only realm where a male citizen could gain public admiration, so important to assuage individual vanity. As such, the Greek *polis* represented a place to commemorate the deeds of great men. Initially, Arendt (1958) argues that the word 'hero' did not refer to someone who is courageous. Its original Homeric meaning was a free man who participated in the Trojan wars, and about whom a story could be told. It was through the storyteller's words that a hero gained immortality, something that the Greeks desired above all else. For example, in Homer's epics, people are seen as showing courage when they are willing to take action. Thus, poets like Homer had a political function, which was to immortalize Greek action. Without the storytelling efforts of poets like Homer, Arendt argues that heroic actions would be lost in the mist of time.

Authority and leadership

In contrasting previous ways of thinking about leadership and authority with modern times, Arendt (1993) contends that nowadays belief in legitimate authority has virtually disappeared. She sees legitimate authority as deriving from an implicit, or explicit, agreement between the leader and her followers. For Arendt, this type of legitimate agreement cannot take place wherever there is a threat of violence or coercion. Furthermore, she maintains that the breakdown in authority is due to increasing secularism, and the ensuing lack of faith in traditional beliefs. The problem, according to Arendt, is that modern society has chosen to stop learning from the past. Yet she argues that without the depth of understanding that one can obtain from the past, we are unable to comprehend current events in their fullness. Thus, it is valuable to delve into history, Arendt contends, because it enables us to understand ourselves through the stories that we share over time and space.

To illustrate her point, Arendt contrasts some modern and ancient understandings of authority within the Western tradition. As an example, for the Romans, authority was based on the notion of tradition, and a veneration of important events in the past. The foundation of Rome acted as a critical form of remembrance for their political actions, since it was the Roman republic that mattered above all else. She maintains it is from the Romans that we get our modern understanding of authority. Arendt argues that the Roman understanding of authority was unknown to the Greeks since, with the exception of the *polis*, the only forms of rulership the Greeks knew was that of tyranny, that is, rule by force, or despotism, which amounted to rule by coercion. On the one hand, the rule of the tyrant can only be enforced through violent means whereas, on the other, despotic rule manifested itself in the absolute control of the head of the household. Both forms of rulership served to negate individual freedom. Thus, neither type of rulership constitutes legitimate authority.

Arendt maintains that neither the tyrant nor his subjects are free because freedom can only arise from a contract between ruler and subject. Such a contract must be freely entered into, rather than upheld by forcible means. A similar problem is evident with the absolute rule that male citizens had in the household. The master/slave relationship is coercive and, in Arendt's view, anathema to freedom. As we saw earlier, it is only in the political sphere of the Greek *polis* that freedom is possible since – at least for male citizens – there was the ability to speak one's mind and appear before others. It was the expectation that citizens openly shared their views with others. It is from this collective sharing that leadership, understood as non-coercive and expressive of all viewpoints, comes into view. Such leadership is for Arendt the essence of power, since it is a coming together whereby people share their ideas and expectations.

For Arendt, power stands in opposition to its negative counterparts, force and violence, which she sees as emblematic of harmful ways of ruling. The problem, she contends, is that liberal thinkers fail to distinguish between these phenomena. As an example, Arendt states that the common term 'all power corrupts' is a meaningless phrase, since it overlooks the crucial distinction between legitimate and illegitimate manifestations of power. In her view, authority represents a positive form of rule, because it is based upon an agreement between the ruler and the people. Conversely, an illegitimate manifestation of power that emerged in modernity is that of totalitarian rule. Totalitarian regimes stand in opposition to human plurality, because 'a polis belonging to one man is no polis' (Arendt, 1985, p. 105). Accordingly, any leadership regime that derives from a sovereign will is not conducive to good government, since it puts the desire of the one about that of the many. Hence, she vehemently disagrees with Rousseau's notion of a government based on one will, because laws of sovereignty deny the basis of human freedom, that is, the ability for people to share their diverse views.

Arendt (1958) argues that leadership functions best when it arises out of individuals working together, rather than directed by a person in charge. A type of *polis* can appear at any time when people come together for a common goal. In our time, we can see an Arendtian-style *polis* emerge whenever there is concerted action taken by groups who are striving for justice. When people come together for a common cause, they discover the strength that comes from collective action. Therefore, collective power has a liberatory quality because it is through the medium of joint action that a committed group of people have the potential to topple dictators and their oppressive regimes that seek to suppress difference.

Social conformity

Arendt (1958) maintains that there is another form of rule that is contrary to human flourishing and that is social conformism, because it can result in an inability to respect and foster difference (pp. 38–50). In her view, social conformism arose in the eighteenth century as part of the massive changes that took place in the move from a feudal to a bourgeois society. Rather than equality for all, the rise of the bourgeoisie brought about an entrenched social conformity. For Arendt, this social conformity created a kind of 'no-man rule' whereby society dictates what we do, and how we think. Within this societal framework, action is subservient to behaviour as people become more inclined to do what is expected of them by wider society, and conform to social rules without thinking. The problem is that, in our desire for societal acceptance and approval, we may turn away from personal values to embrace social standards. When this happens it may become unclear as to what is our individual moral responsibility *vis-à-vis* taking a stance against injustice. This reluctance to take a stand can result in indifference toward the plight of others.

According to Arendt, the fundamental aspect of freedom is the ability to speak and act in the public realm. In late modernity, however, social conformity obviates a deeper notion of authenticity. In her view, individual freedom, understood as a right to celebrate our unique differences, is curtailed whenever we believe we are all equal, but fail to take into account that we are all equally distinct.

Structurally, we see this suppression of individual freedom manifest itself through bureaucracy. In *Origins of Totalitarianism*, she makes connections between totalitarianism and bureaucracy, arguing that both systems disregard uniqueness in favour of a particular way of thinking.

Within a bureaucracy, uniqueness is threatened because each person is seen as expendable. Arendt (2003a) regards bureaucracy as the least human and most cruel form of rulership, because leaders refuse to take responsibility for their actions, and encourage others to do likewise (p. 37). Hence, bureaucracy and totalitarian-like ways of thinking and acting are similar in that both suppress a plurality of viewpoints. As a consequence, these impersonal systems have a detrimental effect on those who attempt to humanize them. Such systematic approaches to social life reinforce inequality because a voiceless, autonomous way of life serves to deny, or suppress, individual expression.

What is demanded in bureaucracy is assent, not dissent. In response to not being able to voice their dissent, people start to feel alienated and, as a result, refuse to take responsibility for their actions, preferring to hide behind corporate policies and institutional rules. One way we see this is with phrases such as 'I'd like to help but I have to follow regulations'. This lack of ownership is indicative of how individuals lose their identity in the bureaucratic speech of what Heidegger (1962) termed 'the they'. Bureaucratic ways of speaking and acting are, in Arendtian terms, damaging to human flourishing because they lead to an increasing social conformity to rules and regulations that we fail to question. Within the context of a healthy work environment, plurality does not mean that dissenting viewpoints are not permitted, but that openness to dissent is often seen as negative in the modern workplace. This is partly due to the hierarchical nature of bureaucracy, whereby institutions prefer conformity to freedom of expression, but also because of a fear of reprisals on the part of many employees. Without the freedom to dialogue and debate with one another, genuine engagement may be curtailed. When the multiplicity of human expression is lost, so too is an ability for genuine interaction.

For Arendt, each of us has the ability to be ethically responsible by reflecting upon what we do. Yet, oftentimes people choose not to take the time to reflect upon their actions. What is more, confidence is privileged over doubt. Yet doubting is a necessary part of the reflective process because it enables us to bring forth alternative perspectives. These diverse perspectives may alert us to the danger of proceeding with a particular decision, and help us guard against unethical decision-making and the dangers of hubris. This is why Arendt (1971) urges us to 'stop and think' about our actions. In many organizational settings, however, it becomes easier to go along with whatever bureaucratic decision is made, rather than take the time to figure out whether or not we agree. But it also means that people must be willing to disregard a leader's request if they view it as unethical, and be willing to take a stand. Only then will we be able to create working environments that are not prone to the alienation, mistrust and obtuseness so common in bureaucratic life.

Conclusion

In this chapter, we examined some of the major tenets of authentic leadership. Through this examination, I have shown how this theory focuses on certain dimensions of leading that serve to preclude others. In their attempt to develop a universal theory, some leadership scholars restrict authentic leadership to a narrow framework consisting of four dimensions, namely, self-awareness, balanced information processing, relational transparency and internalized moral perspective. This framework is too reductive in scope to allow for a depth of understanding regarding the place of authenticity in leadership. As well, there is often an implicit assumption that authenticity is good for leadership. Rather than arguing that authenticity in leadership is necessarily a good thing, we must be willing to interrogate the reasons why sometimes this might not be the case. This requires us to critique prevailing power inequities rather than simply assuming that by adding authenticity to the mix, we will develop good leaders.

Earlier, I posed the question – would a world populated by authentic leaders be a better one? Although some leadership scholars presume that is the case, history teaches us to beware of leaders who are certain they are right, not least because, in hindsight, we observe the negative consequences of that single-minded belief, and the untold suffering caused by such certitude. Thus we need to question whether a leader's authenticity is necessarily good for the well-being of others, and organizations in general. For example, we need to interrogate why it is that authentic leadership has emerged as a topic of interest at the beginning of the twenty-first century. Could it be that a guiding motif of our time is that of distrust, not only of leaders but of one another? A society of distrust emerges, in tandem with a penchant for instrumental modes of thinking that result in a lack of caring for others.

Thinking with Arendt reveals some of the shortcomings with the discourse of authentic leadership, especially the ways in which too much focus on leaders can prove detrimental to others. An Arendtian analysis reveals some of the negative implications with a leadership theory that purport to be about authentic relationships but is limited by its functional approach. It is my contention that one cannot found an ethical theory of leadership based on quantitative measurement, because it is simply too narrow to encompass the scope of human action and thought. In its current form, authentic leadership does not offer us the ethical guidance we need to create a just and harmonious society. Conversely, Arendt shows how our relationships and forms of mutual responsiveness are central to existence. By seeing leadership in relational terms that weaves together diverse perspectives, her work opens up fruitful avenues of investigation. As such, Arendt provides us with an alternative ethical guide for us to reconsider the connections between authenticity and leadership.

The lack of focus on gender and a failure to interrogate how the intersections of identity have a bearing, not only on leadership, but on what it means to be true to ourselves, leaves us with a limited view of authenticity. Ignoring the intersubjective dimension of everyday life can result in leaders becoming separated from daily concerns, and acting in self-indulgent ways to the detriment of everyone else. Put simply, a focus on the self can lead to a disconnection from the world, which may have negative implications.

It is by considering authenticity through diverse perspectives that we will be able to obtain a more rounded view of leadership. In the following chapter, I explore the question of authenticity in leadership through a gendered lens so as to examine how material circumstances and societal assumptions influence gendered assumptions about leaders.

3
Gendered Expectations

In response to an interview question from Günter Gaus, Hannah Arendt (1994a) referred to herself as having old-fashioned views about women leaders. She further contended: 'It just doesn't look good when a woman gives orders. She should try not to get into such a situation if she wants to remain feminine' (p. 3). Arendt's public statements regarding women leaders illustrate some common prejudices. Her stated bias against women leaders is still prevalent in Western society, as a recent survey by Kim Elsesser and Janet Lever (2011) illustrates. In this survey of 60,000 individuals in the United States, while 54 percent of people said that they had no preference regarding male or female bosses, of those remaining participants who expressed a preference, however, twice as many preferred to work for a male leader. Although prejudice against women leaders is lessening, it is still firmly embedded in the cultural imagination. This gender prejudice can have a deleterious effect given that some women leaders may assimilate dominant styles of leadership that merely serves to perpetuate structural inequities in the workplace and beyond.

Prejudice against women leaders is, in part, because they challenge the normative, hierarchical framework. Simply put, women leaders are perceived as out of place in the gendered hierarchy that pervades the higher echelons of organizational and public life, which may be one reason why, in the twenty-first century, we still have such a low percentage of women occupying positions of power. Consider, for example, that out of 159 United Nations member states only 21 have women as either political leaders or heads of state.[1] Although gender stereotypes are changing, when it comes to leadership, it is still the case that men occupy the vast majority of leadership roles within the public sphere, and it is women who have greater responsibilities in the private sphere (Wolf, 2014). To paraphrase Charles Dickens, although individual women leaders may have 'great expectations', it is gendered expectations in society at large that may place limitations on their advancement.

In this chapter, I explore how normative ideas about gender roles shape our understanding of leadership. This is a wide-ranging discussion because I want to look at gender relations from a variety of lenses to see what it tells us about the interconnections among gender, authenticity and leadership. My main contention is that authenticity is influenced by our notions of what constitutes appropriate gender behaviour. In particular, we will see how authenticity is a social construct that is always being contested. In addition, I look at how some women's perceived lack of vision and confidence may negatively affect their ability to move up the leadership ladder. By considering how gendered identity influences notions of authenticity in leadership, we gain insight into societal ideas about leaders. We will see how structural and socio-cultural stereotypes affect our understanding of what constitutes an authentic leader.

In considering how gender influences ideas about authenticity and leadership, we will start by looking at some feminist critiques of authentic leadership and organizational theories. We will see how situated, gendered embodiment has multiple effects on leaders. We will also look at how idealized gender roles, such as that of the 'good mother', may prove a detriment to women's public advancement in leadership. The notion of what constitutes the most authentic role for a woman is complicated by the ideal of motherhood. To begin, however, I want to consider some critiques of authentic leadership in relation to gender, subjectivity and embodiment.

Gender troubles in leadership

Due to the influence of postmodern scholarship, identity, like gender, is perceived to be a fluid concept. From this perspective, it is argued that a person's subjectivity is not static, but changes depending upon situational context (Calás *et al.*, 2013). Thus, the notion that a leader can be authentic on all occasions is disputed. When we look to society in general we see that the notion of gender fluidity has limited impact on societal attitudes regarding gender roles. For example, cultural stereotypes such as the strong leader or the good mother are so powerful that they serve to reinforce traditional ways of thinking, and may unconsciously influence people's notion of what constitutes authentic leadership. I will return to this point in due course.

Amanda Sinclair (2013) claims that a major shortcoming with authentic leadership scholarship is its lack of concern with gender. Even though scholars may not think about the effects of gender, Sinclair contends that, in practice, authenticity is often judged through a gendered lens whereby women leaders' bodies are perceived as a primary indication of their moral worthiness, or lack thereof. But few scholars concentrate on how a leader's performance is filtered through the lens of gender. Instead, what we have are scholarly accounts of authenticity that arise from supposedly gender-neutral cognitive acts. But while scholars perceive authentic leaders in disembodied ways, women leaders are often assessed by their bodily appearance. Issues that are irrelevant to a leader's overall effectiveness, such as being overweight, having visible grey hair or poor dress sense may have an inverse effect on how their leadership is perceived. So while embodiment is often ignored by authentic leadership scholars, in practice, 'gendered bodies are central for leaders and their audiences attributing and evaluating authenticity' (p. 240).

Similarly, Jan Shaw (2010) maintains that authentic leadership scholarship is predicated on a Cartesian mind/body dualism (p. 90). As a consequence, the effect of materiality on leaders' bodies is often disregarded. Such disregard serves to ignore the myriad ways in which leaders are judged based on their physical appearance. A leader's values, therefore, are often considered by others in conjunction with their embodied actions. For instance, our perception of how leaders should look and act will be influenced by social, historical and cultural beliefs. Who a leader is, therefore, will be assessed not only by what they do, but by how they look, in conjunction with societal ideas about appropriate behaviour. But it is not the mind of the leader that matters to followers as much as their embodied actions. What is more, hierarchical systems and power imbalances in society are often internalized, and then reproduced, often in an unconscious way, in our material practices (p. 92). Consequently, discourses like authentic leadership serve to reproduce dominant paradigms about leaders, rather than interrogate them.

Authenticity cannot be seen as something that is self-directed, because it fails to account for how we are influenced by the world. Just as we, in Arendtian terms, bring something new into the world by inserting ourselves through action and speech, so too does the world influence our style of being. One of the women leaders I interviewed summed this up eloquently by stating: 'Just as I influence my organization I have to recognize that the organization influences me'. This symbiotic relationship demonstrates that leaders are influenced by structural concerns, as well as other people.

Rather than a leader possessing authenticity, it is through their interaction with others that authenticity is manifested (Sinclair, 2013; Ladkin and Taylor, 2010). As a result, gender norms will influence our ideas about a leader's authenticity or lack thereof. These gender norms will change over time and place. Furthermore, societal ideals about what is regarded as acceptable behaviour for leaders are also influenced by gendered perceptions. To understand authenticity, we must recognize how gendered norms affect how leaders are perceived. In the case of women leaders, for example, their authenticity is often perceived in ways that focus on their gender presentation.

Yet Sinclair argues that the notion of authenticity appeals to many women. She offers three reasons why this might be so. First, being authentic is regarded highly, since it means that a leader is perceived as possessing integrity, and being straightforward in her dealings with others. Second, building trusting relationships is central to leading successfully, since people hate working for phonies. Third, because many women want to lead differently, authenticity is perceived as a way of leading in line with feminist values. She calls for feminist research that exposes how 'authentic leadership scholarship has contributed to the selective invisibility of some gendered bodies' (p. 249). This means that we acknowledge how the phenomenon of authenticity is socially constructed, and try to understand it alongside gendered norms and negative stereotypes. Furthermore, instead of asking women to 'perform to masculine norms of authenticity we need to move towards a radically different gender-aware understanding of authenticity and its role in leadership' (p. 249). This requires that we acknowledge how structural issues, material circumstances and gender socialization influence how we think about authentic leadership. Let's start with considering the media portrayal of women leaders.

One negative influence on women leaders is the manner in which they are often perceived in the media. In fact, gender bias can be seen in the media coverage that many high profile women leaders attract. For example, a member of Hillary Clinton's press corps remarked that the story which the media picks up on is not about what Clinton says, but on how she looks (Ibarra *et al.*, 2013, p. 67). But the time spent managing one's appearance can actually detract from a leader's larger purpose. Moreover, when someone's appearance seems too perfect, they may be accused of being self-absorbed (Sinclair, 2013). Conversely, too much focus on how others perceive them can actually impair a leader's ability to remain committed to the task at hand. Instead of focussing on gender stereotypes, it is vital that leaders develop a clear sense of purpose from which they direct their actions. This kind of media coverage of women leaders reflects patriarchal ideologies of women's value. That is, women are still valued for their appearance, even in important and powerful roles, because patriarchal ideologies dictate that women's worth comes from their appearance, while men's worth derives from power and status.

Alternatively, consider the manner in which the ex-Prime Minister of Australia, Julia Gillard, was viewed by the media (Sinclair, 2013). Gillard's harsh treatment was partially based on the fact that she was a divorced, single woman in her early fifties who did not have children. Her status as a divorced woman without children meant that she allegedly did not have all the accoutrements necessary to indicate her strength as a moral leader. Not being a good mother quickly transcended into not being perceived as a good woman, as the abuse she received showed. These two examples are indicative of how prominent women leaders are perceived in terms of stereotypical ideas as to what constitutes appropriate feminine behaviour.

Rather than media bias, it is academic bias that is of concern to some scholars. It is claimed, for example, that authentic leadership scholarship fails to include feminine presence or voice (Irby *et al.*, 2002). But not everyone is comfortable with this quest for more feminine voices in leadership research. Indeed, Adrianne Kezar and Jaime Lester (2010) argue that research in women's leadership has a tendency to be essentialist, especially in regard to the supposition that women will be better leaders than men. All this thinking does is to reproduce gender dichotomies (Due Billing and Alvesson, 2000), and reaffirm cultural stereotypes about gender.

Instead, we need to rethink notions of masculinity and femininity as culturally created and reiterated bodily practices. Although some scholars argue that research in organizational leadership is saturated with embodied masculinity (Binns and Kerfoot, 2011), I suggest this is a particular kind of masculinity that views leadership as a form of mastery. As with femininity, masculinity is culturally conditioned. But the avoidance of a detailed discussion on masculinity serves, unintentionally, to reinforce gender binaries.

In many ways, the work of leadership scholars interested in gender has a tendency to replicate some of the essentialist leanings of some second-wave feminist theorizing. That is, a focus on gender, on its own, can lead to a reification of the term 'Woman'. But it is somewhat naïve to suggest that all women are good leaders. Clearly, becoming a leader depends on a variety of factors. This is why I suggest we need to consider the connections among gender, authenticity and leadership through an intersectional lens.

Intersectionality

To comprehend authenticity in leadership as it pertains to gender, we need to understand these issues from a broader perspective. In our inquiry, we require a more nuanced theoretical approach that takes account of gender, as well as other intersections of identity, such as race, class and age. This is where the concept of intersectionality may prove fruitful. The term 'intersectionality', popularized by Kimberlé Crenshaw (1991), refers to how identity is influenced by multiple factors, such as race, class or gender. This alerts us to the need to account for how multiple facets of social oppression and privilege work together. Being cognizant of difference helps us see how the intersections of identity play a role in how we think about leaders. Yet an intersectional analysis, so prevalent in feminist scholarship, is often ignored by leadership scholars who concentrate exclusively on gender.

We must also guard against research that considers gender independently from other social factors because it fails to explain why a minority of women climb up the leadership ladder, while the vast majority of women have not. As an instance, by looking at feminist critiques of gender and work, through an intersectional lens, we may obtain a richer understanding of some of the inherent problems at work.

Stereotypical ideas about gender roles continue to negatively influence women's ability to achieve equal pay, as well as hamper their advancement to higher positions. Recent statistics from a report written by the United States Bureau of Labor Statistics (2013) indicates that pay inequity has stalled. For example, in 2012 American women who worked full-time earned 81 percent of the male wage in comparison with 62 percent in 1979. This is obviously an improvement. However, when we look more closely at those figures, there are important distinctions. Considering age, we note that, in the U.S., young women, aged between 18 and 24, earn, on average, 89 percent of their male counterparts while women aged 35 and older earn between 75–78 percent of their male counterparts. If we factor in race and ethnicity, we see some striking differences between women. For example, U.S. statistics show that in 2012, Asian women earned the highest salaries, followed by white women, who earned, on average, 92 percent of Asian women's salaries. Next black women earned 78 percent of their

Asian counterparts and, finally, Hispanic women earned 68 percent of their Asian sisters. Also, when education levels are considered, both men and women without a high school diploma earned around half of what those with a college degree did. Interestingly, the wages for women without a college diploma have remained steadier than their male counterparts, whose earnings have dropped by a third since 1979 when inflation is taken into account. Clearly, when one takes into account a range of intersectional factors such as age, race, education and class, we see that when it comes to pay, gender is but one salient factor.[2] Hence, an intersectional analysis offers us a wider perspective for understanding structural inequities.

In looking at the effects of class and gender Paula England (2010) notes that although gender segregation has altered, change is not the same across the workforce. Over the last few decades, for example, while middle-class women have made substantial gains in professions such as medicine and law, there has been little advancement for women in traditional blue-collar jobs. In trying to ascertain the reasons why change has been so different across sectors, England shows how, increasingly, middle-class women have chosen different career paths than their mothers. In the latter part of the twentieth century, it appears that many middle-class women chose male professions such as law, business and medicine as a way of gaining financial reward and status, instead of following their mothers into more traditional feminine occupations, such as teaching and nursing. One negative outcome of this movement of middle-class women into masculine professions is a further devaluation of traditional women's work.

While the working lives of middle-class, well-educated women have been enriched by financial rewards and increased social status, this has not been the case for the majority of women. For example, in 2007, 80 percent of American college-educated women were employed versus 47 percent of those with high school qualifications or high-school dropouts (England, 2010). In 1970, the comparable figure for female employment was 59 percent for college-educated women and 43 percent for high school women (England, 2010). These statistics demonstrate that although middle-class women with a college or university degree have made tremendous strides in the workplace, this has not been the experience for women as a whole.

What is perhaps more telling is that in certain fields, such as social work or nursing, there has not been a notable increase in the number of male students. This is because social discrimination is greater for men who choose to pursue female professions (England, 2010). Those men who choose traditional female occupations are faced with a lack of status and financial rewards, as well as social disapproval. Hence, England argues that there is little incentive for men to change careers. One reason for this continuing gender segregation in the workplace, England argues, is that there has been no substantial change in social ideas regarding gender roles. Indeed, the private realm reaffirms gender inequality, which has ongoing implications for the workplace in general, and women's leadership in particular.

Women at the top ... or not

One reason why gender pay differentials still exist, according to Eagly and Carli (2007), is that there remains demonstrable opposition toward the appointment of women leaders at the higher echelons of organizational life. Their assertion is backed up by recent statistics, which show that only 3 percent of the top 100 companies in Europe have female CEOs, with a slightly higher figure (4 percent) for the Fortune 500 companies in the United States (Catalyst, 2012). Statistics also show that women still make up less than 20 percent of senior corporate executives in the United States and Canada (Catalyst, 2012). Similarly, women make up 17 percent of senior corporate executives in Europe, although this figure differs dramatically depending on whether countries adopt quota systems such as in Norway, where the goal of 40 percent of female participations on corporate boards has been reached. Thus it appears it is only when governments are willing to introduce quotas that there is a significant change in terms of gender disparity at the highest levels. However, the introduction of what is called the "golden skirt" legislation in Scandinavian countries has not necessarily led to enhanced working conditions for all women. Those at the top have sometimes benefitted at the expense of women at the bottom.[3]

While some scholars argue that women leaders make a positive difference in the workplace, I want to critically explore this assertion as it relates to ethics. During the last decade, Eagly (2005) conducted a series of longitudinal studies on women and leadership. Her research findings suggest that when women are initially hired to lead an institution, they may act differently than their male counterparts, presumably because of different value commitments. Over the long term, however, this gender difference tends to dissipate. So although female leaders may be more vigilant in regards to business ethics at the beginning of their leadership role/s, this gender difference seems to disappear the longer a woman remains in a position of leadership. This is a problem, states Eagly, because if women leaders take up similar ways of acting to their male counterparts, organizations will not be transformed, and ethical problems will persist. Thus, we need greater understanding as to why women leaders who desire to lead in a collegiate fashion often end up being as autocratic as their predecessors. Drawing from her interviews with 60 women leaders, Marianne Coleman (2010) suggests that a major impediment to gender equity is women's belief in their individual success. Her interview data suggests that women leaders are more inclined to see that success is based solely on their own merit and hard work. Moreover, the women leaders she spoke with were often indifferent to feminist principles, arguing that 'the fate of the individual is their own responsibility' (p. 47). As a result of this expressed indifference, gender equity may be difficult to reach.

It appears, therefore, that placing some women in powerful positions does not necessarily lead to the empowerment of women as a group (Kellerman and Rhode, 2007). In striving for gender equality in the workplace, what has happened is that women's limited ascension to top leadership posts has been conceived in terms of representation when what is required is a troubling of organizational structures. So it may not be enough to hire women as leaders if the desired outcome is gender justice. Rather, it is leaders who are inspired by principles of social justice who are needed if the goal is to challenge discriminatory institutional practices (Morley, 2013, p. 126). But there are significant obstacles to changing organizational structures, some of which we will now discuss.

In the past, some feminists denounced bureaucracy and hierarchy, because of its male-dominated structures of control (Acker, 1990). Many feminists, both men and women, wanted to create organizations that would operate in non-hierarchical ways. Instead of a new kind of workplace, however, the results have been more of the same, that is, a number of women leaders have acted just as badly as some of their male counterparts. Partly, this was because there was a lack of models available for feminists to adequately rethink organizational structures (Smith, 1990). In large bureaucracies in particular, it can be difficult to create an organization model outside of the normative, hierarchical framework.

But large bureaucracies are often intolerant of different ways of leading (Blackmore and Sachs, 2007). For instance, if we look at the changing landscape of higher education, we see that, over the last few decades, there has been a movement to corporatize institutions. Such restructuring places the emphasis on efficiency, accountability and outcomes, which may not always be in the best interest of students, or necessarily lead to ethical action. Indeed, the emphasis on efficiency may lead to an instrumental approach that serves to constrain dissent, something that Greenleaf warned against, as we saw in the previous chapter.

In considering the move toward entrepreneurialism within universities, Blackmore and Sachs maintain there is too much pressure placed on senior managers to concur with the leader's decisions. This shows itself as an unwavering commitment to corporate goals, regardless of any personal misgivings about a particular decision. Rather than authentic engagement what is required is total loyalty, not only to the organization but also to the leader.

Furthermore, the corporatization of universities encourages social conformity in the way leaders dress, the rituals of meetings and the symbolic use of space (Blackmore and Sachs, 2007). Who is allocated the best location, or the biggest office, serves to reinforce institutional hierarchy, and offers a spatial indication into power dynamics. Over time, these power dynamics work to ensure only those who are willing to agree with the leader are likely to retain their positions. This can create feelings of powerlessness on behalf of others in the organization who want to alter this situation but feel powerless to fight against it. We need to recognize how feelings of powerlessness are often tied up with gender socialization (Sinclair, 2007).

What is considered to be appropriate gender behaviour can negatively affect women's agency in particular. For example, role incongruity, that is, the ways in which women leaders may seem out of place, can lead to prejudice. This gender prejudice may take the form of perceiving women as ill-suited for a senior leadership role. In general terms, women are often seen to have less agentic qualities than men. But sometimes when a woman leader behaves in a manner that fulfills common expectations of leadership behaviour by being assertive, she may be evaluated negatively because her action is deemed inappropriate for her gender (Eagly and Karau, 2002). Although male leaders do well by being agentic, women must appeal to communal ideals to be seen as successful leaders. But a relational approach may actually work against a woman leader, since it serves to reinforce gender stereotypes (Eagly, 2005). For this situation to be altered, Eagly and Karau maintain there has to be major societal change, not only in the way that most people perceive gender relations, but also in how we conceptualize leadership.

It is not enough for a woman to 'lean in' and bring her whole self to work, as Sheryl Sandberg (2013) asserts, because this does little to explain how structural inequities in leadership work. Furthermore, Sandberg's assertion that authentic communication is akin to the interaction that takes place on Facebook illustrates how authenticity is often perceived in a superficial way. As a consequence, there is a flattening of a deeper sense of authentic connection in favour of superficial forms of relating.

To counteract this superficiality, Helen Nicholson and Brigid Carroll (2013) suggest it is time to reframe authenticity as a 'social virtue,' rather than an individual disposition (p. 286). Perceiving authenticity as a social virtue serves to promote honest dialogue, but it may also encourage an involvement with broader political issues, rather than a focus on individual concerns. Viewed in this way, authenticity is not about perfecting the self, but about sharing one's aptitudes and gifts with others so as to make the world a better place. Such a revisioning of authentic leadership would require 'leaders, facilitators and researchers to engage in questions about agency, impact, care, responsibility and connection' (p. 298). In turn, this would allow for a more holistic approach to leadership than what we currently have, and one more in line with Arendtian notions.

Another problem, as Nicholson and Carroll note, is that many authentic leadership scholars portray the world as an arena of evil. By focussing on unethical corporate practices or the danger of terrorism, it suggests that evil is omnipresent. To combat the negativity of the world around them, authentic leaders are urged to develop 'inner strength' to deal with challenges more successfully. But this leads to a schism whereby the inner self is defined in opposition to the external world, rather than in relationship with it.

In their leadership development work, Nicholson and Carroll note that the term 'authenticity' is often brought up by leaders. They offer the example of Annie who wanted to rid herself of self-doubt so as to become an amazing leader valued for her ability to effect social change. Annie talks about wanting to be true to her authentic self by finding her voice and not hiding in the shadows (p. 287). Yet Nicholson and Carroll argue that the demand to be an authentic leader can lead to frustration as leaders like Annie try to perfect themselves, rather than recognize that we all have strengths and weaknesses. Moreover, too much soul-searching can mean that leaders are constantly monitoring their actions. Such self-monitoring is unlikely to encourage authentic action, since leaders will be constantly wrestling with internal doubt as to the right course to follow. This is why Nicholson and Carroll argue that we must stop viewing authenticity as an individual virtue and see it instead as a social one (p. 294).

A major obstacle that some women leaders face is establishing personal credibility in an organization unused to seeing women in top leadership roles. Rita Bornstein (2010), the first female Jewish president of Rollins College, has written extensively about the difficulties she experienced as an outsider in achieving Presidential legitimacy. At the beginning of her tenure, Bornstein describes the hostility she faced from some colleagues due, in part, to her ethnicity and gender. For example, she overheard one senior administrator stating that the College was not ready for a Jewish president, let alone a woman leader. Another problem Bornstein faced was that she was not an academic and, therefore, did not fit the stereotypical ideal of President of a higher educational establishment. (Bornstein's major accomplishments were in the field of Advancement, in particular fundraising, which did not provide her with the skill-set that people traditionally expected of a college president.)

Bornstein is candid about the problems that presidents face in regard to constant challenges to their moral leadership. At times, she argues that a president may have to suppress her personal views so as to uphold the values of the institution. Given her presidential role as the person who is supposed to embody her organization's mission, she may need to uphold institutional values that differ from her own. For example, a president might have a pro-choice stance that is anathema to the stated position of her faith-based institution. In such a case, a president would have to resist expressing her personal beliefs, and thus be inauthentic, or express a position that contradicted the organization's espoused principles. These types of situations serve to complicate the issue of authenticity in leadership. Presidents face these ethical dilemmas on a regular basis and yet, according to Bornstein, there is a lack of discussion regarding the complex relationship between institutional demands and a leader's ethical values. It is not just a question of whether a leader is a principled person, but whether those principles are in line with the organization.

There are other contradictions at work in relation to what constitutes authenticity in leaders. For example, although many employees state their preference for working in a caring environment, it appears that most people prefer to be led by strong leaders, since this is perceived as successful leadership behaviour. Hence, some leaders may face a double-bind in that although employees say they want to work in a caring environment, they do not want leaders who exhibit a caring demeanour, because this is regarded as a sign of weakness. This equation of caring with weakness reinforces the belief that organizations require strong, independent leaders. Yet, according to Paul Begley (2006), it is only through caring for the values of others that authentic leadership can occur.

But it can be difficult for men, as well as women, to lead complex organizations in a caring manner. From her interviews with male and female university presidents, for example, Pamela Eddy (2010) notes how leaders incur problems when they attempt to transgress gender stereotypical ways of acting. For instance, she describes a situation where a male president espoused a team-based approach. Rather than seeing him as a collaborative leader, faculty perceived him as weak. Thus, Eddy suggests that people still judge success from an outdated, autocratic, heroic model of leadership that makes it difficult for leaders to deviate from the norm. It is important to look at how gender stereotyping influences leaders.

For instance, although corporations have spent time and money on leadership development to encourage women to take on more responsible positions, Ibarra *et al.* (2013) contend that women are still less likely to occupy leadership positions. They argue that taking on a leadership role requires an identity shift that some women feel uncomfortable with, partly because they are worried about seeming inauthentic. We need to understand why some women's desire to lead is less strong than many of their male colleagues. In the following section, I want to investigate how subtle gender biases in the workplace may influence women's ability to see themselves as leaders. This requires us to see how gender stereotyping is still a factor in the workplace.

Ibarra *et al.* (2013) contend that becoming a leader requires both an internalization of the leadership identity together with a sense of purpose. Gaining a sense of oneself as a leader, therefore, is an iterative practice. Effective leaders, as we saw in Chapter 2, are often perceived as people who possess a strong sense of purpose and pursue goals that fit with their individual principals and the larger societal good. When leaders are able to work in an environment that meshes with their values, they will be perceived as authentic and worthy of others' trust. In gaining trust, leaders are able to build a stronger workplace, as others will be inspired by the leader's purposeful action (Ibarra *et al.*, 2013). All this seems straightforward, but there are constant biases to women's leadership that affect their authenticity, or lack thereof.

One aspect recently identified as a problem for women's leadership is second-generation gender bias. This bias refers to how many younger women are unaware of gender discrimination, even denying it exists (Ibarra *et al.*, 2013). One reason for this second-generation gender bias may be because there has been significant movement in terms of the pay gap between younger workers, as we saw earlier. Although working-class and older women earn substantially less than their male counterparts, the gender pay gap is much less for middle and upper-class young workers. Furthermore, in cultures where the emphasis is on individual rather than collective rights, what happens is that we stop to consider how the injustice that one worker is facing is related to systematic injustices in the workplace and beyond. By putting oneself first, we negate our responsibilities for others, which as Arendt demonstrates is disastrous for the overall well-being of society.

Within many workplaces, there is a strong link between masculinity and leadership (Ibarra *et al.*, 2013). This can create unconscious biases against women leaders. For example, what is regarded as assertive behaviour in men may come across as aggressive posturing in women and, thus, contrary to traditional gender expectations. Conversely, being seen as too feminine may result in a woman leader, while being liked, not being respected. Clearly gender bias has an effect, implicitly or explicitly, on the way that leaders are viewed.

Deeply engrained gender socialization may mean that some women leaders have a harder time being perceived as CEO material. Recently, Sherry Cooper, the Chief Economist at the Bank of Montreal, reported in a radio interview that she had never been considered for the top job.[4] The reason she failed to break through the glass ceiling, she argued, was because she was pigeonholed in her role as Chief Economist. Being good at her job had actually worked against Cooper's ascension to CEO. A different example of how gender stereotypes negatively affect leadership is in regard to Jill Abraham, the former and only female managing editor at *The New York Times*. Although some commentators argued that Abraham was let go because of her abrasive style, Kay and Shipman (2014) point out that toughness is part of the culture of news rooms. The real problem, they maintain, is that women leaders are judged by outmoded stereotypes, which do not allow them to be themselves in the workplace.

In Chapter 2, I noted the importance that leadership scholars attach to vision. Indeed, some scholars maintain that a lack of comfort in sharing their vision is holding many women back from top leadership roles (Ibarra and Obodaru, 2009, p. 2). Although women are perceived as just as competent as men in the majority of managerial tasks, developing a distinctive vision is the area where women leaders express unease, moreover, they are perceived as being less successful than their male colleagues. If more women wish to lead organizations, Ibarra and Obodaru contend, it is necessary for them to become more comfortable with putting forward their own vision. In short, women need to become competent in this area of leadership, which requires a greater sense of self-assurance in sharing their personal beliefs.

Others argue that it is not a lack of vision, but a lack of confidence that is holding women back (Kay and Shipman, 2014). Those who believe that attention to detail and hard work will result in promotion are mistaken since, according to Kay and Shipman, it is confidence that allows one to get ahead in the workplace. In general terms, men are more likely to feel a greater confidence in their abilities to succeed than most women. We see this in the way that men are more willing to put themselves forward for senior roles, regardless of whether they possess the necessary qualifications (Kay and Shipman, 2014). Thus, women need to do likewise if they wish to be leaders. One way for women to show leadership capacity is to take greater risks. It is only through learning from failure that it is possible to succeed. Therefore, risk-taking can enable women to improve their confidence level.

But not everyone agrees with the supposition that confidence is unquestionably good for leadership. For example, Jennifer Binns (2008) contends that a leader's desire for self-certainty may negate ethical transformation, since creating ethical relationships means being open to doubt. Although confidence is perceived as vital to a particular kind of masculine leadership, being open to doubt can overturn the dominant leadership script by providing an openness to consider different perspectives, and create new possibilities. While doubt may seem to be a negative indicator of leadership qualities, it may just as well be an indication of someone who is willing to think about different perspectives before making a decision. This willingness to consider diverse views is an important aspect of a leader who wants to act in a more relational manner.

Idealized roles

According to Connell and Messerschmidt (2005), the continuing gender hierarchy in society alerts us to the asymmetrical position of masculinities and femininities (p. 844). They argue that it is crucial to see gender in relational terms, since femininity is always defined in relation to masculinity. Thus what are considered to be feminine traits will often be in direct opposition to masculine ones. Some of these opposing traits would be strength/softness, individualistic/communal and competitive/altruistic. Thinking in terms of gender binaries serves to encourage social conformity to the prevailing stereotype. Cultural stereotypes perpetuate gender disparities, and are restricting to all. Two prevailing cultural stereotypes in society are the 'good mother' and the 'strong leader'. The good mother is regarded as caring and compassionate, and is someone who puts her family before herself. Conversely, the 'strong leader' is often depicted as someone who is ambitious, determined, and seeks centre stage. This connection between leadership and competitiveness is firmly entrenched in historical connotations of what constitutes strong masculinity (Connell and Messerschmidt, 2005).

Historically, the paragon of womanhood is the bourgeois, self-sacrificing mother figure, who represents the emblem of feminine moral goodness. This ideal is limiting to women, who cannot live up to this cultural stereotype of moral goodness. Hence, this ideal of the good mother may be just as stultifying for women as the idea of the strong leader is for men. The difference, of course, is that one has greater cultural capital within the public sphere, while the other has cultural capital within the private realm. While cultural norms are changing, the notion of the breadwinning father and stay at home mom, prevalent in nostalgic views of what constitutes the perfect family, still shape ideas about gender roles. Yet, as Hill Collins (1994) notes, the ideal of 'good mother' understood as one who stays at home for her children is in contrast to the reality of many women of colour and working-class mothers, who work due to financial necessity. Clearly the dominant ideology of the 'good mother' serves as a conflicting devise in relation to a woman's authenticity.

Thus, one problem for greater participation of women in leadership positions relates to what constitutes the most important societal role for a woman. This confusion leads to an ambiguity as to whether the role of leader is one that women should aspire to. In most societies, a woman's cultural 'strength' emerges as a result of her maternal role. The power of the maternal role is derived from bourgeois notions of the mother as the moral centre of the family. A woman's ability to lead within the public realm may be restricted by this emphasis on the private realm as the place where women excel. The notion of motherhood is in tension with common understandings of a successful leader. This is not least because there is still a strong societal belief in the mother as an altruistic character, an emblem of the servant leader that, as we saw in the previous chapter, Greenleaf identified as critical for the good of society. The problem with self-sacrifice is that it can work to the detriment of a woman's ability to see herself, or be seen as, worthy of leadership within the public realm. This powerful image of motherhood may serve to limit the possibilities available to women.[5]

Many women hold different ideas about leadership, and the effect of gender in particular. We can turn to Arendt for a reductive way of thinking about women leaders. As I mentioned in the introduction, she didn't think the role of leader looked good on women. Having said that, however, Arendt demonstrated leadership qualities. Yet she did not self-identify as a leader, because her traditional views of womanhood served to contradict the image of herself as being one. Arendt's public statements alert us to a significant problem that still exists for many women, which is whether it is appropriate for them to become leaders within a public arena at the expense of their private life.

Societal ideas regarding gender roles serve to influence and restrict how we think about women's leadership. Furthermore, by ignoring how women lead in diverse contexts, for example, through their church, volunteer experience or home management, we ignore experience that is important to society as a whole. If there is only one place whereby leadership counts that is, the work environment, then women are always going to be seen as lagging behind. Moreover, when women leaders are perceived as exceptional, they will be judged as different to the vast majority of women. This is a problem for gender parity since if some women leaders are perceived as exceptions, then it is unlikely that the gender hierarchy that currently exists is likely to change. Unless we move away from the great man (or woman) thinking about leading, we are unlikely to change the firmly embedded gender stereotypes in society.

What is necessary, therefore, is a seismic shift in the ways in which society thinks about leadership. One shift is toward a relational approach to leadership. A relational approach to leadership allows a person to not only acknowledge, but learn from mistakes. Perhaps it is through an attention to relationships that combines a desire for equality and justice with mutual responsibility and care that we may work toward a different approach toward authenticity in leadership. By acknowledging contingency, as well as lived experience, we may be able to think further about the conditions for ethical leadership praxis.

Conclusion

In this chapter, I have illustrated some ways in which gendered expectations have a bearing on leadership. The stereotypes that pervade the ideological constructs of masculinity and femininity in society have an

impact on how we view leaders. I have shown how gendered expectations influence how we think about authenticity. Over the last
50 years, limited progress has been made in terms of gender equality,
and even in statistical terms, this change has stalled (England, 2010).
Although some women have made tremendous strides in terms of
workplace equality, when factors such as race and class are considered
we see how, for many women, pay equity is still a dream. One reason
for this lack of progress is that there is often a cultural lag between
changing ideas and how these ideas take root in society. Thus, it is
important to investigate some of the socio-historical reasons for why
gender injustice still exists.

In 1933, Arendt wrote a book review entitled 'The Emancipation of
Women', where she notes that although women were afforded the
same legal rights as men, they are not valued equally by society
(Arendt, 1994d, p. 67). This gender inequality is evident, Arendt
argued, not only in the fact that women receive lower wages, but also
because the professional woman often had primary care of her household and children. In her words, 'a woman's freedom to make her own
living seems to imply either a kind of enslavement in her own home or
the dissolution of her family' (p. 67). Arendt was astute enough to recognize that the gendered conditions of women's lives had a negative
influence on their ability to flourish in the public realm.

Gender socialization influences the ways in which we perceive
leaders and, in turn, affects our notions of what constitutes authenticity. We need to comprehend how the many skeins of social, political,
historical and cultural forces have a profound bearing on our thinking
about leadership. If, as I argue, gender prejudice is embedded in the
Western cultural imagination, then it may prove fruitful to turn to
history to see what effects gendered notions of authenticity had on
women's ability to lead. This will be the main topic of the following
chapter.

4
Enlightened Virtue

In a famous essay written in 1782, Immanuel Kant argued that it is only when a man is free to make his own choices that he can be said to be enlightened (pp. 58–65). In his opinion, 'enlightened' freedom was composed of three components: the ability to think for oneself; the ability to think from the standpoint of others; and, lastly, the capacity to think and act in concert with one's beliefs. In this chapter, I examine how Enlightenment ideas about freedom related differently to men and women, especially in regards to societal notions of authenticity and leadership. I focus on Western Europe, since this was where modern ideas surrounding authenticity were initially formulated (Taylor, 1991). In tracing authenticity's modern underpinnings to the emergence of bourgeois selfhood, I show how gendered notions of what constituted right conduct served to enhance men's freedom while simultaneously restricting women's agency.

During the Age of Enlightenment, gendered ideas concerning virtuous action served to instruct and divide the sexes. This is evident in a guiding bourgeois motif of the time that states 'the sons of reason should converse only with the daughters of virtue' (Colley, 2005, p. 23). The establishment of gendered notions of virtue was a way for bourgeois society to redefine its moral standards in opposition to their aristocratic counterparts, whom the former regarded as immoral. On the one hand, a man's virtue was exemplified by his character. On the other, a woman's social reputation was deemed as more important than her character. The effects of this gendered discourse regarding virtue, alongside women's economic dependency and lack of political and legal rights, served to constrain women's sense of possibilities. Whereas bourgeois man viewed himself as a relatively free agent within an increasingly competitive public realm, bourgeois woman became progressively more defined by her marital and maternal roles. This had the additional effect of restricting women's sphere of influence to the domain of the domestic, while men were able to develop a more expansive existence through the public sphere of action, ideas and adventure.

As the rights of middle-class men were being espoused, women's agency became ever more constrained by social conventions. These social conventions were underpinned by gender prejudice, as in the case of Rousseau's assertion in *Emile* that it was natural for women to obey men. One way that this female obedience manifested itself was through gendered ideas about caring. For women, caring for others, rather than the self, was regarded as the epitome of feminine virtue. Carefulness became the watchword for middle-class women, as they learned how important it was not only to be selfless, but also to ensure that any pretension to talent was kept quiet. For a woman to profess talent contradicted gendered notions of propriety, and was perceived as unbecoming. This dual legacy of obedience and selflessness affected adversely women's ability to see themselves, and be perceived, as leaders beyond the domestic sphere. It would be wrong to suggest that these social dictates proved wholly insurmountable, as there were women who were courageous enough to brave public censure and enter into public debate, but they remain the exception.

In tracing the routes of this gendered discourse back to the Age of Enlightenment, we see how ideas about what constituted authenticity for men and women evolved differently, partially as a result of the social, legal and political restrictions on women's lives. By examining gender through a historical lens, we see how ideas about masculinity and femininity are produced, reproduced and transformed in different situations (Scott, 1999). Furthermore, this historical understanding helps to shed light on the cultural antecedents of present-day thinking regarding gender, authenticity and leadership. Phenomenologically, by looking to the past I want to demonstrate how time and place affect a societal understanding of authenticity and gendered subjectivity. In particular, looking to history helps us to comprehend how gender roles were conceived of in particular ways, and to consider the effect on women's leadership.

In discovering the historical links among gender, authenticity and leadership, I compare the work of different Enlightenment thinkers to obtain a deeper understanding of the gendered discourse of virtue. I focus on the cities of Paris, London and Berlin, because much of the theorizing about authenticity and bourgeois ideas about gender roles was initially formulated there. After briefly laying out some pertinent historical information, I discuss Montesquieu's *Persian Letters*. This book represents a veiled critique of the French court, and is an exposé of social hypocrisy. Through his description of a changing Parisian society, Montesquieu illustrates how, due to the vagaries of modernity, people's social roles have become more fluid than in the past. This fluidity produced an increased level of anxiety with regard to whom one could trust. Then I turn to Denis Diderot's withering critique of Parisian society. In *Rameau's Nephew*, Diderot captures some contradictions implicit in a moral versus immoral perspective on society.

Next, I consider the work of Jean-Jacques Rousseau, whose ideas herald a new way of thinking about authenticity that places an emphasis on a gendered self. For instance, in *Emile*, he argued that 'everything that men and women have in common belongs to the species, and [that] everything that distinguishes them belongs to the sex' (Rousseau, 1979, p. 358). His theoretical justification for a gender dichotomy was to have a major influence upon notions of authenticity. Put simply, what constitutes authenticity for a man was his strength of character. For a woman, conversely, it was the opinion of others. In effect, a woman's role was performative – that is, she had to act in what was considered to be a virtuous manner. Therefore, a woman's claim to authenticity depended upon the approval of others, whereas a man's claim to authenticity was determined by his self-belief.

After the section on Rousseau, I consider what happens when the Enlightenment dictum to 'think for oneself' runs contrary to social mores. This predicament emerges when women attempt to speak out against gender injustice. Here, I examine the leadership of two women whose action on the political stage was thwarted by societal dictates regarding female virtue. The first leader I discuss is Mary Wollstonecraft, who was regarded as notorious because of her outspokenness and perceived lack of moral decorum. The second example of female leadership is provided by Olympe de Gouges. During the French Revolution, she fought against the establishment of a political system that espoused liberty while, at the same time, restricting access for women to the political sphere. Both exemplify the gender paradox that occurs when women take up the Enlightenment maxim to think for themselves.

Any woman courageous enough to cross the gender divide was regarded in one of two ways. She was either treated as a figure of scorn, as exemplified by Horace Walpole's (1795) epithet 'hyenas in petticoats', indicating that Wollstonecraft's action was unbecoming of her sex. Or she was regarded as having a masculine mind and, therefore, different from other women. This was the case with Olympe de Gouges, whose critics labeled her as a male woman (Scott, 1996). Identifying her acts as masculine was an attempt by her detractors to discredit Gouges by implying her action was unworthy of her sex. What becomes apparent is that whenever women were brave enough to risk public censure, they were accused of acting in a manner inappropriate to female conduct. This gender prejudice had a negative effect on women's ability to speak and act in the public realm that, according to Arendt (1958), is crucial to freedom.

Although gender is an important factor, there are other identity characteristics that have an influence as to how a person's life may be negatively affected by social prejudice. Later in the chapter, I examine the life of Rahel Varnhagen, whose desire for social assimilation was stymied because of ethnic and religious prejudice, as a result of her Jewish identity. Here we will see how social prejudice can have a profound influence on a woman's ability to be who they are within a given context. As a result, a person's ability to engage in an authentic manner is limited due to social prejudice and discrimination.

I also contend that eighteenth-century notions of authenticity cannot be understood without considering the effects of social hypocrisy. The social realm that emerged during this time was, for Arendt (1958), a sphere of inauthenticity, because social dictates encouraged the standardization of human behavior. Rather than the agonistic nature of the Greek *polis*, which she regarded as a genuine space of appearance because citizens were able to enter into dialogue and debate, in the eighteenth century, different mechanisms were adopted to contain the full range of opinion. First, public debate was suppressed by the strict censorship enforced in France and Prussia in an attempt to contain political and social alternatives in favour of the absolute rule of the monarch. Second, the tyranny of social decorum privileged assimilation over the outward expression of differences of opinion, and encouraged hypocrisy. These mechanisms worked to suppress individual freedom.

In exploring issues relating to authenticity within a Western historical context, there are two interconnected threads that are worthy of attention. First, eighteenth-century commentators expressed concern regarding what they perceived as a divergence between being and appearance, that is, the gap between what is and what seems to be. Second, the rapid changes taking place in society led to confusion and anxiety over whom one could trust. Whether a person was or was not who they said they were became of increasing concern as traditional roles altered. The notion of authenticity emerged as a way to counteract this changing situation (Trilling, 1972). But the problem is that authenticity was defined in a prescriptive manner that negates individual freedom.

During the Enlightenment, ideas about freedom fomented social and political dissent. Yet while the ability to speak and act was touted as fundamental to enlightened freedom, for the majority of the population, access to the public sphere was denied. Through political and legal means, freedom was restricted to the fortunate few, that is, men of property. Moreover, one of the harmful legacies of the Enlightenment was that people conceived of equality in abstract terms (Arendt, 1965). This abstract way of thinking had a negative effect on anyone who did not conform to the ideal notion of the citizen. Herein lies some of the contradictions associated with eighteenth-century ideas regarding equality, understood as sameness. Instead of being regarded as a unique entity which, for Arendt, is a necessary component of the full expression of human existence, people were regarded for what they were, something that Rousseau and Wollstonecraft railed against, albeit in different ways.

As I pointed out in Chapter 2, a person's social role is but one component of what constitutes an individual. It is the sum total of a person's experiences, together with identity characteristics such as race, class and gender, that make up who we are. Today, we recognize how a person's social and cultural possibilities can be negatively shaped by prejudice. Although economic and social disparities make a difference as to how a person may experience the world, in the eighteenth century, these social distinctions often went unnoticed because they were not regarded as important. A classic example, as Arendt (1965) notes, is that while the Founding Fathers in America debated what constituted equality of rights for citizens, it rarely occurred to them to ask those whom they saw every day about what they thought. I am referring here to members of the working poor, slaves and women. The reason why these people's views were deemed irrelevant was because, unlike propertied men, they had no political and few legal rights. Since this is a large topic to which I cannot do justice, I omit important aspects such as ideas of empire and slavery from this discussion. Instead, I concentrate on the gendered discourse of virtue and its influence upon cultural ideas concerning gender, authenticity and leadership.

To begin, I offer an overview of some socio-historical changes taking place in Europe at this time, and their effect on the emergence of new ways of thinking about morality and gender roles.

Changing values

In 1750, London was the largest European city with 750,000 inhabitants, while Paris was the second biggest metropolis with approximately half a million inhabitants (Sennett, 1974). In London, many middle-class inhabitants benefited from the wealth amassed from increased trade and commercial expansion. For the fortunate few, there was an increased luxury in terms of the quality and quantity of goods available. As a consequence of their new wealth, the middle class enhanced their social status and, over time, political legitimacy. With this greater prominence in society, the middle class began to redefine the notion of good taste. For example, rather than the large banquets of the past, smaller social gatherings became popular. These more intimate gatherings complemented the increased emphasis on good manners and sociability, especially through polite and witty conversation, as we will see later in our discussion of the salon.

As well, scientific discoveries began to challenge traditional ways of thinking as did new religious sects. In England, along with Protestantism, sects such as the Quakers and Methodists, placed an increasing emphasis on the relationship between the individual and God. Religious belief, increasingly, became seen as a private affair between man and his Maker, rather than something to be regulated by priests. In short, conventional values were challenged by changing scientific and religious discourses, which placed more emphasis on individual self-knowledge and evidence-based inquiry. These changes brought about the erosion of a sacred hierarchy and the fragmentation of traditional roles (Lindholm, 2008).

Increased social mobility, as a result of urbanization and economic expansion, led to a greater anxiety regarding whom one could trust. Judging a person's integrity, or lack thereof, became more difficult as social roles became less well-defined. The desire for authenticity arose out of a perceived need for greater sincerity in social relationships (Trilling, 1972). This search for authenticity was both a response to the vagaries of modernity and a way for the middle class to distinguish their moral standing from that of the aristocracy, whom they regarded as irreligious and immoral.

These bourgeois notions of morality were intrinsically connected to beliefs about gender differences. For example, the idea that middle-class women had a heightened, or more refined, sense of morality than their aristocratic sisters began to take shape, and was to have a profound influence on a woman's ability and desire to go against social norms. For women, individual action was curtailed by what was deemed appropriate social behaviour, with the result that, as Chris Roulston (1998) notes, the Enlightenment quest for self-knowledge was not 'who am I, but rather who must I not be' (p. 187).

In addition, a concern with role-playing became commonplace as observers noted how eighteenth-century city life in Paris and London resembled a stage. We see the phenomenon of role-playing emerging through the eighteenth-century fascination with masquerades, as well as the enthusiasm with which the body was perceived as a mannequin to be adorned with exotic costumes (Sennett, 1974). This fascination with role-playing was also apparent in the increasing appeal of the theatre. Indeed, the ability for an actor to transform himself into a character was regarded with wonder by the *philosophes,* such as Diderot. He was fascinated by great actors, because of what he regarded as their exceptional ability to distill the essence of human feelings. But not everyone shared Diderot's enthusiasm for the theatre. For example, Rousseau (1960) saw theatre as having a corrupting influence since it encouraged artifice, which, he maintained was contrary to the proper, moral values of the emerging middle class.

Through this brief review of some emerging trends in eighteenth-century Western Europe, we begin to see how economic expansion resulted in social and political changes. As a result of these transformations, the aristocracy began to lose its prominent place in society to the middle class, whose increasing wealth gave them a greater say in political affairs. In the next section, I examine how three writers – Montesquieu, Diderot and Rousseau – chart these changes that were affecting social life in France.

Montesquieu

The early 1700s was a period of social unrest in France. At this time, France was primarily an agrarian society. As a consequence of Northern Europe's mini ice-age, there was a series of poor harvests that led to a devastating famine in 1707, and a peasant revolt (Hufton, 1995). This revolt was quelled forcibly by government forces, who offered little assistance to those most devastated by the famine. This seeming disregard for the plight of the poor on behalf of the King and his government was to have major repercussions later in the century.

Until 1715, France was ruled by the conservative monarch Louis XIV. Together with the Catholic Church, the Monarchy used censorship as a method of controlling the spread of radical ideas, making it difficult for writers to disseminate their work. In contrast to France,

England had entered a period of scientific and artistic revitalization. Following Louis XIV's death, the new Regent, Philippe d'Orléans, instigated major changes in French society. Being an Anglophile, he wanted to bring a new spirit of learning to France so as to encourage artistic and scientific advances. As part of his desire for cultural change, the Court moved from Versailles to Paris, which became the centre of intellectual activity in France (Kahn, 2008).

One of the first eighteenth-century writers to explore the connection between the artifice of Parisian social life and its effects on human nature was Baron de Montesquieu, especially in his epistolary work, *Persian Letters,* first published in 1721. Through his comparison of two different locations – Parisian society in the early 1700s, and the fictional depiction of a Seraglio in Persia – Montesquieu shows how social pretensions negatively influence human behaviour. He contrasts the static environment of the Seraglio, where everyone's life is controlled by their fixed roles, with that of the fluidity of Paris, which is regarded as a place of transformation, not just of society, but also of the self.

Montesquieu's main characters are two Persian visitors, the tyrant Usbek and his servant Rica, who act as dispassionate observers of Parisian society, which they find lacking in moral substance. In their letters, they comment on the differences between the Parisians they meet, and their own society. In particular, they note the discrepancy between what people say and how they act. In one letter, Usbek comments: 'I see people here arguing endlessly about religion; but at the same time they seem to be competing over who can observe it the least' (p. 56). What Montesquieu highlights here is the difference between what people profess to believe in, and how they actually behave. In another letter, Rica describes how, when dressed in his Persian costume, he was the centre of attention. Adorned in Parisian garments, however, he is ignored by the people who had previously found him so fascinating. Reflecting upon this situation, Rica asks: 'if clothing and manners make the external man will the inner man change to follow suit?' (p. xvii). In questioning the relationship between a man and his outward appearance, Montesquieu asks his readers to think about how the way a person's looks may have an effect on their assumed moral attitude. He shows us how appearances can be deceiving. For example, at a dinner party, Rica overhears two men conspire on how they can appear witty by laughing at each other's jokes. Similarly, in highlighting the false manners of a young woman, Rica states her gravest concern is not to enjoy herself, but to appear as if she is having a good time (p. 148). What becomes apparent to the visitors is an inconsistency between people's actions and their intentions. Montesquieu seeks to draw the reader's attention to the superficial nature of French society, and how what we perceive on the surface may not be the same as what is.

The Persian visitors also express their disapproval of the profound social inequalities they witness. For instance, Usbek observes that for one man to lead the life of an epicure, a hundred others must work to satisfy his indolence. Yet while he makes disparaging comments as to the inequalities in French society, he refuses to examine the inequalities that exist in his own culture. Usbek also expresses disdain at what he considers to be the shamelessness of Parisian women. Because of these women's perceived lack of propriety in dress and decorum, Rica quips that Frenchmen hardly ever talk about their wives, as they are afraid to speak of them in front of men who may know them better (p. 72).

Allusions to the promiscuous behaviour of women in French society are juxtaposed by the apparent modesty of the Seraglio women. Although his wives write declaring their undying love for him, the longer Usbek remains in Paris the more he exhibits anxiety that they might not continue to obey him. He gradually comes to the realization that a society based on obedience is devoid of genuine relationships. Yet this knowledge affords Usbek little enlightenment, since he is reluctant to change the social order in Persia, even though his power affords him little contentment. To demonstrate concern for his people would mean altering the power structure, something that Usbek will not countenance. Instead, he prefers to rule by force, even while acknowledging that this tyrannical behaviour results in his increasing isolation from others.

Paradoxically, through sharing information about the different ways that women act in Paris, Uzbek's wives gain the courage to revolt against their servitude. When he learns about the anarchic disorder in the Seraglio, Usbek is especially distraught that his favourite wife, Roxana, has committed adultery. In her last letter to him, Roxana explains that she has chosen to commit suicide, rather than await Usbek's punishment. However, before she dies, Roxana wants Usbek to know that her expressions of love were false. Roxana informs him: 'How could you suppose me so credulous as to believe that the sole purpose for my existence was to adore your caprices?' (p. 213). Although she appeared obedient and loving toward Usbek, she felt the opposite. Roxana adopted a loving persona because it allowed her some level of autonomy. She further insists that her mind remained independent, even under the guise of her submissiveness. Here again we see the difference between being and appearance which, as previously stated, was a common motif in eighteenth-century writing.

By contrasting the world of the Seraglio with that of Paris, Montesquieu wants us to recognize that these societies are similar in that both are dependent upon the dictates of the ruler. In the fictional Seraglio, each person has a fixed role, subject to the rule of the Potentate, Usbek. In France, we see that public opinion oscillates, according to the whims of the ruler or the fashion of the times. In either case, Montesquieu suggests that when people acquiesce to a leader's desires, or to the dictates of social conformity, they risk losing their capacity to think for themselves and, concomitantly, compromise their freedom.

Societies which refuse to offer people freedom are tyrannies not only for the slave, but also for the master. Hence, there can be no freedom for the ruler or servant in a hierarchical relationship. It is only by overturning the social order that master and slave can achieve autonomy. Therefore, Montesquieu intimates that it is natural for oppressed people to want to revolt. While *Persian Letters* is a satirical observation of the social mores that existed under the Regency of Philippe d'Orléans, it can also be read as a political allegory. As such, the wives' revolt in the Seraglio serves as a metaphorical illustration of what might happen when a group organizes to defeat the social order. In the end, Montesquieu's work was prescient since, like Usbek's wives, French people rose up against autocratic rule and social repression in the Revolution of 1789.

Montesquieu makes us aware of two different kinds of tyranny: first that of autocratic rule and, second, that of social conformity. In the fictional Persia, Usbek reigns through force, while in Paris rule is maintained through coercion. Arendt (1958) describes both types of society as pre-political since rule by force or coercion serves to suppress dialogue and dissent, and serve to limit personal autonomy. Thus, the potential for genuine relationships is constrained by what she called 'the no-man rule of society' (p. 40) and that of autocratic rule, which are merely mirror images of each other. Thus, autocratic rule and social conformity function to restrict the fullness of human relationships.

For Arendt (1958), then, bourgeois capitalism led to social conformism. This conformism was encouraged by the Enlightenment desire for an abstract notion of equality that, in turn, resulted in a denial of difference. Instead of dialogue between competing views, we see the move towards a social order where everyone is encouraged to behave in a similar manner. One reason for this standardization was the rise of what Arendt (1958, pp. 38–46) describes as the social realm. With the introduction of what she terms 'the social', aspects of what were previously deemed private concerns now appear in the public realm. In her view, the bringing of private concerns into the public realm had a negative influence on the ability of people to excel. This bourgeois privileging of conformity works to suppress excellence in favour of uniformity. When excellence fades from political life, Arendt argues, what is left is a desire to standardize behaviour that served to deny the full range of genuine, human expression in favour of artifice. Another problem with social conformity is that it encourages hypocrisy and cynicism. We will explore this next.

Diderot

What constituted virtuous action as opposed to artifice was a topic of great debate in the eighteenth century. For instance, the *philosophe* Denis Diderot argued that it was the task of the artist to illustrate how vice is evil and virtue attractive (Tancock, 1966). In his satire *Rameau's Nephew*, we see how virtue is explored through opposing viewpoints, that of the virtuous man and the charlatan. The virtuous man is called Moi (me), while Lui (him) represents a literary manifestation of selfishness. (Diderot's playful use of the terms 'me' and 'him' in this context alerts us to how often we assume that it is the other person, rather than ourselves, who is corruptible.)

Published posthumously, *Rameau's Nephew* is ostensibly based on a conversation between Diderot and Jean-Philippe Rameau, the nephew of a famous court musician (Tancock, 1966). This conversation allegedly took place during the summer of 1761 when Rameau was dismissed from his position as sycophant at the house of Bertinhus because, rather than lying – his usual *modus operandi* – he chose to tell the truth.

Each character espouses an opposing opinion on virtue. On the one hand, Lui argues that the good life is about self-enjoyment, obtained through wealth and prestige. For Moi, on the other hand, virtuous living is defined through one's relationships with others, which are far more important than social status or material goods. Their different perspectives lead these characters to disagree on most topics. One example is their heated exchange regarding the value, or lack thereof, of Socrates dying for his beliefs. Moi contends that the judges erred when putting Socrates to death, thus demonstrating not all legal and ethical pronouncements stand the test of time. Lui disagrees vehemently, declaring that Socrates' willingness to die for his principles was a futile act. Risking one's death in order to show one's moral superiority is a spurious act, he argues, because it is life which is our most valuable treasure. What matters most, Lui contends, is to be rich and successful. Therefore, a man should adopt whatever means necessary to obtain his desires, regardless of the cost to others. Although Moi concurs with Lui that life's pleasures are wonderful, he argues that there is an intrinsic difference between happiness and virtue. A virtuous life is preferable, Moi states, because acting morally and caring for the welfare of others is more fulfilling. Yet, in Lui's opinion, such virtuous conduct is downright dull. Moreover, he derides the notion that there can be a singular notion of the good, which he regards as an eccentric idea, common among philosophers, but irrelevant to the demands of eighteenth-century society. Instead, being immoral is the way to get ahead. Lui justifies his sycophantic behaviour as being socially apt, stating: 'Supposing virtue had been the road to fortune, either I should have been virtuous or I should have simulated virtue as well as the next man. But people wanted me to be ridiculous, and so I have made myself that way' (p. 83). How Lui appears to others, therefore, is dependent upon the role people want him to play. In commenting upon his role-playing, Lui remarks: 'I say to myself: Be a hypocrite, by all means, but don't talk like a hypocrite' (p. 82). In adopting diverse personae to suit the situation, Lui maintains that he is not being duplicitous; rather he behaves in keeping with social convention. In his view, only the King does as he desires. Everyone else is just posing.

Although Diderot depicts Lui as a man without scruples, he is also portrayed as an astute observer of social mores far more so than his moral counterpart. For example, in their debate on education, Moi declares his intention to teach his daughter ethics. Lui scoffs at Moi's proposed plan, asserting that ethical instruction is pointless for girls because it is only their attractiveness that counts. In a society where beauty has more cachet than virtue, Lui contends it is training in the art of seduction that is a more useful education for young women. He argues that, if you want your children to succeed, you must offer them a modern education, which means instruction in the art of deceit. Thus, Lui is proud of how his son has developed into 'a thief, a waster and a liar' (p. 108), because his progeny possesses all the right qualifications to get ahead in society.

In *Rameau's Nephew*, Diderot illustrates how, in a society based on self-interest, what passes as virtuous behaviour may actually be its mirror opposite. Paradoxically, it is the person who is able to see through social pretense, and use this knowledge to his own advantage, who may offer us a deeper understanding of human nature. As such, it is the man who is attuned to deceit, not the honest individual who is more likely to succeed in society, because the virtuous person fails to comprehend sufficiently how others may be tempted by vice.[1]

Diderot's work is instructive because he shows us the shallowness of social pretense. One reason why social pretense was so manifest in French society was because rulers like Louis XV preferred the nobility to engage in petty intrigues, rather than allow them to take an active role in affairs of the state (Arendt, 1965). These courtly intrigues fostered an atmosphere of deceit that pervaded society, and encouraged hypocrisy.

In her exploration of hypocrisy, Arendt (1965) notes that the Greek root of 'hypocrite' is play-actor (p. 99). She tries to ascertain why so many eighteenth-century writers remarked on the problem of hypocrisy. After all, Arendt argues, hypocrisy seems a much lesser evil than, say, violence. In reflecting upon this matter, she comments that the problem with hypocrisy is that it is the one human failing that obscures integrity and the development of genuine relationships. Hypocrisy leads us astray in our judgements, since those who profess honest motives may hide dishonourable intentions. Arendt further argues that an emphasis on virtue is also problematic since it can transform people into hypocrites (p. 93). For Arendt, a hypocrite is overly ambitious in that he does not only want to appear virtuous to others, but has to convince himself. But as no-one can be completely sure of their motives, the belief in the certainty of one's virtuous actions can lead to devastating results, as we will see later. Moreover, when we unmask a hypocrite, Arendt maintains, this unmasking may destroy the deception, but does not disclose anything authentically appearing.

Rousseau

Arendt (1958) argued that the eighteenth-century writer who most exemplified the contradiction between authentic intent and inauthentic action was Jean-Jacques Rousseau. He was convinced of the need for virtuous action so as to counteract the negative effects of competitive society. While Montesquieu and Diderot celebrated the liveliness of Paris, Rousseau detested the polite veneer of Parisian society because,

he argued, the superficial façade of polite society masked the fundamental prejudices that existed. Rousseau especially disliked the rich
aristocrat who, he insisted, was corrupted by vanity. In *Emile*, he
declared the rich were 'pitiless and hard toward all the rest of the
world' (p. 510). The social inequalities between rich and poor were
entrenched, not only by the former's wealth, but by how they regarded
the latter with disdain. The poor were not perceived as individuals, but
as a homogenous, expendable group. As such, the polite façade of
French society served to mask the social inequities that existed.

Rousseau contended it was only those who had known suffering who
could fully understand the plight of others. For example, in his
Confessions, he wrote about his alleged mistreatment while under the
employment of the Comtesse de Vercellis. As her secretary, Rousseau
felt judged 'less by what I was than by what she had made me' (p. 83).
Echoing an earlier sentiment expressed by Montesquieu's character,
Rica, Rousseau notes that, in Parisian society, a person's station was
seen as the marker for their self-worth. Yet he was adamant that social
status was no indication of moral worthiness. The problem was that
social inequality was firmly entrenched in the fake morality of Parisian
society. Wherever falseness is the social norm, Rousseau argued it is in
each man's self-interest to be a dissembler.

In *The Social Contract*, Rousseau argued there could only be genuine
relationships when all men were equally free. As with Montesquieu, he
reasoned that neither the position of master nor slave enabled a man
to be autonomous. Therefore, it was each man's duty to rebel against
this unnatural state of affairs by refusing to don the mask imposed on
him by society. By pledging allegiance to a State, rather than a specific
leader, he argued men could ensure their equality. In uniting individual will with the public will of all, Rousseau maintained that moral
freedom would be realized. In making this argument, he differentiated
between man in nature and man in society. For Rousseau, man in
nature is neither virtuous nor corrupt. Although man can be happy in
his natural state, he argued that man can only be a moral being if he is
a member of a society.

The problem was that the competitive nature of Parisian society
encouraged inauthenticity. As a consequence, true intimacy was
debased because, instead of developing loving relationships, which
Rousseau maintained was necessary for virtuous conduct, people
engaged in superficial affairs. Furthermore, while society could offer a
person of means innumerable examples of beauty and taste, each new
desire, instead of bringing satisfaction, created a greater sense of

anxiety. It was only by recognizing the reasons why this anxiety occurred that, he suggested, it might be possible for people to recognize the superficiality of their existence. In order to gain a more authentic way of life, Rousseau asserted society must change.

One way that Rousseau envisaged a just society being developed was through a re-consideration of the role of women. Through their maternal role and virtuous natures, he argued that women could provide a civilizing counterforce to the competitive nature of men. Thus, what was needed to encourage human flourishing was not just reason, but sensuous reason. The way to obtain this delicate balance between the sensuous and reason was through moral education.

Yet the appropriate education Rousseau proposed for boys and girls was demonstrably different. For instance, in his discussion of moral education in *Emile*, Rousseau described how, rather than learning through competition or being taught by rote, a boy must learn through experience. With this personal knowledge, a boy could learn to judge for himself, and guard against falling prey to the prejudices of others. In so doing, a boy would be able to realize his full potential. Moreover, Rousseau argues that if a boy was taught how to be flexible, then he would be better able to deal with changing circumstances while, at the same time, sustaining their core identity. A girl's education was diametrically opposed to the instruction that Rousseau argued boys should receive, as his depiction of Sophie in *Emile* illustrates. Unlike her future husband, Sophie is offered little opportunity to develop her talents, other than through domestic knowledge gathered from her mother. These domestic skills were all a woman required, Rousseau maintained, for her proper place was to take care of the home and teach her children to be virtuous. Even when a woman had genuine talent, Rousseau contends that female modesty requires that she keep such talents unknown, since her glory came from her selfless devotion to her husband and children.

This notion of selfless action as integral to female virtue creates dissonance in that, for a woman to act authentically, she may have to go against society's dictates. In discussing the connections between virtue, authenticity and selfhood, Roulston (1998) highlights how eighteenth-century sentimental narratives, such as Rousseau's *Julie*, depict a character's desire for self-revelation as a departure from artifice. But this fictional self-confession is somewhat dubious, since the declaration is always influenced by the moral strictures of society. Rather than revealing a 'true' self, the self revealed through the language of virtue may be yet another form of masquerade (Roulston, 1998). Furthermore, this fictional portrayal of a feminine self who is self-sacrificing and obedient is intrinsically connected with bourgeois constructions of ideal gender identity.

Hence, femininity and authenticity serve as mutually reinforcing markers that restrict a woman's autonomy (Roulston, 1998). We see this clearly in Rousseau's (1997[1760]) famous novel entitled *Julie, or the New Héloïse*. This novel offers insight into the ideological prescriptions that accompanied emerging bourgeois notions of feminine virtue. The central character, Julie, is a young woman who has an affair with her penniless tutor, Saint-Preux, and becomes pregnant. Although Saint-Preux offers to marry Julie, her father refuses to allow this marriage to take place because he perceives Saint-Preux as socially inferior. Caught between the opposing dictates of familial duty and her desire, Julie asks her lover to comprehend the hopelessness of her predicament. Social propriety tyrannizes young women, she argued, since they are not allowed to show their true feelings. Instead, it was incumbent upon a young woman 'to be false for the sake of duty, and lie for the sake of modesty' (p. 173). In short, the dictates of social decorum encourage falseness that, in turn, negatively affects a woman's autonomy.

Julie's ability to do as she wishes is restricted by the dual constraints of society and familial duty. Since her father will not allow her to marry the man she loves, Julie acquiesces to her father's request to marry his friend, Baron de Wolmar. Together with her new husband, Julie creates what appears to be an idyllic community called Clarens. In this community, each spouse takes on a part emblematic of Rousseau's ideal gender roles. Wolmar's role is that of the stern, rational patriarch, while Julie plays the part of dutiful wife and benevolent matriarch. In doing so, they act in compliance with gender expectations. However, this ideal community is not quite the idyll it seems on the surface. For example, the servants at Clarens are hired as young children because the Wolmars believe that their lack of knowledge of society will make them more obedient. From the day these young children start work at Clarens, they are not allowed to visit their families. Instead, the Wolmars act as their parental overseers. Additionally, to maintain order at Clarens, each servant is encouraged to spy on her fellows. When servants do wrong, they are punished in one of two ways. Wolmar reprimands them in a cold, rational manner; his stern admonishments are designed to maintain control. Julie takes a different approach to punishment; she reproaches the wrongdoer by taking away her love for them. Although the servants may fear Wolmar, they are emotionally distraught at the notion that Julie may cease to care for them. In playing out their roles as stern patriarch and reproachful matriarch, they personify ways of leading that Rousseau saw as conducive to their gender.

At Clarens, Julie endeavours to be the paragon of middle-class female virtue. She is a faithful wife to Wolmar, and loving mother to her children. Yet it is only by sublimating her desire for Saint-Preux that Julie is able to play the part of virtue (Roulston, 1998). Some years following their marriage, Wolmar invites Saint-Preux to visit them so that he can see how virtuous Julie has become. During this visit, Wolmar decides that Saint-Preux should become the tutor of their children. Julie is vexed at her husband's decision, which she perceives as a way for him to exercise his control by forcing her to be in close proximity with her ex-lover, while maintaining appropriate decorum. Writing to Saint-Preux, Julie explains that she does not want him to live at Clarens, as she is concerned about what might transpire. But Saint-Preux pays no heed to Julie's warning, since he is delighted that Wolmar regards him as having the moral fortitude to resist temptation. But Julie starts to question whether her virtuous life may have been as rich an existence as she had previously thought. Her growing anxiety results in a questioning of her choice to forego sexual desire in favour of marital duty. Shortly after writing this letter, one of her children falls into the lake, and Julie jumps in to save her child. Although she is not seriously injured, Julie's health starts to deteriorate. Rather than continuing to live a life of masquerade, and the constant tension between duty and desire, it appears that she chooses to let herself die.

This novel was to bring Rousseau tremendous fame as his depiction of Julie connected with female readers across Europe. On the one hand, his novel served as a moral tract that maintained it was a woman's duty to be selfless. As such, a woman's personal desires must be sublimated in favour of her submission to her husband and adoption of the maternal role. On the other, in his sympathetic portrayal of Julie's plight, Rousseau illustrates the ethical dilemmas regarding the sublimation of passion, and the limitations of a virtuous life. What Julie wants is to be the paragon of female virtue that society demands. But her personal desire is at odds with her wish for social conformity (Berman, 1971).

Rousseau's study of Julie reveals the contradiction between a woman's ability to express desire, and the need to keep in line with gendered expectations of a virtuous woman. These societal expectations serve to hamper the expression of authenticity in favour of conformity. His concept of authenticity thus highlights the imbalance between a person's outward conduct and their innermost desire. Hence, Rousseau demonstrates the contradictions with gendered aspects of appearing authentic to others. In doing so, he points to the complex nature of authentic engagement.

Alessandro Ferrara (1998) argues that Rousseau's conception of authenticity is multi-faceted, because it is composed of three interconnected threads: sincerity, autonomy and intimacy. First, sincerity is the avoidance of being false; second, autonomy means acting in accordance with one's ethical principles; and finally, intimacy in relationships is necessary to foster personal authenticity. Although an ethics of autonomy tries to contain these inner deviations regarding them as unworthy and undignified, an ethics of authenticity recognizes that these deviations originate in emotions and feelings. What is important about Rousseau's notion of authenticity, then, is that it is derived from genuine action, founded on sincere relationships.

Yet, as the fictional experiences of Julie illustrate, genuine action is difficult – even for fictional heroines – because it is necessary to repress personal desire to submit to social dictates regarding what is considered proper for a woman. Hence, there is an inherent paradox in Rousseau's sense of authenticity as inner truth, and his insistence that a woman pay heed to her reputation. His work is paradoxical because, as Lisa Disch (1994a) observes, Rousseau's insights into authenticity are thwarted by his belief that it was a woman's reputation rather than her character that matters.

Rousseau's assertion that the opinion of others was more important than a woman's own conscience serves to undermine the Enlightenment maxim that it was critical to think for oneself. In the eighteenth century, it was only masculine minds that were judged to have the capacity to reason. Women, by contrast, had to conform to social standards concerning appropriate conduct, even when this meant deviating from their own conscience. Although a man was encouraged to have the strength of character to speak out, a woman was obliged to adhere to society's dictates, even when they went against her beliefs. Because a woman was perceived as unable to reason like a man, these social rules were regarded as more important than her own conscience. This gender prejudice was something Mary Wollstonecraft sought to challenge.

Mary Wollstonecraft

In *Vindication of the Rights of Woman*, Wollstonecraft declared that the ideal feminine self that Rousseau wrote about was designed to keep women in a subordinate role. *Contra* Rousseau, she maintained it was a good conscience that should serve as an indicator of a woman's rightful place in society. Wollstonecraft further argued that when women are treated differently from men, this created an environment where false morals rule, leading to social hypocrisy. These gender distinctions served to 'corrode all private, and blast all public virtue' (p. 288). Only a revolution in manners and education could, according to Wollstonecraft, bring about human progress in the manner that the Enlightenment *philosophes* desired. For such progress to take place, gender prejudice needed to be counteracted through rational debate.

Although Rousseau maintained that women should be educated to please men, Wollstonecraft contended that being educated in this way offered them little opportunity for the development of reasoning skills. Consequently, women would never have the same abilities to reason unless they were afforded better education. Moreover, she disagreed with Rousseau's assertion that the extent of a woman's aspiration was to be obedient. It is not the passive, submissive woman who makes an ideal partner, Wollstonecraft argued, but a woman who is willing to be a friend to her husband, as well as teacher to her children.

As well, Wollstonecraft railed against the double standard whereby aristocratic women with influence in society insult other women's character, while continuing to indulge in their own illicit liaisons. Not only is this hypocrisy morally wrong, Wollstonecraft contended, it encouraged a superficial assessment of a woman's character. What was needed was a new moral sensibility that would herald opportunities for women to achieve their full potential. The establishment of 'true sensibility' would encourage a more caring attitude towards others.

Although Rousseau stated that without virtuous women there could not be a virtuous society, Wollstonecraft demonstrated how his ideas were contradictory. For example, she disagreed with Rousseau's argument that the female mind was distinct from that of the male mind. These alleged gender distinctions were not natural, as he maintained, but a result of the restrictions society placed upon women. While many regarded the cultivation of a woman's mind as inappropriate, Wollstonecraft maintained that if women's education continued to be limited, this would be a problem for society as a whole since, without their full participation in public life, it was unlikely that enlightened attitudes would flourish. She argued that it was vital for women to speak out against societal ills. Otherwise, the pervasive false morals would never change. Moreover, as women were the educators of their children, Wollstonecraft contended that their lack of knowledge would set back the cause of progress for society as a whole.

Without alterations to the social, economic and political order, Wollstonecraft contended, women would never be able to reach their potential. Her argument represents a radical critique of social mores that reworked Rousseau's insights into the nature of authenticity, with a political argument for women's rights. She demonstrated the negative effects of living in a morally corrupt society, as well as highlighting the potential for change. Wollstonecraft wanted to carve out a broader social and political role for women. By transforming society into one based on reason and virtue rather than superficiality and artifice, she argued that men and women could participate equally to improve human existence. If a nation wanted women to be good citizens, then, alongside political representation, women needed to receive a liberal education on par with men. This meant the eradication of the notion that the only purpose of female education was to equip a woman for marriage (Hufton, 1995).

Wollstonecraft's views about female education were not commonly shared. Rather it was thought that educating young women to participate in public affairs was unnecessary, since their future responsibilities lay in the private realm. As a consequence, there was great disparagement shown towards women like Wollstonecraft who engaged in intellectual pursuits. Such intellectual endeavours were perceived as inappropriate for their future roles as wives and mothers. Akin to Rousseau, most educators in England argued for a clear distinction between how middle-class girls and boys should be taught. Boys were given instruction that would help them prepare for the demands of a competitive society. Engaging in competitive activities was seen as preparing boys for their future careers. However, educators regarded boisterous action as unsuitable for young women, since it was assumed that a girl's delicate nature would be harmed by competition (Cohen, 2006). As in France, the main instruction that middle-class girls received was how to become a dutiful wife. This supporting role, reinforced by political and legal restrictions, encouraged women to be submissive, rather than to take the initiative and lead. Simply put, men were taught how to take charge while women were instructed in how to be selfless. Neither of these gendered modes of instruction was likely to bring about an enlightened society.

Olympe de Gouges

I want to turn now to explore the life of a French woman who, like Wollstonecraft, was willing to speak out against gender injustice. Olympe de Gouges was a playwright, courtesan and working-class woman who actively worked for social change, especially during the initial events of the French Revolution. She sought to expose the contradiction with the notion that it was natural for men to be leaders, while it was unnatural for women to do so (Scott, 1986). Gouges argued that dividing humans into two groups made no sense as each human being displayed both male and female qualities. To illustrate her point, she described herself as a courageous woman, as well as a timid man. In playing with common ideas about gender roles, she highlighted the hypocrisy of denying women a voice in the political realm. As a result of her action, Gouges was branded a male woman. Although this was intended as an insult, she regarded this label as proof that a woman could reason just as successfully as a man.

Like Wollstonecraft, Gouges maintained that a nation could not be deemed virtuous when it denied political representation to most of its people. If human progress was desired, then she argued it was essential that all people were given the opportunity to share their ideas as to how to improve society. Gouges used the platform of speeches and petitions to put forward ideas about women in politics. In *Declaration of Women*, published in 1791, for example, she argued that social and political change in regard to women's rights was necessary if the Revolution sought to bring about a just society. If the Age of Enlightenment was to be the Age of Reason in fact rather than in theory then antiquated notions of gender roles needed to be changed. Women were not just a homogeneous group, Gouges contended, but distinct individuals who had the ability to think for themselves. By arguing that women could have an active, rather than a passive imagination, she undermined Enlightenment distinctions regarding what constituted the proper roles for women and men. It was only by promoting equality for all that a virtuous society could be attained, yet this was the kind of incendiary idea that proved unpopular with the new political regime.

Freedom from the tyranny of Louis XIV did not herald liberty for all. When the Jacobins took control of the National Assembly under the leadership of Robespierre, those who dared to disagree with the will of the Nation were branded as traitors to the Revolutionary cause. Gouges' statements became increasingly inflammatory as she railed against the Jacobin government, asserting there was no logical reason to deny women political status and legal recognition. But her arguments held little sway in the new constitution. And when Gouges declared it would be better to live under a benevolent monarch than under the new Republic, she had gone too far. In 1793, Gouges was arrested, imprisoned for treason, and guillotined.

The suppression of voices like Gouges was emblematic of what become known as Robespierre's Reign of Terror. In *On Revolution*, Arendt (1965) argues that his tyrannical leadership was, in fact, a terror of virtue, and a reaction to the lack of concern for the plight of the people, as demonstrated by Louis XIV's autocratic rule (pp. 90–94). She differentiates between Robespierre's rule of terror and institutional forms of terror which, as we will see in the next chapter, are distinctive of totalitarian regimes. Arendt states that Robespierre's reign began in good faith. Things went awry when, inspired by Rousseau's political philosophy, he put the cause of virtue above all else, as demonstrated through his compassion for the *malheureux*. Robespierre's rule became tyrannical as his search for truth and the rooting out of hypocrisy took hold. By trying to unmask hypocrisy, and bring the suffering of the masses to light, Arendt contends it was rage rather than virtue that appeared on the political stage. Those who tried to put forward alternative perspectives were singled out, and declared traitors to the Republic. By speaking out against gender oppression, Gouges was just one of many casualties of Robespierre's 'virtuous' leadership.

For Arendt, one of the key aspects necessary for the flourishing of society is the ability for citizens to act and speak freely. But absolute goodness, like absolute evil, can be devastating to the political realm, since leaders who are utterly convinced of their beliefs cannot be persuaded otherwise through dialogue and debate. What Robespierre's leadership meant for the French Republic was the suppression of plurality in favour of the one voice of the State. Anyone who tried to go against the monolith of the State was regarded as an enemy. In addition, those women who tried to take on a public role in Enlightenment politics faced humiliation and danger. They risked their reputations and, at times, their lives to gain a voice on the political stage.

Wollstonecraft and Gouges are examples of eighteenth-century women leaders who tried to change gender prejudice in society through political action. In their desire to be heard, they exemplified Arendt's (1958) notion of virtuosity, in that they had the moral courage to try and alleviate gender injustice. Although both women fought valiantly to change the social order, their ability to do so was thwarted by their lack of social status. Now I want to look at the actions of some women who were better placed in society to take a leading role, that is, the salonnières.

The salon

The eighteenth century created new opportunities for people to meet and share ideas. As the century progressed, there was a flourishing of public spaces. Public life was enriched by discussion in different venues. What was distinctive about the bourgeois public sphere, according to Jürgen Habermas (1994), was that it represented the sphere of private people that came together as a public. Each European city had diverse examples of these new public spaces. For example, at the height of their popularity, London had 3,000 coffee houses, each with its own regular patrons (Habermas, 1994, p. 32). Discussions were wide-ranging, and included topics from art to politics. In the majority of coffee houses, however, unlike that of similar places in the past such as inns, women were refused entry. As a result, they were unable to take part in these public conversations. This lack of female voices contrasts sharply with that of another eighteenth-century phenomenon, the European salon.

Salons emerged in France during the seventeenth century and were to flourish throughout the eighteenth. Most salons were located in Paris and were run by upper-middle-class women. For a short period, the salon flourished in other European cities, notably Berlin. Most salons allowed for a mix of people such as prominent artists and intellectuals, as well as members of the aristocracy. In France, the salon created a public venue for writers to circumvent the strict censorship. Because *philosophes* like Diderot had no political voice, the salons became the civil working space of the Enlightenment (Goodman, 1994, p. 53). These spaces provided an intimate venue in which authors could test their ideas publicly. Women played a leading role in organizing salons. Some prominent salonnières include Madame de Staël (1766–1819) and Julie de Lespinasse (1732–1776), whose guests included the *philosophes*, D'Alembert and Diderot. But not every guest was happy with women's dominant roles in the organization of the salon. In his 'Letter to D'Alembert,' for example, Rousseau despaired of how, due to rules of social etiquette, men were forced to pay attention to women. Such behaviour was demeaning to men, Rousseau argued, since false gallantry was emasculating. His negative assessment of the salonnières was partially because he regarded women's presence as an impediment to the vigour of masculine discussion. Although Rousseau regarded the rarified atmosphere of the salon as restrictive to debate, Dena Goodman (1994) contends that the salonnières created intellectual venues for the dissemination of ideas. Furthermore, the women who ran them were highly intelligent, and exhibited that flexibility of tongue that Rousseau believed gave women an edge in conversation, albeit not in intellect. Clearly it wasn't that women did not possess intellectual prowess but that gender notions of propriety meant there was a limited number of public venues where they could express their views.

The expression of one's viewpoint is a critical component in the ability to flourish in society. Indeed, the Enlightenment privileged thinking for oneself as the most important thing an individual could do. But Arendt (1974) reminds us that a person who is 'liberated by reason is always running head-on into a world, a society, whose past in the shape of "prejudices" has a great deal of power' (p. 10). In what follows we shall see how one woman's life is overshadowed by ethnic and gender prejudice.

The inauthenticity of assimilation

During the period 1780–1806, Berlin salons provided a popular venue for the aristocracy and middle-class intellectuals to mingle (Hertz, 1988). One of the most popular Berlin salons was run by Rahel Levin, a Jewish woman. Central figures of German Romanticism, such as Friedrich Schlegel and Friedrich Schleiermacher, were frequent guests at Rahel's salon. Visitors were impressed not only by her sensibility, but also by her intellect. One admirer described Levin as the most intellectual woman on earth (Hertz, 1988, p. 258). Admittance to her salon depended on a person's ability to behave like 'a cultivated personality' (Arendt, 1974, p. 60). Intimate thoughts and actions were shared within this close knit group of the Berlin intelligentsia who joined together in their desire for a new way of life. People put aside differences in social and ethnic status in favour of scintillating dialogue between like-minded acquaintances within the sheltered world of the salon.

However, the flourishing of the salons in Berlin was a short-lived affair. Following the defeat of the Prussian army by Napoleon in 1806, life in the city was to change dramatically. In particular, Jews were no longer welcome in Prussian society. Previous acquaintances began to ignore Rahel Levin, who despaired of her isolation from society. To combat the risk of becoming a social outcast, she changed her surname to Robert, and told her brother that the Jew must be extirpated from us (p. 130). It was only through the erasure of her ethnic identity that Levin felt able to regain her place in society. After several unsuccessful love affairs, Rahel married August Varnhagen, a match that enabled her to return to polite society. Her husband enjoyed moderate success as a diplomat. In 1813, Rahel Varnhagen joined him in Prague where, for the first time, she experienced a sense of belonging because people regarded her as German, rather than Jewish. Paradoxically, Rahel Varnhagen felt more at home in Prague than the place of her birth, since her ethnicity did not wholly define who she was. Upon their return to Berlin, the Varnhagens hosted a new salon, and established a Goëthe cult. At last, Rahel Varnhagen had acquired her twin goals of rank and marriage, but she found herself discontent. As the wife of a government official, her role was to be her husband's appendage. Rahel Varnhagen realized that she had sacrificed freedom for the sake of social acceptance. Social assimilation had not afforded her the expansive existence of which she had dreamed.

What Rahel Varnhagen was capable of, and what she was able to accomplish, was restricted not only by her gender, but also by her ethnicity. Rahel Varnhagen's desire for social acceptance motivated her to renounce her ethnicity, and live her life pretending to be someone other than who she was. It was only toward the end of her life that Rahel Varnhagen began to regard her Jewishness as something integral to her sense of self, and not something of which she should be ashamed. It was through her acceptance of her Jewish identity that Arendt argues Rahel Varnhagen was finally able to find peace with the world. She did so by recognizing the absurdity of a social framework whereby hypocrisy and prejudice were allowed to flourish, at the expense of a more humane society.

In exploring the ethnic and religious prejudice that existed in Prussian society at this time, Arendt points to the naiveté in which the Jewish intelligentsia sought to assimilate into a society that – for the most part – despised them. An indication of this ethnic prejudice is that Jews were only allowed to work in certain occupations, such as money-lending or the law. The only way for a Jewish person to become accepted socially was to be regarded as an 'exceptional' Jew. One person who made this transition was the philosopher, Moses Mendelssohn. He regarded Jewish assimilation as a logical extension of Enlightenment ideals of progress and equal rights. Mendelssohn argued there was no rational reason for such rights not to be extended to Jewish people. Assimilation was a good idea, he contended, since ethnic prejudice would be lessened when Jews demonstrated what upstanding members of society they were. The trouble with Mendelssohn's argument is that being accepted into society as an exception to one's ethnicity forces a person to reject an integral part of who they are (Arendt, 1974). By forcing someone to integrate by denying their birthright is damaging to the flourishing of human society because it destroys individual uniqueness in favour of social conformity.

Arendt (1974) points to the ethical dilemmas that ensue when people try to assimilate into a society that despises them. She despairs of the political naivety that encouraged people like Rahel Varnhagen and Moses Mendelssohn in their belief that social assimilation was an adequate response to prejudice. She maintains that the human cost demanded of assimilation is too high a price to pay for giving up one's heritage because, in doing so, a person has to give up something of herself. For Arendt, it is the only the social pariah who is able to remain true to their ideals. There is value in being on the margins of society because marginalized people are able to 'instinctively discover human dignity in general long before Reason has made it the foundation of morality' (p. 214). What is critical is not merely going along, but encouraging a more inclusive acceptance of the rights of different people to be who they are. Such inclusive acceptance is, I suggest, what authenticity means for Arendt.

Furthermore, Arendt (1958) notes how self-absorption became a dominant motif of the move toward Romanticism in the late eighteenth century. She viewed the Romantic preoccupation with inwardness as negative because in this focus on the self, there was a shift from the shared concerns of the public realm that had been so important to Enlightenment thinkers. This concern with personal authenticity, and the psychic harmony of the self was to the detriment of an engagement with the world (Benhabib, 1995a, p. 113).

Conclusion

In this chapter, I have considered how ideas about authenticity were influenced by gender and ethnic prejudice. (I have concentrated on the former since the following chapter will focus on the latter.) In the eighteenth century, notions of propriety, together with educational differences, defined feminine ways of behaving in contrast to masculine ways of acting. Gender differences about what constitutes right conduct had an effect upon how authenticity and selfhood were conceptualized and experienced. These gendered notions of virtue worked to enforce particular kinds of female behaviour, such as obedience and submissiveness, which had the negative effect of constraining women's belief in what they could accomplish. Dena Goodman (1994) sees a correlation between female timidity in the eighteenth century and Iris Marion Young's (1990) contention that nowadays women lack trust in their abilities. A lack of self-belief is partially a response to social dictates that encourage women to be submissive, rather than to lead.

In the Age of Enlightenment, authenticity was related to gendered ideas of virtue. Social wisdom decreed that the opinion of others was more important than a woman's own sense of self. There were tremendous barriers that affected women's ability to think of themselves as leaders, which stems from societal beliefs that women should obey their fathers and, later, their husbands. When obedience is perceived as integral to a woman's sense of self, a willingness to take a leadership role is likely to feel uncomfortable and may induce anxiety. Being authentic, according to Arendt (1958), depends upon our willingness to express ourselves in words and deeds. However, the gendered nature of social life barred women from seeing themselves as uniquely able to do so. Although there were exceptions, as my discussion of Mary Wollstonecraft and Olympe de Gouges demonstrates, nevertheless, when a woman has been inculcated to believe that her foremost duty is to be obedient, it will be more difficult for her to obtain the courage to express herself within the public sphere.

Bourgeois ideology privileged some bodies over others. It encouraged middle-class men to view themselves as unique individuals and to participate actively in public life, while limiting a middle-class woman's sense of self to her private role/s as daughter, wife or mother. Thus, the Enlightenment sets up a paradox in terms of gendered notions of freedom and authenticity. For male citizens, new ways of thinking about freedom engendered an open attitude toward their potential possibilities. Conversely, for the majority of people without political rights, the public realm was experienced in a very different manner. Women who tried to break through such gender barriers were held up to ridicule. If authenticity is connected with one's ability to think and speak for oneself, then being ridiculed may negatively affect a person's wish to actively participate in public life. Furthermore, if freedom and human excellence derive from being able to be seen and heard in the public sphere, as Arendt maintains, then being unable to take a commanding role in the public arena will have future repercussions, especially for women's leadership.

For many Enlightenment thinkers, the notion of authenticity was connected to ideas about freedom, not just in the sense of realizing one's own dreams, but also in the sense of envisaging social change. Enlightenment thinkers, as Charles Taylor (1989) contends, believed that rational individuals possessed dignity. Yet, for the most part, the Enlightenment motto: *Sapere Aude!* Have courage to use your own understanding, was thought not to apply to women since they were not regarded as rational, thinking beings (Taylor, 1983, p. 366). As a result, the restricted gender roles available to eighteenth-century women limited their opportunities for self-expression in the public sphere. While men were able to take up positions of leadership, many women who were just as eloquent and intelligent were denied that opportunity. In the Age of Enlightenment, gender prejudice served to limit women's potential for intellectual and personal growth.

Societal beliefs about appropriate gender roles influence ideas about authenticity. I suggest there are vestiges of these historical inequities regarding gendered roles in our current society in how we think about leaders, and the ways in which we may overestimate the talents of some while underestimating those of others. Prejudice toward women leaders is still embedded in the cultural imagination, and has ongoing ramifications in regard to notions of gender, authenticity and leadership.

We have also seen how ethnic prejudice may serve to deny a person's right to be who they are. The 'right to have rights' was fundamental to Arendt's belief in the flourishing of society (Birmingham, 2006, p. 1). In denying people the right to freedom, there is a danger that society may lose a sense of humanity. These ethical concerns will be the focus of the next chapter as we question how authenticity, in and of itself, can guard against unethical behaviour not only in leaders, but communities as a whole.

5
Authenticity, Ethics and Leadership

In this chapter, I explore whether authenticity, in and of itself, can guard against unethical conduct. My interest in this topic emerges from my discussions with research participants. For example, although most women leaders I interviewed regarded authenticity as important in regards to leading ethically, not everyone was convinced. One participant argued that the problem with management theories like authentic leadership is that they fail to account for the problem of a leader's 'dirty hands'. I want to address this issue of 'dirty hands' by considering how authenticity is connected to ethical action in leaders, and others.

In thinking through this issue, I turn to Hannah Arendt and Martin Heidegger. I begin with an overview of Heidegger's (1962) theory of authenticity, because his work is referenced by authentic leadership scholars, albeit in a perfunctory way (Algera and Lips-Wiersma, 2012). A deeper engagement with Heidegger's notion of authenticity could add conceptual depth to current thinking. However, my main argument here is that his conception of authenticity as resoluteness, or inner purpose, as it has been taken up by leadership scholars serves to privilege self over others. Resoluteness is but one of two ways that Heidegger conceptualizes authenticity, the other being care. The latter is of more value to the formation of ethically-inspired relationships. Indeed, the focus on a leader's resolute action may serve to cover over a deeper engagement with others.

Although Heidegger gestures toward the importance of relationships with his concept of *Mitsein* (being with), I argue his notion of authenticity is primarily self-oriented. Conversely, Arendt shows us why mutual responsiveness is central to an ethical stance. This responsiveness requires a willingness to engage with different perspectives to ensure our ethical intent aligns with our action. For Arendt, what matters most is that we take into account our responsibilities for one another. Hence, to act ethically is not necessarily about following social rules, but being prepared to take a stance against injustice. It is paramount to ensure that our actions are not only good for the self, but good for the world in which we live (Arendt, 1958).

I begin with a review of Heidegger's concept of authenticity, then show how Arendt re-envisages his ideas. In comparing these thinkers, I consider how a person's moral stance, and willingness to judge, can be negatively affected through the experience of living under a totalitarian regime. In this regard, I contrast Arendt and Heidegger's actions during the Nazi period in Germany. My contention is that his leadership action, during Heidegger's tenure as Rector of Freiburg University, points to a discrepancy between an authentic vision and an ethical responsibility toward others. Heidegger's (1985) vision was to radically overhaul the university system so as to counteract the scientific mindset that he argued was becoming predominant. However, he was so overly focussed on his authentic vision that his leadership actions proved to be an unethical response to the crises of the time. Thus, Heidegger's willingness to become involved with Nazism was partially a result of his single-minded obsession with a new university system based upon Platonic ideals. But his leadership demonstrates a failure of judgement.

Authentic visions, no matter how deeply felt, may be damaging when they do not sufficiently account for our responsibility toward others. By contrast, Arendt demonstrates courage and commitment in her willingness to fight against a totalitarian regime. In doing so, she highlights the difference between leadership, understood as a collective endeavour, and leadership as mastery.

Heidegger

In *Being and Time*, first published in Germany as *Sein und Zeit* in 1927, Heidegger's purpose is to comprehend the nature of being. By disclosing how we live in the world, he contends we may be able to ascertain the nature of existence. One problem he identifies is that metaphysical thinking has led us to misunderstand the nature of truth. As a consequence, there is too much focus on scientific evidence or theoretical proof. This desire for proof privileges that which can be perceived or measured, rather than what is. *Contra* metaphysical claims, Heidegger contends that the nature of being can only be understood if we consider the question of who we are, both existentially and ontologically. To comprehend the essence of truth, therefore, it is necessary to uncover what has been obscured by metaphysics through a hermeneutic, existential analysis.

Heidegger's account works on two levels. First, there is an investigation into the ontic, that is, surface phenomena. From these observations, he tries to discover what these ontic phenomena may tell us about a deeper, ontological structure. For example, by observing the state of anxiety, Heidegger argues we can obtain a glimpse of authenticity, which represents the phenomenon's 'ground' or ontology. In comprehending the meaning of anxiety, we might be able to comprehend authenticity more thoroughly. By doing so, we will be able to gain insight into the nature of being. That is, we may begin to understand what it means to exist.

A primary aim of Heidegger's phenomenological investigation into the nature of existence is to distinguish the subject 'I' and the 'who' of *Dasein*. The term *Dasein* is comprised of two German words: *sein*, which equals being, and *da*, which means there. By using the term *Dasein*, he wants us to recognize both the constancy of individual being, as well as the ways in which individual existence is influenced by the world. Heidegger juxtaposes the term *Dasein* with the terms 'the they', which refers to our usual way of being in the world. As well, he argues that by focussing on the self, metaphysical philosophers like Descartes failed to address the phenomenological question of 'who'. He contends that, although Descartes thought it was self-evident that 'I' was the same as *Dasein*, this is not the case. Rather, we need to comprehend how what we commonly think is 'I' is, in fact, a 'not I' (p. 152). To illustrate his point, Heidegger maintains that each of us has a core essence that remains constant throughout our lives, and this is what constitutes *Dasein*. The problem is that this core essence is usually covered over, since we live in the world, not as an authentic 'who', but as someone who fits in with others. As he states: 'For the most part I myself am not the "who" of Dasein; the they-self is its "who"' (p. 312). What this means is that most of our lives we act in accordance with the social conventions of the day. As a consequence, '[e]veryone is the other, and no one is himself, and this becomes my way of knowing the world and myself' (p. 165). For instance, we take up the opinions of others while believing each decision we make is our own. One reason why we conduct ourselves in this manner is that *Dasein* is fascinated by the world. It is due to this fascination with the world that we often act without thinking. For instance, we carry out everyday activities without stopping to think about them, and live our lives by compartmentalizing what we do. Such compartmentalization leads to a failure to understand, or even question life's overall purpose. The end result is that we lose our ability to comprehend fully who we are, since our distinctive identity is obscured by the 'they-self'.

This loss of individual agency ensures that people conduct themselves in an inauthentic way without knowing or, in some cases, caring. Such inauthentic modes of existence can be traced back to the phenomenon of instrumental reason, states Heidegger, and the manner in which humans perceive the world as a collection of things. In this instrumental mode of being, we fail to care about the world. For instance, in daily life, we encounter objects without noticing, and become oblivious to our surroundings. We may choose to check our cellphone for messages, rather than listen to the person who is talking to us. Or we might rush off to a meeting, failing to greet colleagues as we move toward our next assignment. Instead of caring about what is nearest to us, we constantly turn our minds to the next activity. Rather than being concerned with the present, we are always oriented toward the future. Ultimately, this leads to viewing the world as merely a means to an end. This instrumental approach to life encourages us to see people and things as objects to be used and discarded at will. If we wish to act in a non-instrumental manner, then we need to think about how our actions affect others. This requires us to recognize the importance of care.

Fundamental to Heidegger's (1962) argument is that Dasein's *Being* reveals itself as care. Through an acknowledgment of care, he suggests that we can begin to engage in the world in a non-instrumental way. For instance, rather than acting in an uncaring way, Heidegger maintains that we need to take a more open approach to the world. One way to do so is by tarrying with things. Such tarrying shows that we care about the world and one another. And this caring awakens us to the possibility of leading a more meaningful existence.

In his investigation, Heidegger distinguishes between authentic and inauthentic ways of caring. For example, an inauthentic form of care involves 'leaping in' and taking over from someone. In acting in this manner, we limit the other person's autonomy. Conversely, an authentic mode of care would be listening to someone's predicament without offering advice, and asking appropriate questions. This allows the other person to find their own solution to the problem. In short, authentic care means allowing others to be who they are, rather than trying to mould them to fit an ideal.

The term 'authentic' in German is *eigentlich*, often translated as 'ownedness' (p. 285), that is, a style of being that is peculiar to me. A difficulty arising from Heidegger's phenomenological investigation is that he uses 'authenticity' in different ways (Taylor, 2005). Sometimes he uses terms like 'inauthentic' or 'authentic' in a non-evaluative manner. Heidegger refers to this undifferentiated way of living as 'averageness' (p. 286). In the mode of averageness, we do not live our lives as either authentic or inauthentic; rather, we spend our time going along with others. Thus, our actions cannot be construed as either authentic or inauthentic, because this binary mode of thinking serves to ignore a third mode of being-in-the-world; that is, the mode of indifference (Taylor, 2005). The mode of indifference is not always bad, since there are activities that we undertake on a daily basis that don't require much forethought. Where it becomes a problem, however, is when we take up social conventions and never stop to think about what they mean. As a result of this lack of reflection, this mode of indifference can result in a lack of caring, and have damaging consequences, as we will see later.

Because we spend so much of our lives going along with others and the social norms that surround us, Heidegger argues that we forget or perhaps misunderstand, what it might mean to live in an authentic way. If we wish to live in a more authentic manner, we need to do two things. First, we must become resolute in our actions and, second, we need to become open to situations. It is worth noting that the German word for resoluteness, *Entschlossenheit*, has two meanings. The first meaning is to be decisive; the second is one of disclosing. These two aspects inform Heidegger's notion of authenticity. On the one hand, to be authentic in a Heideggerian sense requires an open attitude to others and to the world around us. This is the form of authenticity that we would define as care. On the other, authenticity necessitates a willingness to act decisively, and be prepared to stand up for those things that matter to us. Authentic action means aligning with those concerns that matter most, and dissociating from those that do not. It means being aware that to obey without thinking is to lose oneself within the maelstrom of undifferentiated existence.

In the previous chapter, we saw how, for Rousseau, authenticity was perceived in a positive way, as stemming from a willingness to resist social standards so as to seek a more genuine style of being. But this wholeness of being is not what Heidegger means by authenticity, because such a way of thinking ignores how existence is temporal (Taylor, 2005). Hence, the notion of being true to oneself, so often referred to by authentic leadership scholars, is not in alignment with a Heideggerian understanding of authenticity. One cannot 'possess' authentic leadership as in the statement, 'I am an authentic leader'. Rather, it would be more connected to an aspiration, in the sense that wherever possible we try to act in an authentic manner. From moment to moment, our ability to act in an authentic manner will depend upon the circumstances, the response of others, as well as our mood. Furthermore, while our intentions might be authentic, our actions may not be perceived as such by others. What constitutes a genuine style of being is not static, since each of us is influenced by different contexts.

For Heidegger, being equates with time because man's essence is grounded in existence. As such, being and time form co-determining ways of existing in the world. Hence, we cannot think about what it means to be authentic without accounting for how temporality influences existence. He argues that each moment of our lives is an amalgam of past, present and future. When we think about time, therefore, a residue of the past influences current thinking, such that previous knowledge and attitudes have a bearing on present situations. The present moment also includes the future, because we are always-already oriented beyond the present moment toward a future act. The problem is that we may be so focussed on the future that we overlook the present. We need to recognize that time exists in a sense of flux. Understanding temporality in this manner will allow us to better comprehend past actions, present circumstances and decide on future possibilities. It may also help us better understand the temporal nature of mood.

A critical component of Heidegger's phenomenological investigation is to comprehend how moods affect our way of being. He argues that our moods influence the way in which we live in the world. We are always in a mood of some sort, and this influences how things appear to us. Sometimes, we wake up feeling positive, on other mornings, we do not. Because of these changing moods, he argues we are not always in full control of how we feel or how we react. That is, moods colour our perception of events. Consequently, our moods influence the way that the world appears to us, and have an effect upon the way we respond to others.

Certain moods can make us feel uneasy. In the mood of anxiety, for example, we may begin to feel on edge, without realizing why. Phenomenologically, there is a profound difference between the moods of fear and anxiety, since Heidegger argues anxiety is not caused by anything specific. In contradistinction, fear has an object, that is, in the mood of fear, there is something, or someone, that is the object of our dread. Conversely, what threatens us in anxiety cannot be found in a specific place. Rather, the mood of anxiety reveals itself through a vague feeling that we may describe as uncanny. When this anxious feeling comes upon us, we may exclaim that we feel out of sorts, or we do not feel at home. Yet rather than trying to understand what is happening, people tend to dismiss these feelings as irrational. This is a mistake, states Heidegger, because these anxious experiences offer us insight into something valuable.

For Heidegger, anxiety represents the ontic manifestation of the ontological state of authenticity. Thus, if we describe the ways in which anxiety shows itself, we may obtain a heightened understanding about the meaning of authenticity. It is through what he describes as the *Augenblick* (anxious moment of vision) that we may be able to transcend our everyday, undifferentiated existence, and start to live in a more authentic way (pp. 367–368). In the mood of anxiety, we are awakened to future possibility. This is the mode of existence he refers to as resoluteness. In Heidegger's view, resoluteness represents the primordial truth of *Dasein*, because it is an individual response to the call of conscience. As he states, 'resoluteness as authentic disclosedness, is *authentically* nothing else than *Being-in-the-world*' (p. 348). Thus, what is most authentic to *Dasein* is a resolute response to the silent call that emanates from within. It is only in those intense moments when we recognize the inauthenticity of what we are doing that we obtain a glimpse of what it might mean to live a more authentic existence. But such an authentic way of being will differ for each person.

For authenticity to be unique to each person, Heidegger contends that the call of conscience must remain unsaid. To hear the call of conscience, therefore, it is necessary for each person to listen to her inner voice. However, the call's purpose is not to be critical, but to remind *Dasein* of its potentiality for being. This does not necessarily imply that we want to have a good conscience, but rather that we are open to receiving it. When the call of conscience arrives, it is often unexpected and, sometimes, unwanted. Moreover, it is possible for the call of conscience to be misinterpreted as the 'they self'. Nevertheless, the call of conscience is a vital component of authenticity as it is through this desire for a conscience that *Dasein* is able to realize its own potentiality.

Furthermore, it is only possible to live an authentic existence, according to Heidegger, when we come to terms with our own mortality. But facing up to our own death may be difficult, because people who talk about death are considered mawkish. Instead of accepting death's inevitability, he argues that 'the they' transforms anxiety about dying into fear. Such a refusal to accept death represents an inauthentic mode of existence, since it is only possible to face death authentically by owning up to its eventuality. Once we accept our own mortality, this enables *Dasein* to release itself from the illusions of 'the they'. Consequently, it is through coming to terms with our personal mortality that we can move toward a more authentic mode of being. Once we come to terms with our finite existence, we can begin to live in a more genuine way, recognizing that authenticity is not something that an individual possesses but rather something that they aspire toward.

I have discussed Heidegger's concept of authenticity as explicated in *Being and Time* in some detail because his work is referenced by authentic leadership scholars. However, we see that his notion of 'authenticity' is at odds with those looking for more quantifiable definitions. What is important to take from this discussion is that leaders, in aligning themselves with a particular way of thinking about authentic leadership, are not necessarily being genuine. From a phenomenological perspective, adhering to particular leadership characteristics or certain ways of acting does not constitute authenticity. Each situation must be responded to in its own way.

Having a moral script of leadership to follow may not enable leaders to be authentic; on the contrary, it merely encourages conformity to a particular model. In the following section, we see how Heidegger's themes resonate in Arendt's writing. She demonstrates some of the dangerous consequences that occur when individuals conform to social conventions at the expense of ethical relationships.

Arendt

For Arendt (1958), a person's unique identity is to be understood as both relational and embodied because each time we act and speak we do so within an already existent web of human relationships. She re-envisages Heidegger's concept of authenticity through her discussion of uniqueness and plurality. She fleshes out Heidegger's notion of *Mitsein* (being with) to show that human existence is inherently relational. Furthermore, Arendt rethinks Heidegger's concept of authenticity to show that it is natality, not finitude that is central to understanding existence. Natality refers to how, with each act, we insert ourselves into the world (p. 176). Each act is like a second birth since with our words and deeds we bring something new into the world. Her emphasis on natality stands in direct contrast to Heidegger's belief that it is by coming to terms with death that a person starts to realize her potential for authenticity.

In 'What is Existential Philosophy', written shortly after the Second World War, Arendt is harshly critical of Heidegger's work. For instance, she declares that the reason he adopted the term *Dasein*, rather than man, was to avoid a discussion of existential terms like freedom, dignity and reason. Arendt also argues the Heideggerian self is a concept that leaves the individual existing independent of humanity (p. 181). But a self without others is a meaningless concept, she maintains, since the essence of existence is that we live together within a common world. Furthermore, she contests Heidegger's claim that it is through a resolute acceptance of personal mortality and an inward contemplation that people gain access to authenticity. Rather it is through our actions that we show our love for the world.

Arendt (1971) contends that each of us has an innate desire for self-display. She distinguishes between self-display, which she sees as something beyond a person's control, and self-presentation. One reason why self-display is not the same as self-presentation is because appearances can be manipulated. If we think about this in terms of leadership, then we might consider how often leaders appear before the media with a carefully-scripted speech that suggests, on the surface, a particular identity that may be very different to their private personae. The problem as it relates to authentic leadership is that we never really know whether a person is being genuine or not. As Arendt states, 'appearance is by no means the outward manifestation of an inner disposition, if it were, we would probably all act and speak alike' (p. 35). What is crucial to recognize, therefore, is that how we appear externally is not the same as how we appear to ourselves. Rather than an internal, stable self, what we perceive are sensations. These sensations present themselves to us through our constantly changing emotions and moods.

For Arendt, it is our actions, rather than our intentions that matter. Consequently, it is our ethical responsibility to appear to others as we would wish to appear to ourselves. In other words, it behooves each person, if they wish to act ethically, to be consistent in word and deed. In an ideal society, each person would be recognized and respected for who, and not what they are. The problem in modernity, however, is that individual distinctiveness, understood as the ability to speak and act, is covered over by social prejudice. As I noted in Chapter 2, Arendt (1958) maintains that we are inclined to focus too much on what a person does rather than who they are. In becoming a society of job-holders, she argues that we have lost a deeper sense of connection with one another. This lack of connection between people, together with a focus on the self, has led to an increasing alienation from the world. Moreover, the breakdown of communal ties allowed for the emergence of totalitarian regimes.

In the previous chapter, we saw how Enlightenment thinkers were disturbed by how people might act in a manner contrary to their real intentions. That is, writers expressed concern regarding how being and appearance may not be the same. But Arendt (1971) contends that whenever we appear in the world, being and appearance coincide. Hence, there can be no two-world theory that contrasts the depth of being with the surface of appearing. This is why she maintains that scientists and philosophers are in error in their relentless search for the truth behind mere appearances, for it is not possible to move beyond the boundaries of perception to the inner sanctum of truth (p. 26).

Moreover, Arendt was critical of the Enlightenment's stress on equality because it was viewed in an abstract fashion, which offered little respect for difference. An emphasis on equality, understood as sameness, is not conducive to plurality, because it is based on an abstract way of thinking about human relations. For Arendt, human flourishing is dependent upon the ability for each human being to exist in an environment that allows both equality and distinctiveness to appear. In modernity, however, human distinctiveness is covered over by abstract notions of equality that led to standardized ways of behaving. Such conformity can be dangerous for those who are not perceived to be in compliance with social dictates. If a person refuses to conform, this may result in isolation and loneliness. In extreme situations, adherence to a particular conformity may threaten the social fabric to such an extent that humanity itself is threatened.

I have shown how Arendt's work builds upon and, at times, contradicts Heidegger's approach to authenticity. For Heidegger, as we have seen, authenticity arises out of a resolute determination as well as a desire to care. For Arendt, authenticity emerges from speaking and acting with others. In Arendtian terms, we might say that, to be meaningful, authenticity must stem from a caring commitment to the world of others. The way we demonstrate our commitment is through a willingness to play an active part in our communities. Furthermore, she demonstrates how important dialogue and dissent are for a society to flourish. But allowing for a plurality of perspectives runs contrary to some forms of leadership, as we will now explore.

The Leader Principle[1]

In Chapter 2, we saw how the separation of leadership into those who think and those who act brought about a hierarchical way of thinking about human relationships. One reason why such hierarchical thinking is damaging is because it led to the emergence of totalitarianism. Arendt (1951) perceives a connection between the origin of totalitarianism and nineteenth-century imperialism. She contends that empire-building has always been concerned with hierarchies of raced and sexed bodies. Arendt demonstrates how, in the nineteenth century, many democratically-minded European nations were complicit in the creation of race-based thinking. Chief amongst these was England's desire to create an empire based upon trade, no matter the cost to others. Nineteenth-century expansionist policies sacrificed others' lives for greed and profit. This instrumental way of acting, coupled with a complete disregard for human life, opened the way for totalitarianism to emerge in the twentieth century. In short, the destructive exploits of nineteenth-century imperialism led the way to the rise of totalitarianism.

In *Origins of Totalitarianism*, Arendt details the emergence of the Leader Principle, and connects this Principle to the willful destruction of pluralistic society. A significant feature of totalitarian rule is that the only person who takes personal responsibility for any act is the leader. Arendt sees this lack of personal accountability on the part of others as symptomatic of the failings of modernity. She maintains that totalitarian leaders like Hitler led in a different manner from a tyrant. One main difference is that although tyrants use people as scapegoats to maintain power, in totalitarian regimes, everything is based on the will of the leader. For example, in Nazi Germany, the *Fuehrerprinzip* (Leader Principle) decreed that Hitler's word superseded written law. In effect, this meant that Hitler was personally responsible for all official action. In practical terms, this resulted in officials acting as the living embodiment of the Fuehrer in obeisance to his every command. What happens when a Leader claims total responsibility in this manner is that it encourages a lack of personal accountability on the part of others. Moreover, because of this centralized power, it seems to the outside world as if the only person who knows what is happening is the leader. Thus, Arendt was in agreement with Hitler's statement that, without him, Nazi Germany could not exist.

A key problem with the Leader Principle is that these regimes undermine the public realm, since people feel under no compulsion to take responsibility for their actions. Many are at first willing, and later forced, to give up their personal freedom in favour of what seems on the surface to be the stability offered by strong leadership but is, on a deeper level, a breakdown of pluralism, and the concomitant destruction of the social fabric.[2]

According to Arendt (1951), it is not the totalitarian leader's personality that is most important, but his organizational skills. Thus, she disagrees with Max Weber's view that charisma is fundamental to leadership success. What matters is building an organization made up of individuals that are willing to carry out a leader's commands. Arendt observes that Hitler was able, prior to coming to power, to build a loyal following, whereby each follower was indebted to him. She regards this unquestioning loyalty by followers as central to a totalitarian leader's success, because it ensures that no matter what a leader requests there will always be someone willing to carry out the order. It is this absolute allegiance that is so dangerous to the health of society, since someone will always do what the leader requests, no matter how heinous the crime.[3]

What distinguishes a totalitarian state from other forms of rule is that totalitarian regimes are based on the Leader's infallibility (Arendt, 1951). But such infallibility is built upon fabrication. Lies are necessary so that people are convinced that the Leader is intrinsic to their future well-being. Moreover, the Leader's absolute command and total self-assurance seem to offer others a false sense of security. After the humiliating defeat Germany suffered following World War One, Hitler's leadership appeared to offer a positive alternative. Yet although many Germans admired Hitler's leadership, Arendt contends that most sympathizers did not know the full extent of what was taking place. Only the inner elite were apprised of the Leader's objectives. The naive followers expressed their loyalty to the Leader, while the elite carried out criminal activity in a cynical way.

Each totalitarian regime adopts a distinctive ideology to obtain its long-range goal of world domination. In the case of the Nazis, the vision was based on Aryan supremacy. Because the realization of world domination cannot take place within a single lifetime, what made Hitler able to retain power is that his pronouncements could not be defeated by rational argument. Factual truth is denied in favour of the totalitarian leader's vision, which is founded on lies and delusions. Whether the leader is morally right or wrong becomes irrelevant. Under such conditions, knowledge is disconnected from truth since claims to factual truth are no longer considered relevant. This inability for the average person to be unable to tell fact from fiction is, for Arendt, a key to the success of totalitarian regimes.

I have examined Arendt's thinking on the emergence of totalitarianism, and its historical antecedents to offer some context as to why totalitarianism emerged in the twentieth century. Now I want to turn to the question I posed at the beginning of the chapter, namely, how can authenticity guard against unethical conduct? After all, this is one of the major reasons why the concept of authentic leadership came into existence. To address this matter, I want to look at questions of judgement and personal responsibility as they pertain to ethical action.

Morality in dark times

In her essay 'Personal Responsibility under Dictatorship', Arendt reflects upon the controversy that ensued over the publication of her book on the trial of Adolf Eichmann. The controversy raised moral issues she had not anticipated. Briefly, Arendt's detractors argued she was wrong to judge Eichmann, since anyone might have been morally culpable under similar circumstances. Yet Arendt insists her critics are mistaken; what is more, judging is crucial to an ethical worldview. Without a willingness to judge, our world alters without us noticing. To illustrate her argument, Arendt describes how, when she was growing up in Germany in the 1920s, little attention was paid to moral issues because a person's ethical conduct was assumed. In retrospect, she sees this early moral disintegration in German society as a prelude to the abominations that were to follow.

During the 1930s and 1940s in both Germany and Russia, Arendt argues that established moral standards collapsed. She regards this moral decline as more heinous in Nazi Germany, because there was a tacit acceptance from all strata of society to accept a new way of thinking about morality. Controversially, Arendt contends that the true moral crimes were not carried out by the Nazis, who acted out of some perverted sense of commitment to Hitler, but by ordinary Germans who allowed the Nazis to destroy the social fabric. For Arendt, morality collapses when ordinary people choose to go along with a regime they should find morally repugnant.

The first people to accept a new set of moral values are often respectable members of society, thus demonstrating that polite society may not be the best judge of ethical standards (Arendt, 2003a). Another way this moral disintegration is demonstrated is that, at the moment of Nazi defeat, German morality changed once more. What the world witnessed, therefore, was a total collapse of a moral order not once but twice, which begs the question as to how it is possible for society to change its ethical standards so abruptly (Arendt, 2003a).

What this ethical disintegration reveals, she argues, is morality's true meaning as 'a set of *mores*, customs and manners which could be exchanged for another set with no more trouble than it would take to change the table manners of a whole people' (p. 43).

But, if we cannot turn to conventional, societal standards, then where should a person turn at times of crisis? According to Arendt (2003b), religious doctrine does not provide us with such an alternative. In Nazi Germany, religion proved of little assistance in guarding against moral failings, because a person's religious beliefs were perceived as a private matter. Neither can we turn to moral philosophy. Although moral philosophy may teach us how to act in times of peace, Arendt maintains it is not a sufficient guide in a crisis. The most reliable ethical guide at moments of crisis is the Socratic way of thinking, as it constitutes 'the only working morality in borderline situations' (Arendt, 2003b, p. 106). According to Socratic thought, the reason why it is better to suffer than to do wrong is because it is preferable to disagree with others, rather than be in disagreement with oneself (p. 90). From this perspective, the reason not to commit evil is because it would be impossible to live with oneself. This, in Arendt's view, is our best defense against evil.

Critical thinking: An ethical guide

Socrates did not provide his interlocutors with definitions or values to help them direct themselves into the future. However, what he did show us was that having debates about what constitutes justice, courage or authenticity is important (Arendt, 1971). Thus, Socrates demonstrates why critical evaluation of societal ideas is valuable. For example, when we examine concepts in a Socratic way, we see how thinking can undermine 'established criteria, values, measurements of good and evil, in short, those customs and rules of conduct we treat of in morals and ethics' (Arendt, 2003c, p. 176). Thus, what we previously believed to be true is challenged when we stop to question. As such, critical thinking helps us respond in a genuine way, because we are attempting to understand in our own way. By questioning our values and beliefs, we are able to respond in a more caring fashion to new events.

Arendt argues that too much concentration on action ignores a critical function of leadership, that is, reflection, or what she refers to as 'the stop and think'. In distinguishing between the thinking being and the acting self, she contends that when we act we take on a singularity of purpose, whereas when we think we engage in internal dialogue.

Thinking alerts us to the fact that we are what Arendt, following Socrates, refers to as the 'two in one'. In contradistinction to action, when we think, there is an interior dialogue that takes place between me and myself. Thinking enables us to understand, not in terms of knowledge, but in terms of meaning. The purpose of critical thinking, therefore, is to enable us to reflect upon our actions, and to ensure that our ethical intent is in alignment with our action.

The problem when we refuse to hold our beliefs up to critical examination is that we may cling to prescribed customs that are no longer relevant to the political and moral climate of our time. A further danger is that it becomes easier for someone to offer a new moral code that may be in no way ethical. Arendt maintains that 'If ethical and moral matters really are what the etymology of the words indicates, it should be no more difficult to change the mores and habits of a people than it would be to change their table manners' (p. 177). A leader may offer this new 'morality' without people really understanding its full implications. This is why it is so critical to question preconceived ideas about morality and ethics.

For example, there is often conflation among the terms 'ethics', 'morality' and 'authenticity'. (We see this in the authentic leadership literature as Smolović Jones and Grint (2013) have noted.) Phenomenologically, it is important to ascertain the different meanings of these words so as to understand their importance, especially in terms of societal regulation. By considering the etymological roots of these words, Arendt (1971) demonstrates how 'ethos' and 'mores' relate to societal notions of what was considered right conduct in Greece or Rome. What constitutes ethical action or moral behaviour will vary as different societies envisage what is appropriate conduct. The problem when we conform to ethical or moral customs in an unthinking manner is that when faced with a new situation, especially in times of crisis, our customs may not offer us the assistance we need. Thus, we need to constantly question received ideas about moral responsibility.

Responsibility and judgement

In reflecting upon questions of moral responsibility, Arendt (2003b) considers how different philosophers have thought about ethical conduct. For instance, Kant argued that it was necessary to have an imperative to keep the will (an individual facet that she argues was unknown to ancient Greeks) in harmony with reason. This is why he argued that inclinations, both good and bad, were temptations that led one astray. From Kant's viewpoint, people do evil things because of temptation. *Contra* Socrates, he argued that self-contempt was not enough to guard against immoral acts because a man can lie to himself. For Kant, moral conduct is an internal matter; this categorical imperative serves as a moral compass that helps individuals guard against human frailty. To obey the Kantian categorical imperative means to obey reason and, in doing so, remain in harmony with oneself. Indeed, Kant maintained it made no sense to say that a person obeys the laws of nature, since they had little choice. However, with moral law, each person is obligated to obey the laws of the land. When a person obeys the law of the land, he accordingly obeys himself. Yet, unintentionally, Arendt suggests, Kant divorced moral philosophy from religion when he argued that man, not God, was the basis for the law of morality. In placing the duties a man has to himself above those responsibilities he has towards others, this leads to a contradiction whereby it is love of the self, rather than love of others, that compels us to do right. The problem with this viewpoint is that it turns the self into the ultimate standard of what is morally good. As the self can lie to itself and others, it should never be the sole arbiter of morality. Instead, we must look for a more worldly and intersubjective activity, which Arendt argues exists through judgement.

Originally a theory related to aesthetics, Kant's notion of good taste serves as the foundation for the Arendtian notion of judgement. Arendt (1982) regards judgement as exemplary because of its intersubjective nature. Through the act of judging a person, she argues, we are able to expand our perspective to include the viewpoints of others. In judging, one must arrive at a potential agreement that will be in concordance with others. For that concordance to take place, we have to persuade others to our way of thinking. In order to do so, it is helpful to consider an issue from different viewpoints. Being willing to look at a problem from diverse perspectives is why Arendt viewed judgement as the most important human activity to ensure the flourishing of the social fabric.

Having the confidence to judge for ourselves is vital if we are to save humanity from totalitarian-like ways of thinking. Similarly, being prepared to disagree with the dominant viewpoint is critical if a person intends to take a principled and authentic stance. This is especially important in times of crisis where there is no moral guidebook to follow because each situation is unprecedented. In periods of moral upheaval, Arendt maintains it is neither heroes nor saints that are needed, but rather ordinary people who are prepared to speak out against injustice.

For Arendt, an individual's personal quality constitutes their 'moral' quality (p. 79), that is, the moral standard of the self. Yet she is adamant that this personal standard is not wholly sufficient. In addition to this personal moral stance, it is important that there be a moral standard of the world. To understand this more fully, we need to turn our attention to Machiavelli's famous dictum that rulers have to be taught how *not* to be good (Arendt, 1958, p. 77). Machiavelli recognized that what matters is not whether a person's conduct is good, but whether their conduct is good for the world. What attracts Arendt to Machiavelli is that his approach is always political, and, as such, always worldly. From his perspective, it would seem that, at times, wrongdoing is a necessary evil for leaders. Moreover, ethical decision-making is fraught with moral complexities that cannot always be fully understood in the moment. To return to the issue of dirty hands, it could be argued that there are times when a leader has to make decisions that may negatively influence others. Ultimately, what is important is whether a leader's conduct is good for the world. At all times, then, self and world must be taken into consideration if leaders wish to be ethical in their decision-making.

It may be that leaders cannot always choose an ethical path. Sometimes, it may be necessary to choose the lesser evil. But how do we guard against leaders committing evil on a regular basis? Is evil indicative of a lack of forethought? This is certainly the conclusion Arendt (1963) reaches in her study of Adolf Eichmann, where she argues that evil arises when leaders fail to reflect upon what they do. Rather than being radical, as Kant thought and Arendt contends, such evil is merely banal, and emerges from a selfish desire to put oneself first. She suggests that evil acts occur whenever there is an absence of thought. By contrast, when a person engages in thinking, she is grounded in memory. As a consequence, it is impossible for a thoughtful person to do evil because knowing that they have to live with themselves, there will be limits to what they do (Arendt, 2003a, p. 47). For Arendt, a lack of forethought demonstrates a failure to care. This is why she insists that limitless evil is possible only when reflective thinking is absent. Those who choose not to develop the capacity for reflective thought may lose their ethical moorings since they will not be able to reflect upon their mistakes, and make necessary adjustments. For example, without this ability to reflect, a leader may end up taking action that is harmful to others. Arendt (1963) underscored this fact in her study of Eichmann, whom she regarded as evil because of his thoughtlessness. The banality of evil, which she saw as Eichmann's signature, derived from his seeming inability to think about the effects of what he was doing and his refusal to take responsibility for his actions. In questioning Eichmann's thoughtlessness, Arendt asks whether it is thoughtlessness that is at the base of what constitutes evil. She concludes that this is indeed the case. As such, what becomes clear is that leaders must not only be able to act, but also be able to reflect upon their actions so as to ensure that they are responsible for their actions.

Arendt (2003b) insists that an ethical response concerns the individual in his singularity. She sees a correspondence between legal and moral issues, since when someone is brought to justice they always appear as an individual. In a courtroom, the answer that someone carried out an act because he was following orders is never sufficient, because it fails to answer the question of why that particular individual chose to respond in a certain way. But most Nazis brought to trial denied that there was anything personal about their actions, contending that they were merely following orders. This refusal to take responsibility for their actions is, from an Arendtian perspective, an immoral act. While many Nazi officers maintained it was their duty to obey, Arendt shows how a refusal to question a leader's orders will, over time, destroy a person's moral sensibility.

The Nazi fallacy about obedience can be traced back to the Platonic notion that a body politic consists of the ruler who commands, and the ruled who obey orders. In her view, obedience leads to a lack of personal responsibility. *Contra* Kant, Arendt contends that the word obedience has no place in a legal or moral framework. Rather, it is those who refuse to obey, and act out of personal convictions, who demonstrate true leadership in Arendt's view. Their refusal represents a willingness to take a stance and become personally involved in the public sphere. In contrast, blind obedience to a regime shows a lack of personal responsibility.[4]

In this section, we have seen how a willingness to judge is critical to a person's authenticity, especially in times of crisis. In totalitarian regimes, being willing to judge for oneself is necessary if the regime is ever to be overthrown. One problem Arendt highlights is how people went along with the Nazis out of some perverted sense of belief that this regime could bring about a fundamental change in society. But all this compliance did was to usher in a loss of humanity in the face of abject suffering for the Jewish people and other victims of the Nazi

Regime. The devastating changes wrought by totalitarian regimes work to suppress human flourishing in favour of a twisted ideology. This ideological worldview is connected to the Leader Principle, which valorizes one person's vision over the views of others. Such sovereignty negates the dialogue and debate that are necessary conditions of a healthy society.

The danger of authentic visions

Previously, I stated that Arendt's views on uniqueness and plurality are important to counterbalance notions of leadership that place too much emphasis on the self. As an example of her argument, it might be useful to consider Heidegger's unsuccessful attempt at putting his leadership vision into action. Briefly, in April 1933, he was elected Rector of Freiburg University. In his Inaugural Address, Heidegger stated that the purpose of the Rectorate was to provide spiritual leadership to students and faculty. He contended that the essence of a German university could only be revealed when everyone was committed to its mission. To realize this mission, the University needed 'leaders and guardians [who] possess the strictest clarity of the highest, widest, and richest knowledge' (Heidegger, 1985, p. 476). In keeping to a resolute stance, he argued a leader finds strength of purpose. He argued that a transformation of the university was needed so that students obtained the necessary discipline to serve their country. However, Heidegger was not given the opportunity to develop this new kind of university, because his leadership was to prove unpopular with faculty and students. In April 1934, Heidegger resigned from his post.

In describing his time in office, Heidegger (1985) states it was his vision for a different kind of university that propelled him forward, since what mattered was to return the German university to its true vocation. He regards his unpopularity as due to a disinterest in the minutiae of institutional life. Forging positive relationships was less important to Heidegger than establishing a modern university based on Platonic ideals. He maintains that his overriding purpose in becoming Rector was to instill his authentic vision onto the institution. Thus, Heidegger saw the Nazi movement as providing him with the potential to bring this transformation about. While Heidegger admits to being impressed with National Socialism, he explains his decision to join the Nazi Party was for the good of the university.

Heidegger's explanation and initial support of Hitler's regime suggests that he viewed the Nazi regime as offering strong leadership that was important to the well-being and destiny of the German people. Yet he severely misjudged Hitler's megalomania. As such, Heidegger shows a lack of judgement, which was made worse by his refusal to apologize for his act. Indeed, his actions, in support of the Nazi regime, led to him being banned by the Allies from university teaching for a time. One of his actions as Rector, in accordance with Nazi instructions, was to sign a letter dismissing all Jewish professors. This included his friend and mentor, Edmund Husserl. In a letter to Karl Jaspers, Arendt (1985) expresses anger at Heidegger's betrayal of Husserl. She contended that Husserl would have been indifferent if the letter had been signed by someone else, but because his former mentee had personally signed the letter, this proved to be a deep shock. For Arendt, Heidegger had a choice in that he could have resigned, rather than sign the letter dismissing his mentor. But Heidegger's belief in his vision was so strong that he seemed to have ignored how his actions could affect others. In short, he put resoluteness before care.

What Heidegger's disastrous foray into leadership suggests is that strong personal visions, when they do not take the world into account, can lead to self-delusion. This is why leaders cannot rely solely on self-knowledge as their guide. In his desire to promote his vision, Heidegger failed to take into account his own philosophical premise, namely, that caring is fundamental to an authentic way of being in the world.

Courage in action

In contrast to Heidegger, Arendt did not regard herself as a leader. Indeed, she argued that leadership was unbecoming to women (Arendt, 1985). Yet when we review her actions, before and during the Second World War, we see that she demonstrates courage and leadership. Although Arendt (1985) describes herself as apolitical at first, with the rise of National Socialism and the burning of the Reichstag in 1933, she argues it became impossible to remain a bystander. At the request of Kurt Blumenfeld, President of the Zionist Organization, Arendt began attending different events in Berlin, and reading journals to build a collection of what the Nazis were doing and saying. Because of this political activity, she was arrested. During her eight days in prison, she was interrogated repeatedly by a police officer. In order not to give herself or her comrades away, she made up stories. In the meantime, her Zionist colleagues obtained a Jewish lawyer to help her but Arendt decided to send the lawyer away because she trusted her interrogator. This turned out to be a wise decision on her part as charges against her were dropped. Released from jail, together with her mother, she escaped first to Prague, and later to Switzerland. From there, Arendt made her way to Paris where she was to spend the next eight years before emigrating to the United States.

In reflecting upon the Nazi period, Arendt states that what disheartened her most about what took place in Germany was the way that people co-operated with the Nazis. Her particular disdain for intellectuals arose from watching people she knew voluntarily step in line. Arendt argues that there is something about intellectual life that seems to encourage this activity. She states: 'I still think that it belongs to the essence of being an intellectual that one fabricates ideas' (p. 11). Some intellectuals actually believed in Nazism partly because they were trapped by their ideas. It is hard not to read a condemnation of Heidegger's actions in her comments.

Heidegger's authentic vision was so all-encompassing that it led him to forget his ethical responsibility toward others. Conversely, Arendt provides us with a deeper, more relational understanding of the way in which ethics, authenticity and leadership connect. Indeed, I argue that an Arendtian notion of ethical action is founded upon a commitment to others. We demonstrate this commitment, according to Arendt (1958), through promise-making and forgiveness. The reason why it is necessary to keep to our promises is because this is the only way to compensate for the vagaries of action. In terms of forgiveness, Arendt argues that although we can never forgive a heinous act, we can pardon the wrongdoer. Such acts of forgiveness are fundamental to the Arendtian notion of plurality, because they enable each of us to start anew.

Heidegger's lack of judgement in connecting himself with Hitler's regime makes it difficult to decouple his philosophy from his politics. Yet Heidegger's political failings need not outweigh his philosophical insights into the problems of metaphysics. By questioning the place of ethics in metaphysics, Joanne Hodge (1995) argues he opens up the possibility to rethink ethical relations.[5] An ethical investigation requires reflection on matters of genuine import such as personal responsibility and individual judgement. Although it is true that Heidegger shows how it might be possible to detach individual notions of what it means to be authentic from moral notions of right and wrong, it is Arendt who reveals why conventional ways of thinking about morality is potentially damaging to human relationships. I suggest, therefore, that Arendt provides us with an ethically enriched way of thinking about leadership.

Rather than focussing on the leader, Arendt (1958) demonstrates how leadership is a collective endeavour. She argues that the notion of the strong leader is a myth, since it is only through working with people that actions become accomplished. Although a person may experience a feeling of superiority from leading, Arendt (2003b) is adamant that leadership should not be identified with a role, but is context specific – that is, whenever a group converges, a leader will emerge (p. 132). As such, Arendt provides us with a more holistic approach to leadership that stands in contrast to hierarchical notions of leadership, based on a profound unfairness that serves to privilege the few over the many. Instead of concentrating on leaders as exceptional human beings, Arendt contends that it is courageous acts that are worthy of greatness. Accordingly, heroism means having the courage to take a stand publically. This is something that everyone is capable of, rather than the heroic few.

Arendt (2003b) further contends that a leader's success is dependent upon the assistance of others. Seen in this light, as we saw in Chapter 2, a leader is no more than *primus inter pares*, that is, the first among his peers (p. 47). Hence, it is not leadership *per se* that is dangerous to plurality, but leadership understood in the form of mastery. Furthermore, she regards power as productive, since it arises from the collective action of individuals joined together to fight a common cause. The problem is that we confuse the productive nature of power with the negative effects of violence. Power is always about potential that comes from joint ventures. Conversely, tyranny can arise whenever people are denied the basic form of political organization, that is, the ability to speak and act together.

For Arendt, then, successful leadership is about collaboration through dialogue and debate, rather than ruling through command and control. But too often the systems under which we live are not conducive to this kind of leadership. We have seen how spontaneity is suppressed when a society expects its inhabitants to conform. And, in certain circumstances, this conformity can be devastating since it is only when individuals are willing to take a stance against injustice that unethical leadership is likely to be contained.

Conclusion

In this chapter, I have compared the work of Hannah Arendt and Martin Heidegger in order to consider whether authenticity is a useful indicator of a leader's ethical responsibility. In addressing this matter, I have demonstrated how Arendt enriches Heidegger's concept of authenticity through her stress on uniqueness. Each person's uniqueness is crucial to an Arendtian worldview. Such uniqueness has always to be tempered by a commitment to take self and world into account. For Arendt, a world built around the self is insufficient to ensure that we care for one another, and can lead to a lack of genuine responsiveness. By contrast, uniqueness and plurality represent the ethical foundation of our intricate web of human relationships.

We have seen that authenticity may not be robust enough to enable leaders to act ethically. Part of the problem relates to the dangers in seeing one's own view of the world as absolute. For leaders to be ethically responsible, they must be willing to listen to dissenting viewpoints. Further, it is necessary to be willing to put forward a viewpoint even when it is out of step with society at large. At all times, we need to think about what we are doing, and be willing to take a stance. If we do not, as Arendt shows us in her depiction of the moral disintegration that took place in Nazi Germany, our environment may alter without us noticing. When the public arena starts to disintegrate, it becomes easier for people to refrain from taking a particular stance and behave as if they were no more than cogs in a machine. This is dangerous because it can lead to a lack of personal responsibility. In its most dire form, in totalitarian regimes, it results in the destruction of the common world.

Without a shared, common world, there can be no caring relationships. Arendt regards caring as a relationship between self and world, defined by our respect for one another which we demonstrate through our actions. An ethical approach as it relates to authenticity and leadership requires not just an internal sense of purpose, but also receptiveness towards others. Part of this responsiveness necessitates a willingness to think from different perspectives than one's own, as I hope to demonstrate in the last two chapters. Before then, I want to consider methodological approaches to qualitative, phenomenological inquiry.

6
Troubling Method

In the last chapter, I suggested that authenticity requires not just an internal sense of purpose, but also responsiveness towards others. Such a responsive orientation necessitates a willingness to think from different perspectives so as to enrich one's understanding. Arendt described this pursuit as 'thinking without a bannister', an activity that requires a person to move beyond the constraints of their own assumptions. As part of my attempt to 'think without a bannister', and enhance my understanding of the connections among gender, authenticity and leadership, I conducted a qualitative study. The purpose of this chapter is to explore my qualitative approach, which is in the tradition of existential, hermeneutic phenomenology, coupled with a feminist orientation.

I entitled this chapter 'troubling method' because I find distinctions between terms such as method, methodology and theory somewhat perplexing, as it is not always clear to me where one begins and the other ends. Although some social scientists distinguish between these concepts, as someone schooled in the humanities, I find it more difficult to make these distinctions. In thinking about this issue, I am concerned with how obtaining knowledge of a technique – in this case phenomenological methodology – informed my overall inquiry. Thus, troubling method is my attempt to comprehend how my feminist orientation may enhance or restrict phenomenological inquiry, and vice-versa.

As stated in earlier chapters, much of the scholarship on authentic leadership creates the impression of 'genderless' leaders, since it rarely addressing how a person's gender may have an effect on their leadership (Sinclair, 2013). Conversely, through examining descriptive accounts provided by the women leaders I interviewed, I hope to demonstrate how gender has an effect on what it might mean to lead authentically that will add value to current scholarship in leadership studies and in phenomenological inquiry informed by feminist theory. Although feminist phenomenology has found its voice, Linda Fisher (2010) argues feminist researchers must continue to critique and unsettle the phenomenological tradition. I hope to partially answer Fisher's call to action to push phenomenology further so as to obtain insight into the ways in which gender, authenticity and leadership intersect. In what follows, I discuss the actual unfolding of the qualitative component of the research. Two questions concern me. First, what were some assumptions that I took for granted? Second, how does one's epistemological orientation affect the manner in which one employs a particular methodology? I begin by discussing theoretical and methodological contestations as to what constitutes phenomenological research. Next, I explore feminist debates regarding methodological inquiry. Then, I discuss Arendt's approach to methodology, and her emphasis on narrative as a valuable form of investigation. In addition, I provide contextual information regarding the interview process, the research participants and highlight some ethical concerns I encountered. In the conclusion, I consider what I have learned through conducting a qualitative, phenomenological inquiry.

Approaches to phenomenology

I chose hermeneutic, existential phenomenology as my methodological approach as it fits with my theoretical framework that focusses on the situated, embodied nature of social life. In particular, I wanted to adopt the Arendtian concept to 'think without bannisters', which she also describes as visiting. For Arendt, this orientation to research refers to the ability to try and think from different perspectives. It is through a diversity of views that she maintains we will be able to comprehend a phenomenon in a richer, more complete fashion. One problem I face, however, is that Arendt rarely discusses her methodology. On the occasions when Arendt does try to explain her approach, the result is puzzling, as we will see in her response to the historian Eric Voegelin's critical review of *The Origins of Totalitarianism*. This may be partly due to what Seyla Benhabib (1996) sees as two disparate threads weaving through Arendt's work. The first thread reveals the influence of her friend, the essayist Walter Benjamin. Arendt adopted his methodological approach of looking to the forgotten fragments of history to bring forth stories from the past that had been erased so as to dislocate and dislodge commonplace thought. The second thread is that of existential, hermeneutic phenomenological inquiry. We see the Benjamin strand in Arendt's work in her penchant for storytelling as fundamental to comprehending the human condition. The latter strand can be summed up in Arendt's (1985) assertion that the primary reason why she wrote was to understand the given phenomenon.

Arendt's sparse comments regarding her methodological approach may also be indicative of her claim that when we try to clarify what we are doing, we only ever achieve a partial understanding. However, it makes it difficult to discuss her methodological approach in any detail. As a result, I turn to other theorists who wrote in the phenomenological tradition. I offer an overview of the main tenets of phenomenological inquiry adopted by Edmund Husserl and Martin Heidegger to demonstrate how these thinkers differed in their approach. Their methodological disagreements continue to divide scholars engaged in qualitative, phenomenological, inquiry.

It was Edmund Husserl who opened up phenomenology as a form of inquiry. A former mathematician, he was interested in how logical problems are affected by worldly conditions. One of Husserl's aims was to distinguish phenomenology from other forms of scientific investigation. He (1913) maintained that researchers need to suspend their judgement so that the phenomena under question appear as they are. By bracketing off what Husserl describes as the natural attitude, he argued it may be possible to grasp the essence of a phenomenon such that everything significant about it could be described. Central to his thinking is the notion that there is an intentional structure of consciousness. What this means is that each conscious act is oriented toward something, that is, it must have an object.

Husserlian phenomenology offers a way of gathering together diverse phenomenon. What makes his methodological approach of particular importance is that it represents a rigorous attempt to free philosophy from the confines of Hegelian historicism (Arendt, 1994c). As such, Husserl brought a new manner of thinking about the world through his emphasis on the things themselves. Indeed, Arendt (1994c) viewed Husserl as providing a new kind of humanism to guide scholars in their research. Yet his move toward a transcendental phenomenology, that is, the idea that a researcher can bracket off the natural attitude and focus on the structure of consciousness raised problems. Because of this subject-centred approach, she contends that Husserlian phenomenology turns man into what he can never be, that is, the creator of the world.

In contrast to his former teacher, Martin Heidegger argued it is impossible to bracket off one's attitude from one's research, as Husserl asserted, because our moods affect how we orient ourselves toward things. From Heidegger's perspective, phenomenology is not a technique that serves to characterize the 'what' of an object; rather, it is an explanation of the 'how' of research. His approach to phenomenology is hermeneutic; for our purposes here this means that any description is also an interpretation, framed through the lens of the particular researcher. Phenomenology is existential because we are always already, for Heidegger, beings-in-the-world. Consequently there is no transcendental perspective, as Husserl suggests, because each researcher takes up the phenomenon in a different manner that depends upon their particular worldview.

Heidegger maintains we must go beyond metaphysical distinctions toward a deeper understanding of what it means to live in the world. Each researcher will be affected by their situated, embodied viewpoint. Moreover, for Heidegger, phenomenology is not a school where you can learn the right technique, but rather represents an individual way of interpreting the world. Each investigator will be influenced by what they find meaningful which, in turn, may bring to light hidden aspects of a phenomena.

In conducting existential, hermeneutic phenomenological research, Heidegger emphasizes the need to intuitively grasp a phenomenon's meaning. But this is no simple task, since a researcher might fail to grasp the original meaning of a phenomenon. Sometimes, this is because semblances of a phenomenon are misconstrued as the thing itself. For example, a sore throat might indicate tonsillitis, or it could be a viral infection, or something more serious, such as meningitis. Each symptom does not show the illness as is, but reveals itself only in semblances. Because of this revealing as semblance, researchers must be careful not to misconstrue the essence of something by assuming that what appears on the surface constitutes its meaning and ground.

Another way a researcher may misconstrue the phenomenon under investigation relates to how what was once apparent becomes concealed over time. An example of this concealment might be how eugenics, in the early twentieth century, was widely regarded – by intellectuals and members of the general public – as an indication of the superiority of the white race. Because of a change in what is deemed socially acceptable, there may still be people who believe in eugenics, but few willing to share those beliefs publicly. This kind of concealment is, in Heidegger's view, most pernicious since there is a possibility of being misled by the false testimony of someone.

To sum up, for Husserl, phenomenology is a descriptive, rigorous method of inquiry that allows us to let things show themselves as they are. Alternatively, for Heidegger, phenomenological inquiry cannot be separated from interpretation. An important difference between these thinkers is whether it is possible to bracket off one's prejudices, as Husserl maintained, or whether interpretation is a fundamental aspect of phenomenological inquiry, as Heidegger suggested.

With this brief review of the main tenets of phenomenological thought, I now want to consider Arendt's limited discussion on her methodological approach. Following this, I consider how qualitative researchers have taken up these different approaches to phenomenological inquiry.

Methodological quandaries

As stated earlier, Arendt rarely discussed her particular methodological approach. An exception is her 'A Reply to Eric Voegelin' (1994b), where she argued that questions of method and philosophical implications are interconnected. In his review of *The Origins of Totalitarianism,* Voegelin stated that Arendt's book lacked conceptual unity. In her response to his review, she maintained it was not her intention to provide coherence. Rather, her aim was to reveal totalitarianism's main aspects, and to analyse these components of totalitarianism historically (p. 403). In isolating phenomenon across different historical periods, she sought to demonstrate how and why particular ideas emerged at a certain time. However, Arendt found herself in an ethical quandary since, in researching the origins of totalitarianism, she brought to light elements of a phenomenon that she found abhorrent. While she acknowledged that the purpose of historiography is to preserve something for posterity, Arendt contended that the preservation of totalitarianism was the last thing she wanted to do. However, to comprehend totalitarianism in its complexity, Arendt maintains it was necessary to show how it is distinct from other forms of ruling.

Although Arendt concurs with Voegelin's assertion that she is concerned with the philosophical implications of totalitarianism, she argues her phenomenological account is based on fact. She sees the rise in totalitarianism as a result of a loss of consent between people and their leaders, due to the waning societal influence of tradition, religion and authority. Hence, what distinguishes modernity from earlier times, according to Arendt, is that there are fewer common interests, which gather people together. This gathering together has a dual function in that it connects people, while distinguishing them from each other. What made totalitarianism so heinous was that these regimes attempted to destroy human freedom in a manner never witnessed before. Although there had always been immense cruelty in the world, Arendt argues totalitarianism was different in that it tried to eradicate humanity from people through organized means of terror. In stripping an individual of their dignity and self-respect, such as what happened in the Nazi concentration camps, totalitarian leaders were attempting to show how some people were superfluous. Furthermore, the imposition of a singular worldview, often that of the leader, aimed to deny plurality of perspectives. These aspects of totalitarianism, Arendt maintains, make it phenomenologically distinct from other forms of rule.

Arendt further states that generalization is a problem in research, since oversimplification results in phenomenological distinctions being covered over. Instead of seeing what is new about a particular phenomenon, scholars try and explain it by drawing analogies. She regards this practice as indicative of a way of thinking that confuses knowledge with meaning. The only way to comprehend phenomena, in Arendt's view, is to investigate why they appear at particular times, and ascertain what it is that makes them unique. It is through the discernment of a phenomenon's particularity that we will be able to make sense of it. This discernment requires us to use our imagination, which represents our inner compass (Arendt, 1994a, p. 323).

In reasoning why she approached the topic of totalitarianism in a passionate manner, Arendt (1994a) maintains that passion was methodologically necessary given her subject matter. To describe what took place under totalitarian rule in a dispassionate way would, she argues, be comparable to explaining the abject poverty of the British working classes in the Industrial Revolution without showing indignation at human suffering. Hence, by not showing righteous anger when confronted with the despicable conditions of the concentration camps would be akin to removing this phenomenon from its social context (p. 403). For Arendt, therefore, phenomenological inquiry requires researchers to be willing to engage with passion and determination. As well, she suggests that researchers differentiate between similar phenomena if we are to increase our understanding.

Now that we have a sense of the different approaches thinkers have taken to phenomenological inquiry, I want to discuss how their different approaches are taken up in qualitative research. The differences between Husserlian and Heideggerian-inspired research have led to a number of disagreements in regard to how phenomenological work should be conducted, as I will demonstrate.

Qualitative debates

Although there is general agreement amongst qualitative phenomenological researchers as to the importance of providing rich descriptions concerning a particular phenomenon or aspect of lived experience, Linda Fisher (2009) argues that there is great debate about how phenomenological research is carried out. She regards this debate as healthy; however, there are times when criticism turns into confusion, especially as it concerns what constitutes sound phenomenological research. Much of this confusion, according to Fisher, stems from the different approaches adopted by Husserlian-versus-Heideggerian inspired researchers. For example, a common disagreement concerns whether or not the individual researcher can bracket off their individual biases. When a researcher states that they have bracketed off or transcended their assumptions, and then uses hermeneutics as their approach, she regards their research as problematic because it combines two distinctive phenomenological traditions.

A further disagreement concerns how explicit researchers should be about how their embodied subjectivity affects their work. This can be a problem for novice researchers who, according to Fisher, misunderstand how the Husserlian process of bracketing off represents an initial step, whereby subjective bias is acknowledged as part of the project to establish the rigor and validity of the research. Thinkers in the Heideggerian tradition, conversely, regard openness to personal bias as an essential component of research. Fisher argues that research can only be considered phenomenological if it offers an evocative description of lived experience that includes the researcher adopting an open attitude. Furthermore, she contends researchers should tailor their approach to their specific audience, as it is only when readers feel moved by the research findings that it can be said to be a successful phenomenological exercise.

Husserlian researchers, like Amedeo Giorgio (2009), contend that phenomenologists must focus solely on the descriptive account. He maintains that an active imagination is crucial to Husserlian phenomenological inquiry. An inquiry into a particular phenomenon may derive from either a fictional or factual source. What is critical, according to Giorgio, is that the researcher describes a particular aspect of the phenomenon in a meaningful way. The most important aspect of Husserlian-inspired qualitative phenomenology is the descriptive account, which should offer the reader a deeper awareness of a particular phenomenon. In considering the problems qualitative researchers face when trying to retain the richness of lived experience, Les Todres (2007) argues that the roots of this dilemma can be traced back to Aristotle, who held that the form of something cannot be said to exist unless it can be perceived in a particular manner. This raises two interconnected problems for conducting qualitative research. On the one hand, there is a danger in focussing too much on the general structure of a particular phenomenon, because one may lose what is specific to individual experience. On the other hand, remaining too close to the idiosyncratic might obscure what is typical about a particular experience. To avoid this problem, Todres contends that qualitative scholars position their research as a dialogue. Furthermore, by conducting phenomenology in an embodied way, he maintains that it may be possible to evoke the presence of human phenomena. This kind of embodied inquiry is a way to move toward an open stance, respectful of differences.

Todres encourages researchers to bring texture back to structure, because the thicker the description, the more the reader will be able to feel a sense of connection with what has been expressed. Such a rich description needs to work on different levels: it needs to be understood intuitively as well as comprehended intellectually. Yet, because each reader is a unique individual, it is unlikely that every descriptive account will appeal to every reader. Just as writers have their own way of writing so, too, will readers understand in different ways. For instance, I may think that by sharing a particular description, I have provided the reader with insight into the notion of authenticity. However, it is quite possible that while this description may prove informative for one person, another reader may find the account of little interest. I cannot know this ahead of time.

For Heideggerian-inspired researchers like Patricia Benner (1994), interpretation is an inescapable component of the research process. She regards learning the phenomenological method as akin to literary criticism because the researcher is searching for different meanings that can be substantiated by the text in question. Benner argues that there are three narrative strategies that researchers need to take into account. These are paradigm cases, thematic analyses and exemplars. In paradigm cases, the interview is read for a global understanding from which certain topics or events are selected for a more detailed analysis. When you have the paradigm case, it is then necessary to test it against another case to see whether similar concerns manifest themselves.

Conversely, in a thematic analysis, you look for patterns across interviews, moving between parts and the whole of the text. Once you have identified paradigm cases and themes, then exemplars that display similarities or dissimilarities need to be discovered. Stories will come through which act as exemplars that capture important meanings. Thus, we see that there are different ways of reading interview transcripts, because meaning flows from an array of traditions, contexts and experiences.

In terms of my own process, I used a similar approach to that outlined by Benner. First I read the transcripts one by one to obtain a general idea, and then I identified cross-cutting themes. This iterative process took place over several months. Over time, I was able to further hone in on exemplars that I thought captured important insights concerning the interconnections among gender, authenticity and leadership.

Benner maintains that phenomenology is different from a Marxist 'hermeneutics of suspicion' or a psychoanalytic reading that tries to reveal the underlying truth, because phenomenology tries to examine pre-understandings and to confront otherness, silence and commonalities. This includes the researcher's pre-understanding. Indeed, she argues that having research questions challenged is part of the process. In this regard, my own research questions altered over time as a result of conversations with others, and undertaking pre-interviews. I realized I needed to develop research questions that were broad enough to allow for diverse viewpoints to emerge. Hence, I modified my initial questions accordingly.

Hermeneutic research requires us to bring our prejudices into the open so that we become aware of how our biases influence our interpretation. According to Anne Kinsella (2006), this connection between understanding and qualitative inquiry is a result of researchers' desire to comprehend the various facets of lived experience. As most qualitative researchers are concerned with questions of understanding and interpretation, Kinsella argues that such research is implicitly hermeneutic. In her view, qualitative research constitutes a co-mingling, since a hermeneutic inquiry requires the researcher to be willing to think with head and heart so as to be open to questioning. When the researcher adopts an open stance, the reader may discover something about the researcher that the latter did not anticipate.

That being said, each researcher, in taking up a hermeneutic phenomenological inquiry, will have a slightly different approach, because their life experiences will influence their work in some way.

These issues are not only pertinent to phenomenology but also to feminist concerns regarding qualitative inquiry, as I will now demonstrate.

Feminist concerns

According to Sandra Harding (1987), the desire for a feminist method arose from a perceived need to correct distorted accounts produced by traditional methodologies. She maintains it is necessary to distinguish method from methodology. For Harding, method relates to a particular way of assembling evidence or a technique, while methodology is an approach to inquiry. In drawing these distinctions, she claims that there are three categories of method. The first category is interviewing people; the second is observing people's behaviour; and the third is examining historical documents. Arguing against a specific feminist method, Harding contends that preoccupation with method may overlook more important questions concerning how we live in the world.

Methodology, in Harding's view, represents a theoretical approach to the way in which research should be undertaken. Yet many social scientists, as a result of their training, may not consider the theoretical assumptions behind their methodological approaches. Rather, social scientists tend to perceive methodological issues in relation to specific methods. Thus, a common approach taken by social scientists is to address methodological issues when they teach methods courses. By contrast, philosophers tend to raise methodological and epistemological issues when they talk about scientific method. Harding maintains that neither of these ways of thinking is adequate; hence, it is necessary for feminists to devise different approaches. Although there are valuable connections to be made among epistemology, methodology and research methods, Harding suggests it is not by concentrating on the latter that we will ascertain what is distinctive about feminist research.

When considering questions of epistemology, Harding notes that feminists have shown that many theories have often taken 'man' as the arbiter of knowledge. This male-centeredness has led to a narrowness of thinking about how we live in the world. As we saw in a previous chapter, some leadership scholars maintain that authentic leadership is an example of this tendency (Sinclair, 2013; Wilson, 2013). Harding contends that feminist analyses can enrich methodological accounts by revealing how women's ways of being in the world differ, not only from each other, but also from traditional male accounts.

As a result of second-wave feminism, new ways of thinking about methodology emerged, such as that provided by Dorothy Smith's (1987) 'sociology for women'. Her methodological approach, which is influenced by phenomenology, especially the work of Maurice Merleau-Ponty, offers researchers a different means of looking at aspects of lived experience that had previously been ignored. Smith shows how women's experiences of a phenomenon offer a different perspective, one which has often been obscured. She further maintains that it is not enough for women to become leaders of institutions, because it does not deal with structural limitations that affect a leader's ability to connect with people in a caring manner. Instead, it is important to adopt methodological approaches that serve to destabilize existing organizational structures. In this way, we may obtain a richer comprehension of how hierarchical relations dominate our lives. For example, Smith's conception of the 'relations of ruling' (1990, pp. 14–19), understood as the myriad ways in which organizational structures and systems of power are interconnected, offers a means to understand how gender relations are examined in the workplace. Few researchers have placed gender at the forefront of their inquiry into the relationship between authenticity and leadership, yet a focus on gender may offer insights that are otherwise overlooked. This is not least because it allows us to recover concrete experiences that may have been covered over by a narrow way of thinking about phenomena.

In a feminist inquiry, it is important to develop research approaches that help mitigate power imbalances between the researcher and interview participant (Alcoff, 1991). To do so, we need to consider how the perspective of the situated knower influences how we conduct our research. For example, when interviews are conducted with a lack of understanding of cultural difference, this can lead to a distorted version of the experiences of others. In trying to alleviate power inequities, Maria Lugones and Elizabeth Spelman (1983) suggest that researchers become friends with their interviewees for only when genuine and reciprocal dialogue takes place between 'outsiders' and 'insiders' can we trust the outsider's account. When interviewing people, they maintain it is important for feminist researchers to develop an atmosphere of friendship and openness. A vital component of human life is talking about personal experiences, since being silenced is a form of oppression. It is vital, therefore, that researchers be cognizant of the power relations between researcher and interview subject, and how their methodological and theoretical approach may work to silence others.

Although I concur that a researcher must be responsible for her actions, and guard against power imbalances, the problem is that in the interview process things unfold in the moment. There is little time to reflect on one's responses, other than giving oneself a metaphorical kick in the shins on those occasions when one interrupts someone. This is where practice and theory diverge because, no matter how good one's intentions might be, there is an inherent unpredictability in the research process. There are times when things just go awry. I will return to this point in due course. But at this juncture, I want to turn to consider interviewing in greater detail.

Interviewing – Theory and praxis

When researchers fail to consider how theory influences praxis, it may lead to under-theorized and poor quality interview data (Roulston, 2010). Hence it is important before embarking on interviews to think about how theory and practice intersect. For example, theorizing about a particular methodology might involve considering how the data is to be collected, the role of the interviewer, which participants are chosen, the theory underpinning the interviews, and how the final conclusions may be judged. In Roulston's (2010) view, theory is a process whereby we construct concepts and ideas about the world. In relation to interviews, the purpose of such theorizing is to consider, ahead of time, what issues relate to one's research design.

In terms of the research design for a phenomenological, qualitative study, Sandra Thomas and Howard Pollio (2002) maintain there are two important criteria in relation to eligibility. First, the participant must have some experience of the particular phenomenon being studied, and second, the participant must be willing to talk about the phenomenon. They further argue that the ideal number for a phenomenological study is between eight to 12 participants. Although some researchers argue for multiple interviews, Thomas and Pollio contend this is unnecessary provided that the interviewer has conducted preliminary interviews to test her questions, and become aware of her own presuppositions, as these will affect her interpretation of the research findings. In my own study, I interviewed ten participants; I also did single interviews since I had spent several months conducting preliminary interviews to test my questions, and to try and become aware of some of my presuppositions.

When conducting phenomenological research, Max Van Manen (1997) contends that it is important to keep each of the four existentials in mind, that is, spatiality, corporeality, temporality and relationality.

I thought about how I might do this as I was putting the research questions together, as well as during the interviews and, afterwards, when I was looking for themes arising from the interview transcripts. First, spatiality represents an important component of how we interact with one another. I considered spatiality by asking research participants to describe instances where they felt most comfortable leading and, conversely, to describe those times where they felt ill at ease. A good example of this from the interview accounts is one research participant's detailed description of the feeling of 'shrinking' when she found herself in situations where she felt unable to speak out. (I will discuss this account in more depth in a later chapter.)

Corporeality represents the second existential, and refers to how our interactions are always embodied. In relation to corporeality, I asked participants to describe any physical or emotional sensations they experienced when they felt they were acting in a manner that they perceived as true to themselves, or in an inauthentic way. Most interviewees described a recurring physical sensation they experienced, such as a tightening of the chest or a sinking feeling in the pit of the stomach, whenever they were faced with difficult situations. It appears that these recurring embodied signals serve as a reminder that something about a particular situation made them feel uneasy in some way. It is interesting to note, however, that two of the women leaders I interviewed reported experiencing no bodily sensations when they were in an anxious state. I sensed that neither of them was keen on answering the question. I am not sure what to make of their responses other than to wonder whether they have trained themselves not to pick up on bodily cues.

Temporality, the third existential, is non-linear because past, present and future are interwoven. Over time, some experiences take on greater meaning, while others recede into the background. There were numerous examples when interviewees related how past events had a profound influence on their lives. One of the most poignant was one research participant's recollection of being made homeless, as a result of her mother's illness, and inability to pay the rent. Her experience of living on the street influenced this leader's research on prisoners' rights, as well as her desire to try and be responsive to others in her leadership.

The fourth existential, relationality, can be seen from the diverse examples that interview participants offer to others who influenced their own thinking about authenticity and leadership. Some interview participants described mentors they had worked with, or how they tried to encourage others to be successful. Several women mentioned how a particular action by their mother had a tremendous influence on their desire to lead. Stories that they told about a childhood event seemed of especial significance.

Storytelling was a central component of Arendt's interpretative phenomenology (Disch, 1994a). For example, she argued that there were limits to what philosophy could teach us; thus, storytelling helps us fill in the 'worldly' gaps. Hence, storytelling makes us aware of the material reality that abstract theory overlooks. I want to explore how narrative helps us better understand the world.

Narrative

For Arendt (1958), storytelling is intrinsic to comprehending lived experience, since it is through narrative that we make sense of our lives. Each person has a narrative that is unique to them, although Arendt was adamant that we can never be the author of our life story. Rather, as all action is ephemeral, she argues we need storytellers to record what occurred since 'without speech to materialize and memorialize the new things that appear and shine forth, there is no remembrance' (p. 204). Narrative gathers together the two aspects fundamental to an Arendtian notion of subjectivity, that is, action and speech. The primary task of the storyteller is to narrate the actions of others. Storytelling, as Julia Kristeva (2001) notes, offered Arendt a way to re-create the connection between philosophy and politics that was lost following the death of Socrates. Thus, Kristeva sees Arendt's use of narrative as a radical response to Heidegger's attempt to essentialize and rationalize being.

Arendt argues that storytellers are able to put themselves into the minds of others without taking a definitive stance. In doing so, storytellers offer us a plurality of viewpoints from which to assess a particular action. For actions to have meaning there must always be a spectator to engage and respond. Consequently, we need others to interpret our actions through storytelling and remembrance. From an Arendtian perspective, stories are plural in the sense that they are multiple, but also unique in that they belong to someone. The reason why Arendt places high esteem on narrative is because it allows us to memorialize action.

Although Arendt sometimes apologized for using storytelling to advance her argument, Lisa Disch (1994a) maintains this was somewhat disingenuous because storytelling allowed Arendt to make a judgement. Arendt's predilection for storytelling is not because she views it as a way to pass on tradition, nor as a way to express oneself. Rather, the storyteller, through the framework of visiting, is involved in a practice of situated critical thinking. However, storytelling is always an interpretation of events; hence, Disch suggests that we need to be wary of making essentialist arguments or calling for a privileged standpoint through narrative.

The purpose of storytelling is to ensure that there is a space where individuals feel able to participate (Vasterling, 2007). Although science and philosophy help to establish facts, Veronica Vasterling argues that we need narrative to make sense of the world. Even qualitative research is not rich enough, in Vasterling's view, to offer the depth of understanding that can be gleaned from a good story. Furthermore, she expresses concern that storytelling is being undermined by scientific studies conducted by experts. When expert accounts take over from narrative, all that we are left with is rationalization, which may serve to suppress the intangible web of human affairs. The problem with rationalization is that expert accounts may result in the privileging of one voice over others. In doing so, we lose a plurality of perspectives, and the deeper understanding that a multiplicity of accounts offers.

Jonathan Gosling and Peter Villiers (2013) seem to concur, contending that 'management theory is appallingly obscure about the experience of leading' (p. 1). Instead of exploring moral complexities, many scholars focus on the positive aspects of leading. As a consequence, inherent ambiguities and inconsistencies in leadership praxis are cleared away in favour of a consistent pattern. We have seen this tendency in the manner in which leadership scholars define authentic leadership through four dimensions (self-awareness, balanced information processing, relational transparency and internalized moral perspective). This desire for consistency leads to a uniformity of meaning. Such uniformity may obscure what is meaningful about a phenomenon, because we focus on similarities instead of particularity. In a phenomenological exploration both must be kept in view.

Research process

Turning to the selection of participants, interviewees were recruited for this study in three ways. First, I sent an email to university Presidents, Vice-Presidents or their equivalent that belonged, like I did, to an organization called Women's Education Worldwide.[1] Second, I used a 'snowball technique' whereby I discussed my research with eligible candidates and asked them whether they wished to take part in the study, or knew of anyone else who might like to be involved who fit the profile – female, senior-level administrators, preferably Presidents, Vice-Presidents, or equivalent, who worked in the higher education sector. In the end, ten women took part in the study. These women leaders worked in three different countries – the United States, Canada and the Philippines. As well, two research participants came from the Caribbean – one from Trinidad, and the other from Jamaica.

Most women interviewed had worked in universities for several decades; the majority had been faculty members before moving into administrative roles. Two interview participants had worked in the corporate sector before embarking upon a university career. Five women had extensive experience leading at least one educational institution. The other women leaders were in charge of major portfolios such as external relations. The participants' ages ranged from early forties to late sixties. Additionally, the women interviewed came from a variety of disciplinary backgrounds in the humanities, social and applied sciences.

Table 6.1 lists salient details about each research participant.

With the exception of one interview conducted via SKYPE, interviews were conducted via telephone. I found that the lack of visual stimuli helped me to concentrate. These auditory encounters worked well for me because, as a visual learner, I often find there are too many visual cues. Conversely, with the telephone, and the concentration that is required to do a successful interview, there were fewer distractions. The lack of visual cues, however, meant that there may have been physical responses to particular questions that were missed that would have been pertinent to this inquiry.

Table 6.1   Research participants

Name	Role	Age	Country of origin
Alison	Leadership Director	50s	America
Claire	President (retired)	60s	America
Dianne	Vice-President	40s	America
Jane	Associate Vice-Provost	50s	America
Jennifer	Former Director, Diaspora Centre	60s	Trinidad
Jill	President	50s	America
Kate	President	50s	Canada
Laura	International Project Leader	60s	Jamaica
Olive	President (former)	60s	America
Teresa	President	60s	The Philippines

I began each interview by asking the participant what name she wished me to call her as a way to establish a sense of connection. In each case, the participants told me to call them by their first name. I then asked two questions asking them to describe what the term authenticity meant to them, and what the term authentic leadership brought to mind. Some interview participants seemed to have expected questions like these as they responded quickly. On other occasions, participants expressed concern about their lack of theoretical knowledge of the term 'authentic leadership'. When this occurred, I tried to put the woman at ease by explaining that it was their experience of leading I was interested in, rather than an academic knowledge of the term. As we moved further into the interview, participants said things like 'now I see what you're getting at', or 'I guess I do know more about this than I thought'. It was as if, through the interview process, we were bringing to light an understanding that was already present but that the interviewee had not previously recognized. This seems to me an example of the way phenomenology works to bring to light understanding that the person already had, but of which they may not be fully aware.

I had a specific question to elicit responses as to how their personal narrative influences their desire to lead in a manner that each participant regarded as authentic. On several occasions, interviewees described instances where their mothers had played influential roles in instilling not only a sense of doing right, but a belief that they could lead. Additionally, during the interviews, I discovered that four of the women came from working-class, low-income households. The dimension of class enriched the study. Further, three interviewees self-identified as women of colour. Their insights into racial issues as it relates to authenticity serve to deepen my understanding of some complexities regarding the intersection of race, gender and leadership.

Occasionally, during an interview, a research participant mentioned religion. For example, one woman described how Buddhist thought influenced her ideas about authenticity. Two other participants mentioned Christianity. One of these participants was enthusiastic about her early leadership experiences in her church. The other participant who mentioned religion was less enthusiastic due to negative childhood memories. Thus, for some women, religion provided an early path to thinking about authenticity and leadership. For others, religion served to reinforce patriarchal systems of oppression.

Turning to the practice of interviewing, on the one hand, an interview is similar to a conversation in that there is an oscillation between questioner and respondent. On the other hand, it is different since the interviewer sets the pace with the questions she poses. The researcher has an unfair advantage in that she knows the questions because she has the research guide in front of her. In some ways, this restricts the conversation due to its linearity. But sometimes the interviews that go off track may offer useful insight, especially if a researcher is willing to reflect on the reasons why the interview might seem to have failed. For instance, in one interview, a research participant found my questions exasperating. She declared that all we were doing was going around in circles as I kept asking her the same thing but from different angles.

Phenomenologically, I suppose that was exactly what was happening, but my approach was not one with which this person was comfortable. I found myself becoming somewhat irritated by her negative responses. I thought the spirited defense of my research would culminate in the end of the interview. Instead, her attitude softened, and she seemed to become genuinely interested in the project. There was a change in the timbre of her voice, and she began asking questions and sharing stories. Here are two examples from the beginning and end of the interview that illustrate this change of attitude.

My problem is I'm not into this whole framework. I'm sure that your study is going to be very interesting, but you're talking about leadership in ways that I don't normally think about so I'm having trouble getting into your mindset.

As we started out, I was thinking you know that this is going to be a very difficult conversation because this seems to me speaking a different language or too simplistic or whatever. But as we got into it, you've really made me think.

The best way I can describe this interview experience is as a kind of thawing. It seemed to me we entered into the kind of dialogue and dissent that Arendt argues is crucial to understanding. In this particular situation, discord, rather than concord, brought about a deeper connection between us.

In other interviews, there were times when a participant, in the midst of describing a specific instance, hesitated. When I asked a follow-up question to delve further, sometimes the interviewee remained silent. At times, hesitations and silences may illuminate something that dialogue fails to do. If the researcher pays attention to silent gaps, she may obtain a glimpse of something that is hidden from view. For instance, as I read across the transcripts, I realized that no-one mentioned how sexuality or disability may have affected their personal leadership. Conversely, participants talked freely about race, class and gender issues. I mention this to illustrate that there are still many things which are not discussed openly that may have a bearing on our lives. But interviewers have a responsibility not just to knowledge, but also to the people who are involved in the research. But what constitutes ethical action is not always clear-cut, partially because of how our own prejudices may adversely shape our interview approach.

Reflexivity and ethics

Feminist theory, like phenomenological inquiry, makes one aware that it is important to be cognizant of how one's situated perspective shapes the research process. Yet although I am aware of some of my prejudices, I also have blindspots. What this means in terms of the interview process is that there is an ambiguity inherent within any research endeavour, because each person interprets the world from a different, situated perspective. As Arendt (1965) tells us, we can only know ourselves in ambiguity. We are each differently situated and, hence, perceive the world in a distinct manner. Thus, each interviewer will approach her work differently.

In thinking about the relationship between interviewing and ethics, Patricia Benner (1994) argues that an ethical stance is one that respects the interviewee's experiences, while also staying true to the text. One way I approached ethics was by encouraging research participants to give me feedback at the end of the interview as to whether they felt that there was anything that we had not spoken about which they considered important.

Another way of considering ethics in terms of interviewing is for the researcher to be critically reflexive of prescribed methodologies, individual knowledge and social context (Benner, 1994). I tried to reflect upon my research questions and methodological approach to ensure that as a white, heterosexual, feminist researcher, I did not misappropriate the voices of others. I took field notes, before and following each interview, so that I could explore my reactions to what was unfolding, as well as reflect upon my pre-understandings. This reflexivity enabled me to delve deeper into my own assumptions regarding gender, authenticity and leadership, and the ways in which this prior understanding is contested by study participants. Furthermore, if the researcher's views are not changed in some way, Benner argues that the process is insufficient, since the data has been limited by a refusal to reason in transition (p. 112). I have included below some of my field notes from the interviews to demonstrate how reasoning in transition worked for me.

Field notes – August 15

Today's interview was much more difficult. For one thing, SKYPE didn't work again. I don't know why. She seemed very curt at first. No curt isn't the right word but I felt that she was too much in her head. At one point, I thought that it would be over very quickly but then I began to really hone in on what she was saying. I spoke a lot more than in the first interview but this was a necessary tactic in order to draw her out. And it worked, I think. She had problems with the question about comfort – something about that word displeased her almost. I also felt at times that she was interviewing me but then I thought well that's fine, if we think about it as a conversation, it's good for me to have to explain what it is I think I am doing.

The most interesting answer I thought was related to her background where she talked about how learning to act had enabled her to find her voice and to get out from a patriarchal household as a young woman. But all in all, I have to give myself a pat on the back for making the interview work. She also said that she liked the questions and that they had made her think. I still need to go deeper with people, but this interview showed me how hard that might be on occasion.

Field notes after transcription

This was a much better interview than I thought it was. What I saw as her negativity was just her way of approaching questions. She is a thoughtful person; hence the long pauses. It was because she was thinking about the questions that it seemed to me as if she wasn't interested. This is the problem, I guess, with telephone interviews. But this also says a lot about the way I jump to conclusions about people without having enough information – something that I accuse others of doing, but now I see that this is the way that we ordinarily go about the world.

Field notes – August 24

This was the first interview I conducted in the afternoon. It was only 4:30 p.m. but for some reason I wasn't really looking forward to it. The other interviews had gone well if one discounts the issues with technology. I found it difficult to get her to talk. This is the second time this has happened. This time it was not due to a reticence but to a lack of openness. It did not appear that way on the surface because she answered without hesitation. I got the sense that she had answered similar questions in the past. She was very sure of what authentic leadership was making no distinction between personal authenticity and authentic leadership. It was only at the end of the interview when I pressed her that I found that she had left her last institution because of a moral dilemma. She was very pleasant but I sensed a lack of connection between us. She was very clear, honest and open but her answers to the embodiment questions were non-existent. How can someone not have a bodily response?

Field notes – After transcription

Again, I've misread an interviewee. This was a really thoughtful and honest appraisal of her notion of authentic leadership. It means so much to her not least because of her working-class background. It is becoming clear to me that the people who this concept appeals to, have, at one time or another, been or felt themselves to have been on the margins.

Reviewing these field notes, it is fascinating to see how quickly I made assumptions that upon reflection were not necessarily an accurate representation of the interview. Conversely, they also show how quickly I gained confidence doing interviews. In the end, much of the information that I read about conducting interviews only made sense to me after I had gone through the process. This suggests that reasoning in transition is an iterative process whereby theory and praxis unfold over time. Since reasoning is our attempt to understand some phenomenon, it does not end.

Conclusion

Troubling method, in the end, has led me to a consideration of what constitutes an ethical process, and how one shares research findings in an ethical manner. In the role of the interpretive researcher, I see my task as creating a dialogue between myself and the participants' lived experiences. The difficulty is how to conduct interviews in an ethical way. Helen Fielding (2011) suggests that an ethical approach requires us to make sense of what we do according to a reality that consists of multiple perspectives and voices. Reality, as Fielding notes, is always evolving and dependent upon a particular situation. It is this ever-changing contingency that forms the basis for our ethical, embodied relationships. But what constitutes developing ethical relationships within the context of interviewing? In other words as someone schooled in the humanities, what did I learn from the experience of interviewing? I think that the most important thing I learned was that of the complexity with regard to a researcher's ethical responsibility in representing another's account. The way I have decided to deal with this ethical quandary is to be clear that this is my particular interpretation. After all, this is the basis of research that is grounded in an existential, hermeneutic approach. Or so it seems to me. If one holds to Arendt's way of approaching research, each scholar must be willing to offer up her own insights, and make judgements accordingly. In this chapter, I have shown that through conducting a qualitative research project, I encountered ethical issues I had not anticipated. In laying out my methodological approach and offering some reflections on the process, my aim has been to explore my own pre-conceptions, as well as to show how feminist theory and existential, hermeneutic phenomenology intersect.

In the following chapters, I consider some narratives and themes that flowed from the interviews I conducted.

7
Telling Tales Out of School

In a letter to her friend the novelist Mary McCarthy, Arendt (1995) states 'I wish you would write about what it is in people that makes them want a story ... Life itself is full of tales' (p. 129). For Arendt, narrative enables us to find meaning, and gain a sense of who we are in relation to others. In this chapter, I explore the situated, embodied nature of leadership through the narrative accounts provided by ten senior women leaders in higher education. My main purpose is to show how these diverse accounts offer insights into the interconnections among gender, authenticity and leadership.

My original research concerned the ways in which senior women leaders describe their experiences of authenticity (or lack thereof) within an institutional context. What emerges from these research findings is a more expansive way of thinking about leadership. These women's accounts serve to complicate the notion of what constitutes an authentic leader, and run contrary to most scholarship on authentic leadership, especially in regards to the importance of self-knowledge. In particular, these research participants demonstrate how leadership is a relational enterprise, founded upon mutual respect and trust. Viewing authentic leadership through a relational perspective allows us to see previously hidden aspects of leadership. For example, these women's accounts highlight how gender differences reinforce hierarchies in subtle and sometimes not so subtle ways.

To begin, I provide a brief description of each leader before turning to the women leaders' narrative accounts. I share two or three descriptive accounts from each participant. To allow these women's stories to be foregrounded, my commentary will be minimal. I bring these women's narratives into conversation with Arendt to see what insights can be garnered about the connections among gender, authenticity and leadership.

Kate is President of a large educational institution in Canada. Previously, she held a series of administrative positions, including that of Vice-President.

Jane is an Associate Provost at a major institution. A full professor, she has been at her current university for more than two decades.

Dianne is a Vice-President of a large women's college, and the youngest person I interviewed.

Alison developed the leadership program in her university and is also a freelance consultant. She had extensive experience in the corporate world before moving to higher education.

Claire recently retired from her role as President of a women's college. She has extensive experience in the university sector in a variety of administrative roles.

Olive has extensive experience leading co-ed and single sex institutions. She is now a Professor at an Ivy League institution.

Teresa was, until recently, the President of a large university in The Philippines. She has also worked in North America for the World Bank.

Jill is the President of a women's college in the United States. Previously, she served as Vice-President in a major university.

Laura was a Vice-President of a major Ivy League university. She currently works at a college in the United States.

Jennifer was, until recently, Chair of an institute dedicated to Diaspora Studies. She has also served two terms as Chair of Department. Originally from Trinidad, Jennifer lives and works in the United States.

Crossing boundaries

Kate is the President of a large educational institution in Canada. She was the first woman, as well as the youngest person, to be hired as President at her current institution. Authentic leadership, in her words, is about being genuine; but also she states 'there are pieces of your life and your world that it's important that you don't pour out in a leader role'. Here, Kate highlights the importance of keeping boundaries between one's public and private life, something that Arendt saw as critical to a person's ability to function successfully. Kate went on to describe some of the problems that can ensue when a leader allows their professional and private lives to become fused.

> I used to say that XXX was unloved and unlead. Part of the problem was that the leader before me had his heart broken by the institution. He wasn't able to do what he wanted to do, and it just genuinely broke his heart. So for the last two years, everywhere he went, everyone knew how much he had fallen out of love with the institution, and how badly it had hurt him. I think he needed for the good of XXX to keep that to himself. ... There are aspects that you need to be able to control. I don't find it inauthentic; I just think it's responsible to keep some things out of that public arena.

Here, Kate illustrates the need to separate one's public personae from that of one's private self. This separation between public and private was something that Arendt regarded as critical to human flourishing. The problem if we remain only in the light of the public sphere is that we may lose a sense of depth, and even reality, since we forget that we play a role in our social lives.

Yet the separation between how a leader feels, and how much she shows to others is informed by cultural ideas about leaders. Being confident, for instance, is regarded in most Western societies as a positive leadership trait, while showing disillusionment is perceived as negative. Kate's comments suggest that the previous incumbent's expression of sadness was inappropriate given his leadership role, because it had a negative effect on staff morale. In her view, a leader has to inspire others. To illustrate her point, Kate describes her first meeting as President where she tries to engage faculty and staff to share her vision.

> I needed to build the case for change. I had to get them to start thinking that we needed to do things differently, but we could do it together. It was through stating the case in the most honest and blunt way I could. ... It was about refocusing the whole institution. That day was the first sort of laying it out catalyst, and then the job was to engage people and to be challenged. I really did go anywhere I was invited, and listened to everyone who had an opinion. I did come with a plan, and a vision, because although leadership requires humanity, kindness, sincerity, and passion, there's also a need to deliver. That day I said this is the plan we are going to follow, and here's how you can get involved. I was very nervous ... but I truly believed that if we worked together we could turn the place around. I had an hour and a half to garner a sense of excitement about where we could go, what we could do, and how we

could all be in this together. I'm extraordinarily lucky that XXX rallied to that, and we are a fundamentally different place than we were.

Here, Kate describes how important it is for a leader, not just to have a vision, but to encourage others to become enthusiastic about organizational change. Getting employees to align themselves with a new institutional vision was critical to her success. Kate also mentions how nervous she felt; yet, she was determined to present a confident image. Her description is in line with Arendt's assertion that it is not what we feel inside that matters but how we present ourselves to others. Courage comes not from a lack of anxiety or nervousness, but a willingness to exude confidence. This shows how a leader must, at times, demonstrate qualities that are in contrast to how they feel. Kate didn't regard this as inauthentic, but as a necessary requirement of being a leader.

The vision thing

Jane is an associate provost at a public university in the American Midwest. A full professor, she recently moved into an administrative post, where she is responsible for gender issues. Jane describes authentic leadership as 'being aware, as much as possible, of who you are and bringing all the pieces of that to your job, to your leadership so that other people can bring great ideas forward. And, to me, that's what an authentic leader really does'. She contrasts her view of what constitutes authenticity in leadership with what she describes as 'command and control' leadership.

> The command and control kind of leader is not particularly authentic because they are not making room for other people to be authentic themselves, and to bring what they can, all that they can, to the process. A command and control person is saying I don't care what else you have, what I want from you is this, and it better be exactly my way. ... That's what we have a lot of at the administration level at the moment. ... They want to be able to check the box that says we collaborated, and we asked opinions, but they don't actually want to hear those opinions, and they certainly don't want to act on them.

In her negative assessment of what Jane calls command and control leadership, she reveals how important it is not only to ask for opinions, but also to be open to hearing what people say. Jane indicates her unwillingness to operate in this manner may negatively affect her future prospects for advancement. In listening to her account, I was reminded of Arendt's insistence that dialogue and debate are critical aspects of plurality, and central to human flourishing. The type of leader who is unwilling to hear others' divergent opinions is displaying a form of mastery that, although on the surface asks for input, is not interested in listening to different perspectives.

Earlier, Kate described how important it was to obtain the support of others in order to put forward her vision. In her next description, Jane discusses problems when leaders put forward visions that do not obtain sufficient support from others.

> We hired a new Director for the School of XXX. The Search Committee decided that they wanted a visionary, and that's what they got. But the visionary was completely incapable of doing straight administrative work, which is okay; you can hire somebody else to do that. The real problem, in my mind, was that this person assumed that her vision was shared, and made no effort to explain it to anybody, to convince anyone that this vision was good, to even ask anybody else if they had any other ideas, or would like to have input on the vision. She just marched off on this vision, and spent four years trying to convince the university about her vision. The rest of us [were left] sort of looking at each other. And you know what? That's not really what we wanted to do. I'm not sure she ever really figured that out. At the end of her four-year term, she asked to retain the job and they said 'no' because she had alienated so many people by not being at all interested in what anybody else thought. Yet I know she thought that she had consulted. She really believed that everyone was on board with this vision, but she just didn't have the first clue how to go about listening to other people. My sense is that the reason why she didn't dare ask anyone else is she wasn't really that confident; that is, she wasn't authentic enough to allow herself to open up to other possibilities. So she grabbed on to this vision ... it gave her something to cling to, and to aim for, and helped her to keep a shell around everything else so that she didn't have to hear from [others], or hear things that might not be comfortable to hear, or try to incorporate ideas that were unfamiliar or alien to her.

Oftentimes, leaders are hired because they have a specific vision as to where the organization should be headed. In Kate's description, she explains how she spent a great deal of time trying to get others involved and enthused. Conversely, Jane demonstrates the problems that can arise when leaders try to impose a vision on others. When a leader clings to a vision without gaining the commitment of others, this may lead to unresolved conflict which, in time, may result in the leader's termination. What Jane's account brings to light is how much leaders are dependent upon others for their success, or lack thereof.

A question of values

Dianne is Vice-President of External Relations at a college in the Pacific North West, and the youngest person interviewed. Authentic leadership, in her words, is about consistency of behaviour in keeping with a kind of internal compass. To demonstrate authentic leadership, Dianne argued that a person must take a stance against unethical leadership behaviour. She offers the following example:

A staff member came to me expressing discomfort with something that was going on with my manager. My manager was doing something that was making my subordinate uncomfortable. For me, it was a matter of integrity, principle and ethics to deal with this situation in a forthright way. [This] ended up involving a sexual harassment suit or claim. For me, it was a big moment of saying that I claim to adhere to the values and laws related to a sexual harassment free workplace. Here I was confronted with a very awkward situation; how will I live up to my principles and my responsibilities? I received advice from the University Ombudsman [who] gave me a menu of options. I decided to pursue the most aggressive, and turn the situation over to people who had more expertise. It was hard; it led to a year of unpleasantness. But it was something I had to do. I had to figure out the best way of doing it, and [offering] the best support for this staff member in this really uncomfortable position. I was very sorry for her that I was putting this forward at this very high level. It was uncomfortable for her, and we had to have a number of conversations about it. But, ultimately, she felt valued that we were on the same page from a value perspective, and that we really mean what we say when we talk about a harassment-free work place. It developed a high level of trust for us, and mutual loyalty that has endured. I certainly think about my relationship vis-à-vis my manager in this sexual harassment situation, especially his lack of authenticity, integrity, and ethical standard. He violated the sense of being a common shared team.

Here, Dianne illustrates how it is not enough to adhere to a set of values, it is necessary to act upon them. In this instance, she was faced with the problem of dealing effectively with a claim of sexual harassment. Dianne also demonstrates the importance of caring for another's predicament. Such caring requires mutual support that, in turn, develops loyalty and trust. In this extract, we see how essential it is for leaders to stand up against immoral behaviour in the workplace.

Since the time of the sexual harassment suit, Dianne has worked at two different universities. In what follows, she contrasts an experience of disengagement at one institution with her current experience where she feels her input is valued.

> At my last employer I felt hesitant about speaking up. I did not feel that I, or anyone else, was given the benefit of the doubt in those leadership/team meetings. There was a very specific place or agenda that a couple of people were driving, and it seemed like – for the rest of us – our participation was for show. Over time, that had a very inhibiting impact for me. I became less engaged, and less likely to share ideas, or offer input, or even attempt to play a meaningful role setting organizational direction and priorities. By contrast, in my current position, I very much feel that colleagues recognize the value I bring even when it is a topic outside my particular scope. It is a great source of meaning and gratification for me that I can take part in the sessions about other areas – not just my own – and that my input is valued. It doesn't mean everyone agrees with me, by no means. [Laugh].

In juxtaposing these different work experiences, Dianne demonstrates the problems that ensue when leaders do not provide an environment where dialogue and dissent is respected. As we saw with Jane's example, when leaders ask for input when contrary views are not wanted this can prove counterproductive, since employees recognize that leaders are being disingenuous. As a consequence, this can lead to employee disengagement. Conversely, when meetings are open to different viewpoints, Dianne argues it allows for more engagement. It does not matter that people disagree with her ideas; what counts is that people are willing to listen to her perspective. In turn, this engenders a sense of being valued. Her account highlights Arendt's point about the importance for leaders to act in a responsive manner. When different viewpoints are shared openly, the discussion generated will help the organization, and its people, to flourish.

Authentic relationships

Alison is responsible for a university leadership program in The Rocky Mountains. Her path to leadership was different from others I interviewed in that, for most of her career, Alison was employed in the corporate sector, rising to Vice-President in a large high-tech corporation. She decided to leave the corporate setting because she 'wanted to provide something that was more transformative for people'. Since leaving the corporate sector, Alison has developed and facilitated leadership programs for an international not-for-profit organization and a university. In response to a question about authenticity and leadership, she replied:

> It's not that either you're an authentic leader or you're not. It's really a kind of an orientation toward a path. I don't think it's a steady state. I think it is something that people aspire to, and every once in a while they are able to be authentic. To me, that is when they are synchronized in what they are doing, what they are saying, what they are thinking all match, and where they are also in touch with the world. It's all about being in relation to others. Having authentic relationships means being genuine with one another, creating clear expectations, talking with one another about the relationship, rather than just enacting the relationship, and having meta-conversations about how we are doing what we are doing are all very important elements.

For Alison, authenticity is not something that can be possessed but rather flows from an alignment in values, thought and action. This alignment results in what she terms synchronicity, which appears to be founded on genuine relationships whereby each person is clear about what is expected from them.

Later in the interview, Alison described her discomfort with her family's gender dynamics, and how learning to act helped her discover her voice.

> In our family, the men were the more kind of verbal, outgoing ones and the women were more in the role of being the audience. ... When I was in high school, I wanted to find my own voice. I entered into a theatre class and learned about acting and improvisation. Those were just wonderful ways for me to really discover my authenticity, although it was kind of odd because I was discovering myself through other people, through playing roles as an actor.

I discovered existentialism in high school, and I learned about authenticity. It just became a theme for me in my life. It's something I have pursued ever since in many different ways.

What I find fascinating about Alison's description is that she highlights how it was through role-playing that she found her voice. This role-playing enabled her to develop a different sense of self that was not confined to the gendered roles in her family whereby it was the men who took centre-stage. In addition, Alison described how her spiritual beliefs play a profound role in her desire for a deeper sense of connection with others. For Alison, building relationships is critical to her comprehension of authentic leadership. As she states:

> Relationships are extremely important because they are the glue or the connection that allows us to be in this dispersed, networked environment and still remain connected to one another in ways that are meaningful ... You can have rules, or guidelines, or even customer service agreements, or whatever construct that you want to have that you think is creating connection with people, but without authentic relationships it really lacks heart, resilience and a feeling of continuity.

Here Alison reinforces Arendt's notion of the importance of plurality, gained through creating deep connections between people. What is critical is that authentic relationships cannot be forged through a 'one-size-fits-all' pattern but need to arise organically from the interaction among people seeking a deeper sense of engagement with the world.

Leading with integrity

Olive served as President at two higher education institutions. Of all those interviewed, she was the most critical about the notion of authentic leadership. In her words:

> I have problems with authenticity as a measure of the quality or aspirations of a leader because authentic to me sounds like its simply drawing attention to the alternative that you would be somehow hypocritical or flawed. ... I prefer integrity because I think you can show integrity even as you deal with different situations in different ways if your personal balance, your moral compass are still strong. But authenticity, to me, doesn't convey what I think leaders need.

The problem with linking leadership to authenticity is that, for Olive, it suggests that leaders might act in a hypocritical way. This is why she prefers 'integrity' as a way to describe what she regards as an ethical approach to leading. Additionally, in her description of what it was like to be a President, Olive reflects:

> It's an exhilarating, demanding, sometimes frustrating, kind of job. It was a pretty demanding kind of role and, therefore, there were times when you felt somewhat off-balance. Often, you weren't sure about the direction you ought to be taking, making decisions that seemed the right ones but had certain, potential problems that you couldn't avoid or hadn't foreseen. ... I thought about trying to do the very best I could as a leader of two institutions that I deeply valued. I thought about trying to honor the post, and honor those institutions and be fair to the people with whom I worked, and advance goals that were valuable for the people involved as much as I possibly could. It never occurred to me that this was either true to myself or not true to myself.

Olive illustrates how demanding the role of President can be, and how important it is to remain alert. But she also shows how the idea that leaders are aware of how they are acting at all times is erroneous. Olive next describes how, initially, the role of President seemed strange to her.

> It didn't seem to me at the outset that this could possibly be me; as a sort of an ordinary young woman college professor from XXX, or somebody from the South, or whatever, it just didn't fit. It didn't seem easy at the start. Maybe your word comfortable is relevant here, but that feeling didn't persist, or it didn't impede my being able to do my work, and maybe following out of what you've been saying, when it stopped feeling that way, when I sort of felt well – for better or for worse – this is what the President of XXX is like ... I was at the point that you would call authentic leadership. At the time that I was going through all this, I was also spending a lot of my energy trying to be an effective president. So I didn't spend a lot of time wrestling with it. But, as I look back, I think it's probably true that there would have been some point at which it's like an out of focus picture that comes into focus, not all of a sudden, but gradually where you sort of see doubled vision of something, something happens where everything sort of fits together. As I look back on it

that may have been the way it was. I would certainly probably never have been able to explain it that clearly at the time. But I think something like that was going on.

Here Olive uses the metaphor of 'double vision' to describe how being a President, over time, started to feel more of a fit for her. As she became more used to the role, she describes it as similar to 'an out of focus picture coming into focus'. I find this metaphor striking as a way to illustrate how something that at first seems strange to us becomes familiar over time. We often refer to how people grow into the role, and Olive's description demonstrates how leading an institution becomes easier with practice.

It seems that leading authentically depends upon a person's circumstances, relationships and experiences in the world. This is why trying to determine what authentic leadership is misses out the how of leading. And it is this 'how' of leading that demonstrates how different people will lead in diverse ways. What it means to be an authentic leader, therefore, will be influenced by each person's particular set of circumstances and worldview. Thus, it is not surprising that the women I interviewed had very different viewpoints on whether authenticity was a useful descriptor of what it meant to them to lead.

Thinking things through

Teresa recently stepped down from her role as President of a university in The Philippines. Like Olive, Teresa explained how difficult it could be to remain focussed, given the demands of the Presidential role.

> You have to deal with different personalities and motivate teams in spite of personal differences. When you are working with people, conflicts arise as to how you do things, or even in terms of getting the fair amount of commitment. A lot of leadership work is conflict management. ... I like to think about how to solve problems, and how to establish parameters. For example, how do you organize and get the rest of the staff on your side. Although this may be a problem for others, I have a gift for thinking things through, thinking about various ways to solve such problems.

Here, Teresa relates her leadership success to her propensity for 'thinking things through'. Considering a problem from different points of view enables her to decide upon the best course of conduct.

Later in the interview, Teresa reflected upon the ethical dilemmas that arise from a leader's positional power.

I question what my motives are for reacting in a certain way. For instance, you know you are President but then you realize you cannot dictate [laugh]. You have to persuade people even if you have authority. Sometimes that could be addictive, no? You know you have the power, but you cannot do as you want. So at that point, you examine yourself to see why am I reacting that way to certain things that I hear, or certain ways that people react to you?

Teresa is honest about the danger when a leader becomes addicted to power, and, rather than listen to others, choose to dictate. To avoid this temptation, Teresa suggests that leaders need to examine their actions, and reflect upon why they are acting in a particular way. This strikes me as similar to Arendt's 'stop and think', which she sees as a necessary component of an ethical approach to leadership.

A sense of possibilities

Jill is President of a women's college in New England. She spent most of her career at a public university, first as a faculty member, and later in a series of administrative positions, culminating in Vice-President, Research. Authenticity in leadership, according to Jill, is about leading in a manner that reflects personal values. She described how the challenges she faced as a young woman were influential to her leadership.

I grew up in a single parent household with a mother who dropped out of school at the age of sixteen to marry my father, who was in the military. ... I lived with [my mother], and worked with her in the summers in a light switch factory. I saw how institutional or organizational cultures really perpetuate and reinforce classism and sexism. There were no men in the factory. The only men were in the loading docks, or in the catering trucks, or in the boss's office. All the workers were women doing piece work. Yet I saw through my mother, in her role as a shop steward, how you could confront head on those issues of classism and sexism, and it engendered in me a sense of possibilities in terms of women's leadership.

In this narrative description, Jill shows how the factory in which she and her mother worked was divided on gender lines. Although though there was gender prejudice within the workplace, through her mother's union activities Jill saw there were leadership avenues open to women. Then, she described her difficult decision to forfeit a scholarship to look after her mother, who had become seriously ill.

> I attended two years of community college before my mother became chronically ill. I needed to be a care-giver for her. ... That had an impact on my perceptions of social justice, and what it means to live authentically. I lived for a time on the streets with my mother, who was homeless, and got to know that people often don't have control over the circumstances of their lives through no fault of their own. My commitment to looking at prisoners' rights emerged from that as well – the extent to which society's failure to protect people from preventable harm mitigates when the victimized become the victimizers. I have seen how people have been marginalized, and disenfranchised, and how they act out. So I try to lead with a sense of empathy and a commitment to social justice, and access to education for people from all socioeconomic backgrounds.

Jill's experience of homelessness had a profound impact, not only on her decision to do research into prisoners' rights, but also in her determination to lead in a caring manner. For instance, she described how she tried to create a more humane work environment as a result of employees' comments about a lack of engagement.

> When I came to XXX, the structure for faculty meetings was different from what I was used to. ... The faculty meetings were set up so that the President sat in the front, and the faculty was in this auditorium. It was a very patriarchal, hierarchical structure. Junior faculty expressed concerns about how College meetings extended beyond the time when child care ended. The other [issue] was that they felt unengaged with respect to shared governance. The first issue was easy. I said we could subsidize day care until the meetings end. The other issue I suggested we dealt with by having faculty facilitate the meetings. This was proposed at my first faculty meeting. It was voted down because there was a comfort level with the way things had been done in the past. I said my commitment to authentic leadership and feminist principles argue against this kind of structure, but I'm happy to accede to your will if this is what you want. But it was, I guess, a willingness to say this is important to me to at least raise the issues with respect to hierarchy.

Jill's attempt to incorporate changes to facilitate younger scholars' engagement at faculty meetings was unsuccessful. Her failure to get adequate buy-in reveals how difficult it can be for leaders to make structural changes when they do not obtain sufficient support from others. This example illustrates how the leader's ability to change organizational practices is dependent upon a willingness from other people to do likewise.

Situational leadership

Laura was previously employed as Vice-President at an Ivy League university in America. She left that prestigious university to work at a college for African-American students where she heads up an international science and education project. Laura describes how her childhood experiences were fundamental to her leadership.

> I came out of a type of society where the designated heads of households were not necessarily those of management. It was a dominated society in rural Jamaica; men may have had the leadership roles but, I know and I saw, that women, my mother included, managed things, and changed the dynamics of things. My mother, who did not finish high school, grew up in a strange kind of time warp in rural Jamaica. ... Colonial society was dying. There was a move from rural to urban and large land owners were becoming land poor. I grew up in a transitional society, and for me to survive, I had to figure out ways to make the transition. I had to be comfortable with change.
>
> Early on in life, I lived in a world of my own. I was lucky enough to have space, maybe because it was structured by all of those male expectations. Although I recognize there are boundaries set for women, you know, we should be nurturers, I also understood from early interface with smart women, who are always around, we just have to change our definition of smart. The women who ran institutions in my village or my teachers, they had purpose, and value and integrity. ... I come to authentic leadership through that kind of quiet recognition of how powerful situational leadership can be. I grew up in a rural setting, and I had freedom. You see, sometimes, you conceptualize the situation from which you come from as being deficient. It doesn't have elaborate schools, and so on, but leadership, having people follow you, being recognized as having a set of ideas that you can change something were an early part of my view of the world.

Here Laura describes how it was the women in her village who were the quiet leaders who got things done. Thus, she demonstrates how it is not always those in powerful roles who are the ones who get things accomplished. Then, Laura described her experiences as a student abroad.

I was accepted as an international student as part of a gesture to do good and to reach out to the poor. ... I actually had very little money when I went to university but, for some reason, I didn't seem poor because I was on a quest. For my whole life what I originally thought were disadvantages have turned out to be advantages. ... I had women role models who kept saying to me you must defy the gods. Being poor is not necessarily a disadvantage. Being a black woman is not alone a disadvantage, because it allowed me to be aware of who I was as an individual, and to be strategic in my thinking. Other women who were not minorities were going there for the ride because the environment said to them come along for this ride, you are entitled to it. My difference kept saying to me it is required of you to give back, to be authentic. I am always aware that I'm looking forward, but I have one hand reaching back.

In describing what she initially viewed as the disadvantage of being a poor, black woman, Laura shows how she altered her views. Laura was able to obtain the courage to succeed even when she felt isolated and wounded by racism. But it was the knowledge that the women from her village were encouraging Laura 'to defy the gods' that helped her persevere, and become a successful leader. She views her success as partially a result of the support from women role models from her village. Chief amongst these role models was her mother:

My mother was a situational leader. ... She would say to you: Oh no, my child, I'm not a leader. I'm just a simple, rural woman trying to make sure the church and the poor children are taken care of. She was, in fact, a powerful woman. A storm blew down the church; a hurricane tore it down. She rebuilt it. She had an after school program, she fixed the pipe organ so I became a classical musician. I played the piano. I've done so all my life. ... It's my mother who made it possible for me.

Although her mother described herself as a simple, rural woman, in Laura's eyes, her mother was a powerful role model because she took action to improve the community's well-being. Thinking about Laura's account, I was reminded of Arendt's claim that it is during times of crisis that people show how courageous they are. In Laura's description of how her mother set about rebuilding the church following a devastating hurricane, we obtain a glimpse of how a woman takes on a leadership role in her community because she cares.

Authentic leadership

Claire retired recently from her role as President of a women's college. Prior to her presidency, she served in a variety of administrative roles in universities in North America and Europe. In Claire's words, 'an authentic leader must think and act in the context of her values'. As with Laura and Jill, Claire's mother was an important role model in shaping her daughter's leadership values. Claire describes a particular event from her childhood that she found meaningful:

My mother came from an affluent Greek family who, for a variety of complex reasons, forfeited the family's wealth to come to the United States. She was raised to be thoughtful and open to the ideas of others, as well as to people of other races and cultures. She observed and considered many things that others in her day did not. When I was ten years old, we lived in XXX – at that time a highly segregated small city – home of many of the old woolen mills. Catholics dominated the town, primarily French Canadians, Irish and Italian Catholics, as well as Ukrainian Orthodox. Nearly all activities and enterprises were based in the many local churches that were themselves divided by religion and ethnicity. The Boy and Girl Scout troops the churches housed were also homogeneous. My mother – who had been a girl scout years before – noticed this situation and didn't accept it as normal or desirable, as most people did. She said to me: 'I don't believe this was what Juliette Gordon Low envisioned when she founded girl scouting years ago. Her vision was to create an environment in which girls would develop skills, confidence, and understanding of others in the company of girls and women leaders who have different beliefs and come from many cultures.'

Mom found a few like-minded women who offered the Unitarian Church hall for the troop meeting place, and assisted in getting the word out to prospective girls. The response was strong and immediate. First of all, African American, Hispanic, and Jewish girls who had no troop to join before seemed to 'come out of the woodwork' to join the new troop. As news about the new troop and its vision spread, girls from existing parish-based troops asked to join. When the new troop totaled fifty girls, another one was started to accommodate the demand. The troops quickly became known as the best ones in town. Watching my mother – who always described herself somewhat disparagingly as 'just a housewife' – accomplish something so transformational was a powerful, early learning experience for me. To some extent, throughout my entire career, I've followed her example at the schools, colleges, and universities in which I've served. She wouldn't put it in these words, but in effect, Mom taught me about authentic leadership.

Claire's mother offered her a powerful example of leadership in action. We see how Laura and Claire's mothers spoke of themselves in a self-effacing manner as 'just a housewife', or as a 'simple, rural woman'. For their daughters, however, their mothers' actions proved how it was possible to move beyond the gender stereotypes of their environment, and for women to take on a leadership role. In each case, we see how leadership emerges when individuals are willing to act to improve their communities, primarily because they care.

Later in the interview, Claire juxtaposed the positive mentorship she received as a school teacher with her negative experiences as a woman leader in university administration.

I started my career in the comparatively comfortable setting of public school teaching in which I became confident about my leadership ability and felt accepted. However, initially, higher education was another story altogether. It was very challenging to be what can only be described as an 'outsider' on formerly all-male terrain. It was much more difficult to help create educational access and equity for women, girls, and students of color, when I, myself, had to work to be accepted by my colleagues as a 'deserving' peer. However, in the end, these personal and professional experiences only heightened my resolve and sense of purpose.

In describing her positive experiences in a school versus university setting, Claire indicates how the former gave her strength to overcome negative setbacks. As a woman leader, the marginalization she experienced strengthened her determination to succeed. Again, we see how being marginalized may, paradoxically, offer a person valuable leadership lessons.

Leading as an outsider

Until recently, Jennifer was Chair of an Institute dedicated to African Diaspora Studies. Born in Trinidad, she currently resides in the United States. In our discussion, Jennifer recounted how her experiences in a church helped her develop leadership skills.

> I was a leader in my church. I ran things like the women's bible studies groups. I tried to incorporate this idea of being humble, understanding the needs of the people, listening to each and every one of them, and making them feel valued as individuals. I tried to develop a democratic style where it wasn't my ideas alone. I was leading but, at the same time, people were also involved. I would listen to what they had to say and try, so far as it was possible, to incorporate their ideas. When I became Director of the African Diaspora Program, I used the same approach, not only with the faculty who worked and taught in the program, but the administrative staff, and also the students. ... I felt, for example, that faculty couldn't understand and teach about the African Diaspora successfully without experiencing that Diaspora. So I started a faculty trip each year where we'd go to a different place in the African Diaspora. ... We were not just a team, we were a family. It was not like I'm up there, and they are down there. That's one thing I don't like about a lot of leaders.

Here, Jennifer shows the importance of developing an atmosphere where others are encouraged to express their views. One way she tried to develop a positive community was through organized trips whereby faculty could learn more about Diaspora by visiting different places, and sharing meaningful experiences. She contrasts her success in this situation with other experiences.

> Part of successful leadership, is what you do and how you approach it. But part of it is also who you are. And who you are is a composite of a lot of things. The difficulty that I found at XXX was leading from a position as the outsider. That creates its own problems, not of your making, but it leads to either some people will accept you and overlook your difference, your diversity, and others will not. In those cases, regardless of what you do, you can't please all of the people, all of the time. There will be detractors so I just had to keep, just keep on my path, and not let these things make you lose focus.

You know, I will always be the outsider. I can't change who I am [laugh]. I don't intend to.

To me, an authentic leader has to understand the culture that you are working with, and also become responsive and sensitive. I learned very quickly that you don't compare, you don't say: 'Well, when I was teaching here this is how we did it.' Or 'When I was leading in this space this is how I did it,' because people become resentful. So I learnt very carefully that you don't compare; you accept people for who they are, and you work with the conditions that you are faced with.

Jennifer illustrates the importance of a leader being responsive to the situation that she finds herself in, rather than assume that what works in one context will work in another. This requires a leader to refrain from making comparisons between organizations, and be willing to accept people as they are, rather than as she might wish them to be. But leadership also requires having the courage to act, as she shows in her next account.

As a single mother, I have had to find my voice and an example of that – even when I was not technically in a leadership position that people looked to me as a leader – was when my son was in kindergarten. [The School] kept sending these notes when they wanted to take them on field trips. The notes would say '[W]e consent for our child to go on this outing.' All the mothers were complaining but nobody spoke up. Eventually when one of the notes came home I crossed out 'We' and 'put I/We'. I added a P.S. at the bottom that said in future create an option for single parents. I was called into the Principal's Office. I said to her: 'Though I am a single parent and a woman, you have to respect me.' The next time the slips came home they had the 'I/We' on them. The other single mothers came and thanked me and told me they didn't have the courage to speak up. But someone has to have the courage to speak up. To me, that is leadership.

I began this chapter with Kate's example of feeling fear but displaying courage; again, in Jennifer's example we have a demonstration of a person being willing to speak out against perceived injustices. Arendt argues that courage is not the absence of fear; rather, a person displays courage because they have decided that this is how they want to be seen by others. Such a demonstration of courage is, for Jennifer, at the heart of leadership.

Conclusion

What emerges from these narrative accounts is a diversity of viewpoints about the interconnections among gender, authenticity and leadership. For some of the women I interviewed, gender alone was not sufficient to explain how they conceived of authentic leadership. Thus, we see how the intersections of identity can influence ideas about leadership. Additionally, a consistent thread was the importance of leading by being cognizant of, and willing to learn from, others.

These narrative accounts also illustrate how childhood experiences have a lasting effect on present and future action (Madsen, 2006). As such, they alert us to the importance of thinking about leadership in a much more expansive manner in order to understand how people lead in diverse situations. In particular, three women noted how their mothers' actions shaped their ideas about leadership, and shows us how early childhood experiences can have a profound influence on our thinking.

For most participants, authentic leadership emerges out of a situational context whereby someone cares enough to try and change a situation that they regard as unfair. These accounts point to the importance of building caring relationships. Although I recognize the dangers that stem from seeing care as a feminine quantity, there are also dangers in ignoring care. Indeed, a focus on care is missing from much of the scholarship on authentic leadership. If authentic leadership is concerned with the well-being of others, then clearly what is critical is a leader's responsibility to care for others, regardless of gender. If we want society to flourish then we must recognize how caring leadership does not only emerge from a person's social role, but also from their actions in the world at large. By considering leadership alongside questions of authenticity and gender, we gain an understanding about what motivates leaders, and the importance of building relationships. In the following chapter, we will consider the interconnections among gender, authenticity and leadership by exploring particular themes that arose from the interviews.

8
Themes

In this chapter, I draw together salient themes that emerged from the interviews with women leaders. The first theme concerns the conflicts that arise when institutional objectives are at odds with personal convictions. The second theme relates to care and relationships. Gender and embodiment constitutes the third theme. Intersectional identity constitutes the fourth, and anxiety represents the final theme. Then, I briefly discuss two outlying themes that have phenomenological importance. Finally, I bring together the different strands of this discussion to consider how these women's descriptive accounts shed light on the interconnections among gender, authenticity and leadership. Throughout, I connect these themes with Arendt's reflections on leadership.

One problem I have already identified with regard to scholarly accounts of authentic leadership is the attempt to 'fix' meaning. In Chapter 2, I demonstrated how scholars privilege four dimensions of authentic leadership, that is, self-awareness, relational transparency, balanced processing and internalized moral perspective. This way of thinking, I suggest, is not robust enough to explain the interconnections among gender, authenticity and leadership. Moreover, when we try and define a concept like authenticity, we attempt to crystallize something that is essentially fluid. In the attempt to pin down meaning, concepts like authenticity may lose their significance. Theories like authentic leadership must be left open to contestation. Hence, these thematic responses are not offered as an alternative to the four dimensions of authentic leadership, but to illustrate there are different ways of thinking about this concept.

Questioning authenticity

I began each interview by asking research participants two questions. First, I asked interviewees to tell me what came to mind when they thought about the term 'authenticity'. Second, I asked them to describe their immediate response to the term 'authentic leadership'. (Figures 8.1 and 8.2 represent the collated responses to these two questions. When a word appears in larger typeface, this means the word was mentioned more often across the different responses.)

Figure 8.1 'What is authenticity?'

The term that appears most frequently in response to the question 'What is authenticity?' is 'values', closely followed by the term 'integrity' and 'self'. Other words to appear across multiple responses were 'consistency' and 'awareness'. From these women leaders' combined responses, then, authenticity appears to relate to adhering to particular values, practicing integrity through being consistent in one's actions and having an awareness of the effect those actions might have on others.

By contrast, answers to the question 'What is authentic leadership?' generated a greater range of responses.

Figure 8.2 'What is authentic leadership?'

The most common word used to describe authentic leadership was 'genuine', followed by 'listening' and 'journey'. It is noteworthy that no-one used the term 'self' even though this word appeared often in responses to the question 'What is authenticity?' From these collated responses, it appears that authentic leadership is perceived, by these women leaders, to refer to a genuine engagement with others. This genuine engagement was sometimes described as a willingness to listen respectfully, in other responses as responding to others in a respectful manner.

What also emerges from participants' responses to this question is the connection with movement, expressed as 'journey'. This idea of authentic leadership as a journey has been remarked upon by several leadership scholars (George *et al.*, 2007). What we see is that, for these women leaders, authenticity is perceived differently to authentic leadership. The former seems to be concerned with self, and has an inward orientation. The latter term is more outwardly oriented and, as such, has a relational component.

Although there were similarities in participants' responses to authentic leadership, there were also divergences. As I mentioned in the previous chapter, one participant disliked the term 'authentic leadership', because it suggests that some leaders are deliberately inauthentic. Instead of authenticity, she preferred the word 'integrity' to describe a genuine way of leading. Alternatively, the other nine women leaders might be placed on a continuum with some regarding authenticity as central to their desired way of leading, while others viewed it as an ideal to strive toward. At one end of that spectrum, Alison describes authentic leadership as a practice that people can aspire to, rather than a steady state. On the other end, Laura was convinced authentic leadership exists since, in her words: 'I have lived it'. From their responses, we observe that these women leaders have different ideas that stem from their diverse life experiences. This suggests that specific life experiences, alongside social location, influence the manner in which people conceptualize authentic leadership.

Institutional challenges

I want to turn now to a discussion of themes. The first theme I consider is the clash of personal versus institutional values, which was a recurring motif across most of the interviews. Jill described her frustration at being unable to change an organization's unfair policies.

> I started an initiative to make SATs optional because I believed that they are discriminatory. There were gender and class biases inherent in the standardized test that we used to get into the university, and

into certain schools. I had some true supporters, but there were many people who were opposed. I failed ultimately in my objective. ... It was frustrating and so I left the institution. ... I didn't want to work in an institution that didn't share the same values.

Jill's frustration at the decision not to change discriminatory policies led her to leave an institution that she had worked at for two decades. Her example shows how leaders must choose between upholding personal values and complying with the institution's policies. Other women leaders also described how they too gave up the fight for institutional change, choosing to seek new career opportunities, rather than stay in an environment that did not allow them to remain true to their principles. For example, Kate describes a dilemma she faced at one educational institution, when she was under pressure to admit an unqualified student. She expresses her discomfort with what she saw as a disconnection between what is said to be valued, and what takes place in reality.

I was working for a President who talked a lot about integrity in leadership. I received an email from him saying he'd been called by a priest in XXX about a student who was trying to get in to the College and would I deal with it. In a nutshell, this priest wanted to get this young woman into our nursing program, despite the fact that she didn't qualify. He described her as a nice, good Catholic girl, so I should just let her in. I encountered this situation several times in XXX. ... I remember going back to the President because I was disheartened that, despite the conversations about integrity and values, I felt a not so subtle pressure to do what was being asked of me by the outside people. I found it extraordinarily difficult to be asked to bend rules, ignore a policy, or do something out of line with my values.

Kate reveals some of the difficulties in working for an organization where the values espoused in theory are different from everyday practice. In particular, being asked to ignore policies so as to favour particular students was anathema to Kate and contrary to her idea of leading in a genuine way.

Although some women described experiences of moral angst as a result of institutional practices that negated their sense of fairness, others expressed contrary views. For instance, Olive argued that a leader's primary responsibility was to support the institution and not to agonize over ethical dilemmas. Leaders have a duty to act for the greater good, she contended, even when this meant acting contrary to personal principles. To illustrate her point, Olive described an instance when she had called in the police to break up a peaceful student demonstration because she judged the students' actions to be potentially harmful to the rest of the College community. Olive made this decision even though she agreed, in principle, with the students' cause. For Olive, this was not a comfortable decision to make but necessary for the overall well-being of the campus community. In this case, Olive saw her primary leadership duty as ensuring the safety of the community, which meant acting contrary to her personal principles.

In many accounts, women leaders described the challenges that came from taking an ethical stance. In Dianne's account of the sexual harassment case, mentioned in the previous chapter, she reflects upon whether the values she espouses in theory were ones for which she was willing to take action.

Arendt (1958) argues that who we are is defined by our actions. Yet it appears that oftentimes a leader views her actions through the lens of what is deemed socially acceptable. This may mean that for pragmatic reasons a leader concurs with majority opinion. On the one hand, this decision may be a positive outcome if it has been arrived at following dialogue and debate. On the other, it could be negative if a leader acts in accordance with group think, at the expense of personal principles. I view this as a concern in relation to authenticity since what a particular group may think is morally good may not necessarily be the case. Leaders, just like the rest of us, need to stop and think about what they value, and the reasons why. This requires an understanding of how caring is a crucial component of leading authentically.

Care and relationships

Turning to the second theme, from these descriptive accounts there seems to be a strong connection amongst leadership, authenticity and care. For example, some participants contended that when a leader encourages an atmosphere of openness, it is more likely to bring about a trusting environment. It takes time, and sustained effort, for a leader to build meaningful relationships. But it also requires a leader to be candid about the reasons for unpopular decisions that, in turn, means being willing to listen to points of contention. As Jill notes:

> This type of leadership requires transparency and ongoing dialogue
> with different groups. It is vital for a leader to lay out the choices,
> and then identify shared values, and then prioritize in a way that

reflects those values. This is crucial for authentic leadership, because if people do not understand why we are making these decisions then there's suspicion, and mistrust, which creates a toxic culture. However, if a leader makes decisions while keeping people informed, this creates collegiality and collaboration in the face of adversity.

Here Jill shows why it is important for leaders to ensure that people are both expected, and empowered, to make decisions. Empowering others creates an atmosphere of collaboration and consensus-building. To avoid mistrust in the workplace, it is necessary for a leader to have the courage to share organizational problems so that employees work together collectively to find solutions. When a leader develops an atmosphere of trust, it can lead to shared governance and mutual respect, fostered through meaningful conversations.

Jill's sentiments echo Arendt's contention that caring means allowing others to express themselves freely. One way to ensure that different viewpoints flourish is for a leader to welcome dialogue and debate. However this cannot be done in a superficial manner. If leaders are seen to be asking for opinions, but not engaging with dissenting voices, this may prove counterproductive because employees may become dis-affected by what they perceive as a lack of respect to their ideas.

There were several occasions when a woman leader spoke about the paradox of wanting to act in a caring fashion, and the institution's expectations that the foremost priority was to lead in an efficient manner. Others described the tensions that surfaced regarding the quandaries they faced in regards to leading ethically, and adhering to institutional priorities. Some participants described how they were made to feel as if their leadership style was out of step with institu-tional objectives. In this regard, Teresa notes how caring for the welfare of others contradicted the more fiscally-minded position of her institu-tion. Similarly, Jane described how being sensitive to the needs of others was unlikely to result in promotion in her university. In both instances, we see a tension between institutional priorities and what these women regard as a more caring approach to leading.

For example, Teresa describes a conflict she experienced when insti-tutional priorities and workers' demands were at odds.

I always had the welfare of the employees in mind but this is not the institutional position. So there is an internal conflict that says you have to reserve the resources of the institution. It's a difficult thing being authentic, right?

Teresa's example reveals the dissonance between institutional priorities, and her desire to care for her employees in a more humane way. What this dilemma points to is the difficulties leaders face in trying to act compassionately within the fiscal and hierarchical constraints of a bureaucratic system. Leaders are not always able to act as they choose since they must abide by Board decisions, not all of which may promote a caring workplace. At times, an ethical way of leading is at odds with institutional desires for efficiency and cost-cutting. These are everyday dilemmas that leaders have to deal with. These dilemmas point to some problems with regard to seeing authentic leaders as both efficient and ethical.

Other participants made a connection between feminist practice and caring leadership. In fact, Jill suggested that a feminist ethics of care was crucial to her understanding of leadership. Several women mentioned how becoming a leader was a vehicle for them to try and effect a more just environment. As Olive stated 'I wasn't interested in just being a college president to be a president. I had no ambitions for that at all, but when XXX asked me to think about it, I mainly did it because I cared a lot about advancing the cause of women's liberation'. Other research participants also argued that it was their feminist principles that encouraged them to lead in a caring way. What we must be cautious about, however, is the supposition that just because someone espouses feminist principles this will mean that they have a caring approach to leadership. Therefore, we need to be cautious about suggesting that espousing feminist principles necessarily results in the eradication of injustice. An interest in the structural and social effects of gender may encourage a leader to act in a more caring way, but this might not always prove to be the case.

A sense of self

Some research participants described how being self-aware enabled them to build a rapport with others. In this regard, Alison maintained there is a symbiotic relationship between authenticity and understanding one's own capabilities.

> One thing that interferes with authenticity is having an idea about yourself that's not accurate and trying to live up to that. So what I am trying to get at here is being aware of one's capacity and one's capabilities – not to say that you can't continue to grow and learn, but knowing something about your strengths and areas when you

can contribute and being able to continue to track that, rather than fall into trying to become someone that you are not.

For Alison, being self-aware makes it easier to lead in a caring manner. Her views would seem to align with authentic leadership scholars. However, knowing who we are is not a simple task. In reflecting on her leadership experiences, Teresa offers a contrasting perspective: 'You were asking are you true to yourself when you are doing this or that? That's always a question. I don't know. Sometimes, you could see that it's you but, in other instances, it's not very clear.' Teresa suggests that because leaders are often reacting to situations, and making snap decisions, it can be difficult to know whether you are acting in a manner in accordance with your principles. Her assessment resonates with Arendt's (1971) assertion that self-knowledge is always a partial understanding.

Furthermore, Kate acknowledged that her public and private personae were somewhat different. In her public role as leader, she carries herself in a confident manner. Yet those who know her well – close friends and family members – regard her as a shy person. She imagined her colleagues would be surprised to learn of her shy disposition. Kate's distinction between her private and public selves mirrors Arendt's belief that we take on a personae whenever we act within a public context. Thus, the notion that we are always the same within one context or another is not borne out from this study.

Just as leaders influence institutions so too do institutions influence leaders. As Kate states, 'I have to understand that just as I want to change the institution, the institution and the role changed me.' This statement is interesting for it shows how leaders and their institutions transform each other. This transformation can be good or bad in that sometimes people become caught up in the leadership role. For example, Claire states:

> I'm remembering an exchange I had with a colleague some years ago. He'd just taken a college presidency, and I had not yet gotten to that point in my career. I remembered him talking about what it's like to be a college president, and I thought to myself afterwards – he's posing! He was primarily talking about how he would act in new ways to be presidential and be taken seriously. A few other colleagues also seemed to begin to behave differently when they became presidents – posing is how I describe it. I think the most

effective leaders are those who remain authentic – true to themselves, and their personalities, and don't try to have a 'make-over'.

Claire argues that leaders who indulge in leadership makeovers will be
less successful because others will see through their disguise. But other
women spoke of the institutional pressures that leaders face to perform
in a particular manner, as Kate explains: 'Sometimes, people try to be
the leader they think the organization wants or expects and that pulls
them away, or they get trapped into feeling they have to lead in a
particular way. In the long run it destroys your soul.' Instead of leading
from one's unique strengths, trying to conform to some kind of leadership ideal may have a deleterious effect. This is why Kate argues it is
important for leaders not to take up new leadership trends just to
appear *au courant*. For Kate, how leaders do things matters as much as
what we do. This connection to the 'how' of leadership emerged
several times, and indicates how important it is for a person to lead in
a manner that feels right for them, while being cognizant of their
effect on others.

Although some research participants talked about how concern for
their employees and students' welfare was central to questions of
authenticity in leadership, others remarked how responding in a compassionate manner was sometimes regarded as a sign of a leader's weakness. It seems that there is a delicate balance between wanting to lead
in a caring way, and institutional pressures to perform leadership in a
particular manner. These issues have a distinct bearing on what it
means to be an authentic leader.

Gender and embodiment

A prevailing theme arising from several interviews is how a woman's
appearance can reinforce gender stereotypes. This creates additional
burdens as women try to conform to some kind of ideal, as Jill notes:

> All of these expectations about what it is to be an effective woman
> leader the men never have to think about including wardrobe
> issues. It's a challenge to have to think about all of these things.
> That people will judge me based on whether I have my nails done,
> whether my hair's done, whether I wear a particular dress, my
> weight, all of these things.

Several women leaders referred to how 'wardrobe issues' could play a
negative part in how they are perceived as leaders. This brought to

light different ways in which women leaders may be undermined by stereotypical assumptions regarding how the ideal woman leader is supposed to look. Any deviation from what is considered culturally normative may prove prejudicial to her leadership.

It appears that it is not enough for a woman leader to do a good job; she also has to make a good job of herself. For some women leaders, the connection between their appearance and their leadership capabilities was a source of ongoing frustration. Some leaders expressed irritation at how a focus on their appearance detracted from what they were saying. Kate offered a striking description of this type of gender stereotyping.

> I have done presentations to rooms where because of the grace of the audience they've jumped up to their feet, and it's been wonderful and spontaneous and amazing. Then I've walked off the stage and had a man say to me: 'That was fantastic, that's wonderful, but where did you get your suit? I'd like to buy one similar for my wife'.

Such trivial comments, however well-meant, reinforce gender hierarchy by discounting a woman leader's words in favour of her appearance. In this situation, a woman leader's attire has become the defining factor in how she is perceived. This focus on the leader's body serves to undermine her actions. At times, too much emphasis on how a woman looks can prove detrimental to her leadership. Although I am not suggesting that men do not have to conform to a leadership dress code, I do think that a woman leader's figure is read more carefully. As a consequence, too much attention to her wardrobe may work to undermine a woman's credibility as a leader, while too little may lead to cries of derision (Sinclair, 2013).

Yet, at other times, Kate regards being a woman as advantageous to leadership, especially in regards to showing emotion. Following the accidental death of a faculty member, she described how being a woman leader gave her an opportunity to publicly express grief. In her words,

> When I was standing up in front of our folks welcoming them back, and talking about XXX, the tears were rolling down my face. I was broken-hearted, and everybody knew it. I think that was easier, more accepted and, to some degree, expected because I was a woman.

Here we see how societal notions regarding appropriate gender behaviour enabled Kate to openly express her emotion. This open expression of grief was expected because she is a woman, but may be less acceptable from a male leader. The problem is that if a woman does not show an appropriate response, she may be accused of a lack of empathy, whereas a man may be perceived as weak. In both instances, we see how a leader's physical response to a particular situation is influenced by gender socialization.

Intersectional identity

Through listening to these women leaders' accounts, it became apparent that gender on its own was not sufficient to understand these women's experiences of authenticity, or lack thereof. Many times in the interviews, women made reference to class, race and age. Thus, gender needs to be understood within the broader context of intersectional identity. For example, Laura argued that being a black woman in a predominantly white environment helped her to gain a sense of who she was as a unique individual. Being on the margins gave Laura strength, she argued, because it allowed her to keep connected to her past. But being on the margins is not always a positive experience for a woman leader. For instance, Jennifer spoke of how she had to hide the knowledge she learned in Trinidad, since it was perceived as irrelevant by her North American colleagues. Jennifer was adamant that she experiences ongoing racism because of her outsider status. As a result, from time to time, she told me about her struggles with depression. Clearly, being on the margins can work as a positive and negative influence for women leaders.

A person's class origins were also something that some interviewees stated had an effect on their leadership. For instance, Jill described how some alumnae express surprise when they learnt of her working-class origins remarking on how strange it seems that someone from her background could be so eloquent. This negative allusion to her working-class origins had the effect of making Jill feel like an imposter. Claire also talked about how her working-class origins made her aware of injustice, and encouraged her to fight against prejudice in her work.

It is noteworthy that it was only those women who identified as black or working-class that talked about these issues. For middle-class white women, therefore, gender may have a greater effect on leadership, because their relative privileged position in society makes them less aware of other intersectional issues.

In these interviews, age was viewed as both a positive and negative attribute in relation to leadership. While there has been a lot written on the negative societal prejudice against older women, for many of the leaders I interviewed, maturity afforded them a greater sense of confidence, as Jane notes:

> When I was younger, I was only comfortable if I could control the situation, and now I'm much better at being comfortable letting the situation become something, and just letting or waiting to see what it's going to become, and working with that rather than trying to force it into some particular direction.

Allowing situations to unfold organically is one way Jane became more comfortable with the contingency. Other participants described how, when they were younger, they were more likely to conform to the rules. As they matured, however, women described gaining the courage to speak out. As Jane explains: 'I spent a lot of time in my younger years trying to be the way that I was supposed to be ... this is how a professor is; this is how a graduate student is, rather than thinking about who am I? And what do I bring to this?' Here we see that age coupled with gender socialization can have a negative influence on some women's ability to speak their minds.

Interestingly, two women used the same phrase to emphasize what they saw as a barrier to women's leadership, namely, that women had to learn to get over themselves. But this took time. Some participants described how when they were younger they had not taken up opportunities because of what they now see as uneasiness with success. As they gained confidence and maturity, they were more open to possibilities. Thus it appears that it is only with maturity that some women realize their full potential. There are other ways age has an effect on a woman's leadership, as Kate notes:

> I had a humbling moment when I was negotiating my contract with the Chair of the Board. I told him what I expected, and he said that's a lot of money for a young girl like you. I was forty. This was my first one-on-one with the Board Chair. I was tempted to say and if I were a man would you have even thought of making that comment?

Kate's attempt to negotiate her salary is belittled by a person who has power over her. In their negotiations, the Chair of the Board used terms like 'young girl' to bring Kate into line with what he considers to be appropriate expectations, given her age and gender. Rather than her leadership capabilities, her relative youth and gender was used to offer her less compensation than what Kate regarded as acceptable. So we see that age can have positive and negative influences on a woman's ability to speak out, partially a result of gender socialization.

These different experiences of race, class and age alerts us to the need to pay attention to other social factors beyond gender. For these women, gender on its own is insufficient to explain the connections between leadership and authenticity. Finally, it is noteworthy that none of the interviewees mentioned disability or sexuality in relation to leadership, which may illustrate how some topics are still not discussed openly, at least in these interviews.

Anxiety

Anxiety is the final theme that comes out of these interviews as important to understanding gender, authenticity and leadership. Some women described occasions when their self-assurance was negated by anxious feelings. Dianne offers a striking example of this angst when she described an instance when she chose to remain silent following repeated attempts to put forward views that ran contrary to her colleagues on the senior management team. When Dianne senses this is not the case, the result is a sense of unease and a reluctance to speak out.

> When I said shrinking, I was sensing the opposite of that sort of not owning the space that I could or should own. Taking up a smaller corner of that and trying to be – maybe trying is the wrong word because that sounds conscious – but ending up being less influential, both in physical presence and in impact. When I have been in situations where I feel uncomfortable, or devalued, or disempowered, I have been a smaller version of myself, quieter, and less impactful.

The decision to speak, or remain silent, derives from learned experience of what is perceived as appropriate behaviour. I suggest that silence is intrinsically linked to gender hierarchy in a way that works to encourage some people to speak while discouraging others. When anxiety results in silencing, it allows some bodies to gain prominence while others recede into the background, as Dianne's account illustrates. This kind of workplace interaction 'allows spaces to become territories, claimed as rights by some bodies and not others' (Ahmed, 2004, p. 6). For some women leaders, a refusal to speak out resulted in a growing sense of anxiety. This anxiety shows itself on the body. In Dianne's account her decision to refrain from speaking results in a feeling of 'shrinking'. The anxiety provoked by this feeling allows her to recognize how she reacts physically to being marginalized. Alison also mentioned how tension in the workplace could cause anxiety:

> I feel uncomfortable when there are expectations that are hidden or unstated or when there's a mismatch between what I think I am to be doing or what I think we have agreed on and the way things are unfolding. So that feeling of discomfort is usually something that triggers me to move toward more authenticity ... I experience it in my body as tension, as anxiety.

As we saw in Chapter 5, Heidegger regarded anxiety as the ontic expression of authenticity. Clearly for these women leaders there is a deep connection between feelings of anxiety and a greater awareness of self. This shows itself through physical responses to particular circumstances. These embodied responses will differ depending upon the person and the situation. Nevertheless, they offer insight into how being marginalized has physical effects.

Another issue to emerge in relation to anxiety was learning how to overcome hostile environments. As Claire explains, 'I had to learn how to deal with not being loved and to stay focused on the long-term good. That wasn't easy'. A willingness to be unpopular was, at times, the only way these women leaders told me it was possible to remain true to their principles. Having the courage to go against the will of the majority seems, therefore, to be an integral component of how these women viewed authentic leadership. However, submissiveness in childhood may mean that some women are reluctant to take a stance, especially in a hostile environment. At times, therefore, there may be a dissonance between a woman's learned behaviour, and her desire to act. Such passivity may have a negative effect on a woman's ability to lead. Again we see how gender socialization, such as being brought up to please others, can have a detrimental influence on a woman's leadership.

Outlying themes

I want to turn to outlying themes that have phenomenological importance. At the end of each interview, I asked each participant if they had anything they wanted to add. Here are two responses; the first from Dianne.

> Sometimes we can burn a lot of political capital by taking against the majority when it has to do with something that's important to you from a principled or valued point of view. As a woman, one of the challenges for me is thinking how I can maintain my organizational power while, at the same time, acting and influencing the organization in a way that is in keeping with my internal compass.

Dianne reveals how she is constantly reflecting upon the balance between keeping organizational power and taking principled action. This is an ongoing challenge that requires us to measure how our leadership action aligns with our principles. But Dianne suggests that being a woman may make it harder to balance institutional power with personal principles.

At the end of another interview, Olive returned to the question of leading ethically. In her words,

> I wouldn't want to give the impression that I think that it doesn't make a difference whether leaders have a moral compass or whether they are trying to behave as ethically as they can. I think it makes a profound difference. I just don't think it's always easy to describe what moral, or immoral, leadership is, particularly if you are trying to do it through the familiar lens of private, personal ethical decisions.

Here, Olive expresses how important she perceives leading ethically to be. But she also shows that describing what constitutes moral, or immoral, leadership is complex. What constitutes authentic leadership may be much easier to describe in theory than it is within the context of everyday life.

Conclusion

By focusing on particular themes, we have seen that, for some women, authentic leadership is about a genuine engagement that requires a willingness to listen to others. For others, a genuine approach to leadership depends upon being consistent with personal values. Some women emphasized caring while others focussed on the need for a strategic approach. What becomes clear is that authentic leadership evokes different things for different people. This multiplicity of perspectives is due to the fact that each of us is unique. That unique identity is made up of social factors, as well as embodied lived experience, which will influence the way that we lead. These factors will influence gendered perspectives of authentic leadership.

For most of these women leaders, there is a strong correlation between wanting to lead in a caring way, and a desire to be authentic in their leadership. Such openness shows itself through our embodied relationships with others. This relational approach to leadership is fundamental to creating an environment where others will be able to flourish. It requires leaders to welcome different viewpoints. A relational approach to leadership is fundamental to addressing the problems of instrumental ways of being that focus on a means-ends way of thinking. This is why it is important, as these women leaders' accounts show, to think about leadership beyond an institutional framework. And this is why, as Jennifer states, 'We have to explode the idea of being a leader as a thing created by a position'.

From these women's narratives, we see how leadership is influenced by a variety of factors such as gender socialization. At times, this can lead to a dissonance between learned behaviour on the one hand, and a desire to act in a manner consistent with her values on the other. Leaders, just like the rest of us, have to choose between acting in accordance with institutional practices and upholding personal principles. Sometimes, people will make a decision in line with their values, at other moments they may not do so.

What is clear from these thematic accounts is that authenticity cannot be contained within a conceptual framework of leadership that denies difference. This is why a theory of leadership, based on authenticity, cannot take its cue from the self. For now, I leave the final word to Jennifer:

> I just want to re-emphasize that you lead, not just for your own personal embellishment and self-aggrandizement, but with the goal of moving the community forward. That should be your primary focus as a leader. That, to me, is authentic leadership.

9
Concluding Remarks

This phenomenological investigation has revealed some significant shortcomings in current accounts of authentic leadership. I have argued that a focus on specific quantifications is not robust enough to explain the concept of authentic leadership. Indeed, current definitions of authentic leadership remain problematic in part because of the tendency among some leadership scholars to define and constrain the ways in which authenticity reveals itself. Such thinking is troubling since it ignores how the intersections of identity, as well as cultural contexts, affect the theory and practice of leadership. This way of thinking about leadership privileges the universal over the particular, what Arendt (1958, p. 289) termed the 'Archimedean worldview'. Such abstraction is not a useful way of conceptualizing how leadership works, particularly within everyday life. Rather, it is through our intersubjective, embodied relationships that we define ourselves. These meaningful encounters always take place within a world of others.

Arendt's insights offer an important correlative to problems inherent with the concept of authentic leadership, and what I see as its overemphasis on the self. I suggest, therefore, that an Arendtian analysis can enrich current scholarship, especially because of her stress on the myriad ways in which leaders must be responsive to others. As such, Arendt offers us an alternative, ethical guide.

Furthermore, by exploring the intersections among gender, authenticity and leadership, we have seen how social conformity influences our ideas about leaders. An important insight to emerge in this regard is how thinking from the margins offers insights into leadership. Thinking from the margins has taken different forms, such as considering a diversity of sources, as well as interviews with women leaders. As a result, we have an enriched understanding of the manner in which the concept of authenticity is affected by gender socialization, and the ways in which it influences leadership.

Although my original intention was to concentrate on the connections amongst gender, authenticity and leadership within an institutional setting, this was not where the interviews led me. It became apparent that leadership within the context of an institution was only one aspect of how these women conceived of what it meant to be an authentic leader. They spoke on a variety of topics, such as politics, racism, family and the interconnected ways that their lived experiences shaped their ideas about what it might mean to be an authentic leader. A common thread weaving through these different conversations is that leadership needs to be conceptualized outside of hierarchical frameworks. Rather than focussing on a person's position in an institutional setting, it is important to redefine our notions of what constitutes leadership, and show how different situations call for diverse kinds of leaders. This is a more expansive way of thinking about leadership, and complements Arendt's idea that leadership is situational.

Too often the focus on leadership is where most of us think power resides, that is, the public realm. This can lead to a very narrow idea of what constitutes leadership. For instance, by making institutional life the centre of attention, it is possible to underestimate, or even ignore, the important leadership work that is carried out in the home, family, volunteer or church groups. This situated knowledge, if considered at all, is perceived as less valuable than the business of leadership. Furthermore, the seeming disregard for other spaces/ways of leading may be linked to a Western obsession with hierarchies based on considerations of profit and prestige. Hence, ways of leading that do not have a monetary value attached to them may appear to have less cache.

It is only by reconsidering what it means to be an authentic leader beyond the confines of the work environment that we can see how gender plays a role in our understanding of what constitutes leadership. Ignoring the intersubjective dimension of everyday life has negative implications because it can result in leaders acting in self-indulgent ways to the detriment of everyone else. Indeed, the differentiation between the few and the many have led to disastrous consequences. Whether it's the banking crisis or the negative effects of globalization, it is apparent that some leaders are failing to reflect upon, or care about, how their actions negatively affect others, something Arendt regarded as a necessary requirement for a just society.

In the introduction to this book, I mentioned that a secondary research aim is to understand why, at this particular historical juncture, the theory of authentic leadership has emerged. My sense is that this desire for a theoretical justification to teach leaders how to act authentically arises from our cultural fixation on the self as opposed to broader concerns. However, a focus on self-interest can lead to an increasing alienation from the world. And this is dangerous not just for leaders, but also for the rest of us.

Perhaps, then, it is authentic engagement, rather than authentic leadership, that is needed. This is why I concur with Charles Guignon's argument (2004) that we must view authenticity, not as hopelessly 'essentialist' as some postmodernists suggest, but as a dialogical means of trying to build authentic relationships. Indeed, the key to understanding whether authenticity is a helpful way of thinking about leadership is to recognize that authentic relationships are at the heart of the matter (Eagly, 2005; Ladkin and Spiller, 2013).

Instead of dismissing the concept of authentic leadership altogether, however, I want to reframe it as an ambiguous, messy endeavour that cannot be conceived of in terms of behavioural competences but as a non-instrumental engagement with others. Each situation will call for a different response. These new situations will need a different way of framing leadership, which is why conforming to a particular style of leading which may be socially acceptable may not be adequate for the situation's needs. This is why leadership needs to be questioned, rather than merely prescribed. Hence, a genuine approach to authentic leadership cannot work from a script, since each situation will unfold differently.

Arendt shows us why dialogue and debate is critical to human flourishing because, if leaders are unwilling to listen to different opinions, they will be unable to lead in a manner that enables others to thrive. To allow individuals and their societies to prosper, what is necessary is a respect for one another made manifest through the encouragement of diverse viewpoints. It is only by allowing these dissenters to voice their opinions that a leader can start to get people to think through their disagreements with each other and, hopefully, reach a potential solution. There is no saying that resolutions will appear as if by magic. However, if authentic engagement is the centerpiece of an organization, then it is more likely that people will share their concerns. This is why it is so important for leaders to build an organizational structure where people feel that they can speak openly, while being respectful of others. Perhaps it is respect for one another that is the most important value of authenticity in the workplace and beyond.

The ongoing creation of shared, albeit constantly contested, values require us to rethink authentic leadership in organizational terms (Heil, 2010). We need, however, to recognize that no one leader can revitalize broken systems. It is the organization itself that must change. This change necessitates a living demonstration of common values. In order to move toward a shared understanding, we need to be open to dissenting viewpoints. These conversations about where the organization is and where it wants to be cannot just take place when a new leader is appointed, or when a strategic plan is needed. Rather the conversations about what matters to the organization must occur on a regular basis if people are to become more fully engaged with the organization's mandate. A word of caution is necessary, since, as Peter Fleming (2007) tells us, authenticity in the workplace may be a ruse, a way for organizations to get the most out of their employees.

Today, the 24/7 experience of modern-day employment, and the precarious existence that many workers experience, brings to mind a neo-feudalist environment where only those at the top profit. This is a lamentable state of affairs. If living well means to be connected to others in a wider sense, through community work and family life, then being connected to the job 24/7 is hardly likely to offer a kind of experience that feels desirable. Rather, the likelihood is that people will become depressed as to their inability to take control of their lives. But this 24/7 mentality leads to a convergence of the public and private such that there is a 'flattening' of individuality (Crary, 2013). As such, there is little if any space left to provide the necessary sustenance we require to sustain ourselves beyond the avaricious, and potentially damaging, light of consumerist society. Without the ability to cultivate our singularity in our private lives, we become estranged from the world. This estrangement is damaging to human and societal flourishing. But this does not mean that we should not do our utmost to build a society where an ethics of authentic engagement is defined by recognizing each person in their singularity, as who they are and not as who we want them to be.

In *Being and Time*, Heidegger maintains that each person's life is shaped partially by things outside of her control, not least because we begin life, not as we choose, but as a being who is thrown into the world. As a result, our freedom is, to a certain extent, limited by our social position. Yet Arendt (1955) suggests that he may be in error. As she states:

> Heidegger is wrong: man is not 'thrown in the world'; if we are thrown, then – no differently from animals – onto the earth. Man is precisely guided, not thrown, precisely for that reason his continuity

arises and the way he belongs appears. Poor us, if we are thrown into the world!

For Arendt, we are always guided in our entry into the world. This guidance takes many forms; an important aspect is that of parental supervision a child receives. Through the interviews I conducted we have seen how important maternal guidance, in particular, was to some women leaders' ideas about authenticity in leadership. Rather than resoluteness, so uppermost in the literature, at a deeper level, it is care, in our relationships, communities and beyond, that we need so much. Unlike Heidegger, Arendt (1958) offers us hope as she suggests that we have the freedom to change the world and begin anew. I suggest it is through an emphasis on caring for others, rather than resolute action that we best see the potential for positive change both within and around us.

This inquiry started by looking at authentic leadership through an institutional lens so as to see how senior women leaders described authenticity, or lack thereof, within an institutional context. I wanted to ascertain the conditions whereby women leaders described a tension between their desire to act in what they perceived as a genuine manner, and the limitations of the institutional environment. What stops me feeling uneasy about this directional change is that phenomenologists' pre-conceptions need to be challenged. If this does not happen, then research is not sufficiently hermeneutical in scope (Benner, 1994). In order to take into account different perspectives, we must be open to challenging our own assumptions. My research certainly unfolded along different lines than I had envisaged. In particular, the research participants' descriptive accounts enriched my understanding of the role of authenticity in leadership in ways that I had not anticipated. These women leaders' narratives, in conversation with Arendt, led me to an understanding that it is necessary to broaden our enquiry about authentic leadership from institutional life to how we live in the world. Through the sharing of words and worlds, I have been guided back to what I had always known but had sadly forgotten.

In conclusion, if we wish to understand the ways in which gender, authenticity and leadership interconnect, then, we must broaden our inquiry to take into account concrete, lived experience. Only then will we be able to comprehend whether authentic leadership offers us an ethical framework that is robust enough for our times.

Notes

Chapter 1   Introduction

1   Arendt spoke at a conference in her honour in Toronto in September 1972; this quotation is purportedly taken from her speech (Betz Hull, 2002, p. 36).
2   For more on Arendt and uniqueness, see Gardiner (2013).

Chapter 3   Gendered Expectations

1   It is noteworthy that only 17 percent of women in member countries hold cabinet positions. However, the figure ranges from more than 40 percent in Nordic countries to a 16 percent average in the Middle East or North Africa. Moreover, those that are in positions of power usually have a portfolio of family or social services. See The United Nations (2014) 'Facts and Figures' for more information at www.unwomen.org.
2   Latest figures from the European Union suggest that member countries have very different pay differentials. These range from as low as 2.5 percent in Slovenia to as high as 30 percent in Romania. On average, in the European Union, women earn 16 percent less per hour than men. Considering gender through a global lens may also prove instructive. For instance, *The United Nations Global Gender Gap Report* (2013) measured the gender gap in terms of four differentials: Economic Participation and Opportunity, Educational Attainment, Health and Survival, and Political Empowerment. Out of 136 countries, Iceland came first. What is noteworthy, however, is that some countries in the Global South had better showings in terms of gender parity than some of their wealthy Northern counterparts.
3   Paradoxically, Carli and Eagly argue that women exert greater influence in the workplace when they exhibit lower levels of competence than they actually possess. This would suggest that behaving in a duplicitous manner pays dividends for some women. For instance, as a way of gaining attention, some women request assistance from their male colleagues when such guidance is not required. Clearly, engaging in such behaviour is not likely to be conducive to authentic action.
4   CBC interview on *The Current* with Anna Maria Tremonti, May 2014.
5   It will be demonstrated through the descriptive accounts by some women leaders, that when they were asked to think about authenticity, gender and leadership, participants chose to relate stories about their mothers' action. In their eyes, she was the person who epitomized the core values they regarded as authentic.

Chapter 4   Enlightened Virtue

1   Because of its scurrilous nature, this work was only published after Diderot's death; yet it had a major impact on other thinkers. For example, Hegel was so enamoured with Diderot's exposé of social mores that he made use of this fictional account in the *Phenomenology of Spirit*, where he inverted the commonplace notion of what is noble and what is base (Trilling, 1972). For Hegel, Lui represents the triumph of the human spirit over moral orthodoxy.

Chapter 5   Authenticity, Ethics and Leadership

1   Arendt sees a connection between abstract notions of equality and negative forms of leadership. She maintains that what makes a tyranny distinct is that everyone is equal except for the tyrant.

2   Arendt (1951, pp. 473–479) often conceives of politics in terms of spatial metaphors as Benhabib (1995b) has also noted. For instance, Arendt likens constitutional government to a space where the law is like a hedge placed between buildings. The space provided by this metaphorical hedge allows for dialogue and debate which, in turn, enables human flourishing. On the one hand, Arendt argues that tyranny is akin to a desert where the tyrant's will to dominate functions like a sandstorm that overtakes travelers. On the other, totalitarianism acts like an iron band of terror that compresses people together until it appears as if there is no opposition.

3   Another salient feature of the totalitarian state that Arendt notes is mobility. Constant changes of direction by the Leader ensure that people are kept off-guard. Members of the elite are constantly changing. These alterations in personnel enabled Hitler to ensure rival factions did not seize control. In this way, the Leader proves that he is not only infallible, but indispensable. Yet while there is mobility within the system, for the majority of citizens, freedom of movement and speech is constrained.

4   Arendt (2003a) maintains that guilt and innocence can only be applied to individuals. Hence, she is fundamentally opposed to the notion of collective guilt as it can result in a feigned equality. Furthermore, collective guilt may lead to a lack of personal responsibility on the part of those individuals who commit immoral acts. For Arendt, collective guilt is a misnomer, because no moral, individual and personal, standards of conduct will ever be able to excuse us from collective responsibility.

5   Hodge further maintains that Heidegger shows how acting in terms of having predetermined ends is unethical, since it subordinates human relations to instrumental ways of relating. By viewing the world in instrumental ways, we objectify things, and truth, rather than being a question, becomes a matter of certainty. For instance, current versions of ethics that proliferate in medical, educational and political environments are linked with specific outcomes, and this serves to obscure a deeper understanding of ethics as care.

Chapter 6   Troubling Method

1   Women's Education Worldwide is an international network made up primarily of women's colleges.

Bibliography

J. Acker (1990) 'Hierarchies, Jobs, Bodies: A Theory of Gendered Organizations', *Gender and Society*, 4, 2, 139–158.

S. Ahmed (2004) *The Cultural Politics of Emotion* (Edinburgh: Edinburgh University Press).

L. Alcoff (Winter 1991–1992) 'The Politics of Speaking for Others', *Cultural Critique*, 20, 5–32.

P. M. Algera and M. Lips-Wiersma (2012) 'Radical Authentic Leadership: Co-creating the Conditions under which all Members of the Organization can be Authentic', *The Leadership Quarterly*, 23, 118–231.

M. Alvesson and S. Sveningsson (2013) 'Essay: Authentic Leadership Critically Reviewed', in D. Ladkin and C. Spiller (eds) *Authentic Leadership: Clashes, Convergences and Coalescences* (Cheltenham: Edward Elgar), pp. 39–55.

H. Arendt (1951) *Origins of Totalitarianism* (New York: Harcourt Brace Jovanovich).

_____. (August 1955) *Denktagebuch*, Notebook 21, Section 68, http://www. hannaharendtcenter.org, accessed May 6, 2013.

_____. (1958) *The Human Condition* (Chicago: The University of Chicago Press).

_____. (1963) *Eichmann in Jerusalem: A Report on the Banality of Evil* (London: Penguin Books).

_____. (1965) *On Revolution* (New York: Viking Compass Books).

_____. (1971) *The Life of the Mind*, M. McCarthy (ed.) (New York: Harcourt, Brace Jovanovich).

_____. (1974) *Rahel Varnhagen: The Life of a Jewish Woman*, R. and C. Winston (trans.) (New York and London: Harcourt Brace Jovanovich).

_____. (1982) *Lectures on Kant's Political Philosophy*, R. Beiner (ed.) (Chicago: The University of Chicago Press).

_____. (1985) *Correspondence: Hannah Arendt and Karl Jaspers 1926–1969*, L. Kohler and H. Saner (eds), R. and R. Kimber (trans.) (New York: Harcourt Brace Jovanovich).

_____. (1993) 'What is Authority?' *Between Past and Future: Eight Exercises in Political Thought* (London: Penguin Books), pp. 91–143.

_____. (1994a) 'What Remains? The Language Remains: A Conversation with Günter Gaus', in J. Kohn (ed.) *Essays in Understanding: 1930–1954* (New York: Harcourt Brace and Company), pp. 1–24.

_____. (1994b) 'A Reply to Eric Voegelin', in J. Kohn (ed.) *Essays in Understanding 1930–1954* (New York: Harcourt and Brace), pp. 401–409.

_____. (1994c) 'What is Existential Philosophy?', in J. Kohn (ed.) *Responsibility and Judgment* (New York: Schocken Books), pp. 163–188.

_____. (1994d) 'On the Emancipation of Women', in J. Kohn (ed.) *Essays in Understanding 1930–1954* (New York: Harcourt and Brace), pp. 66–69.

_____. (2003a) 'Personal Responsibility under Dictatorship', in J. Kohn (ed.) *Responsibility and Judgment* (New York: Schocken Books), pp. 17–49.

_____. (2003b) 'Some Questions of Moral Philosophy', in J. Kohn (ed.) *Responsibility and Judgment* (New York: Schocken Books), pp. 49–147.

_____. (2003c) 'Thinking and Moral Considerations', in J. Kohn (ed.) *Responsibility and Judgement* (New York: Schocken Books), pp. 159–193.

B. J. Avolio (2013) 'Foreword: Some Transparent Reflections on Authentic Leadership Theory and Research', in D. Ladkin and C. Spiller, *Authentic Leadership: Clashes, Convergences and Coalescences* (Edward Elgar), pp. xxii–xxviii.

B. J. Avolio and W. L. Gardner (2005) 'Authentic Leadership Development: Getting to the Root of Positive Forms of Leadership', *The Leadership Quarterly*, 16, 3, 315–338.

B. J. Avolio, W. L. Gardner, F. O. Walumbwa, F. Luthans and D. R. May (2004) 'Unlocking the Mask: A Look at the Process by which Authentic Leaders impact Follower Attitudes and Behavior', *The Leadership Quarterly*, 15, 801–823.

B. J. Avolio, J. Griffith, T. S. Wernsing and F. O. Walumbwa (2009) 'What is Authentic Leadership Development?', in P. A. Linley, S. Harrington and N. Garcea (eds) *Oxford Handbook of Positive Psychology and Work* (Oxford: Oxford University Press), pp. 39–51.

B. J. Avolio and K. Mhatre (2011) 'Advances in Theory and Research on Authentic Leadership', in K. S. Cameron and G. M. Spreitzer (eds) *Oxford Handbook of Positive Organizational Scholarship* (Oxford: Oxford University Press), pp. 772–783.

B. J. Avolio, F. O. Walumbwa and T. J. Weber (2005) 'Leadership: Current Theories, Research, and Future Directions', *Annual Review Psychology*, 60, 421–439.

B. Bass and P. Steidlmeir (1999) 'Ethics, Character, and Authentic Transformational Leadership Behaviour', *The Leadership Quarterly*, 19, 2, 181–217.

P. T. Begley (2006) 'Self-Knowledge, Capacity and Sensitivity: Prerequisites to Authentic Leadership by School Principals', *Journal of Educational Administration*, 44, 6, 570–589.

S. Benhabib (1995a) 'The Pariah and Her Shadow: Hannah Arendt's Biography of Rahel Varnhagen', *Political Theory*, 23, 1, 5–24.

_____. (1995b) 'Feminist Theory and Hannah Arendt's Conception of the Public Space', *History of the Human Sciences*, 6, 2, 97–114.

_____. (1996) *The Reluctant Modernism of Hannah Arendt* (London and Thousand Oaks: Sage).

P. Benner (1994) 'The Tradition and Skill of Interpretive Phenomenology in Studying Health, Illness, and Caring Practices', in P. Benner (ed.) *Interpretive Phenomenology: Embodiment, Caring, and Ethics in Health and Illness* (Thousand Oaks: Sage Publications Inc.), pp. 141–167.

M. Berman (1971) *Politics of Authenticity: Radical Individualism and the Emergence of Modern Society* (New York: Athenaeum Books).

M. Betz Hull (2002) *The Hidden Philosophy of Hannah Arendt* (London and New York: Routledge).

J. Binns (2008) 'The Ethics of Relational Leading: Gender Matters', *Gender, Work and Organization*, 15, 6, 600–620.

J. Binns and D. Kerfoot (2011) '"Editorial: Engendering Leadership:" Dedicated to the Spirit and the Scholarship of Joan Evangeline', *Gender, Work & Organization*, 18, 3, 257–263.

P. Birmingham (2006) *Hannah Arendt and Human Rights: The Predicament of Common Responsibility* (Bloomington and Indianapolis: Indiana University Press).

J. Blackmore (2009) 'International Response Essay Leadership for Social Justice: A Transnational Dialogue', *Journal of Research on Leadership Education*, 4, 1, 1–11.

J. Blackmore and J. Sachs (2007) *Performing and Reforming Leaders: Gender, Educational Restructuring, and Organizational Change* (Albany: State of Albany).

R. Bornstein (2010) 'Women and the Quest for Presidential Legitimacy', in D. R. Dean, S. J. Bracken and J. K. Allen (eds) *Women in Academic Leadership: Professional Strategies, Personal Choices* (Sterling, VA: Stylus Publishing), pp. 208–238.

C. Branson (2010) 'Ethical Decision Making: Is Personal Moral Integrity the Missing Link?', *Journal of Authentic Leadership in Education*, 1, 1, 1–8.

C. Brightman (1995) (ed.) *Between Friends. The Correspondence of Hannah Arendt and Mary McCarthy 1949–1975* (London: Secker and Warburg).

J. MacGregor Burns (1978) *Leadership* (New York: Harper and Row).

M. Calás, H. Ou and L. Smircich (2013) 'Woman on the Move: Mobile Subjectivities after Intersectionality', *Equality, Inclusion and Diversity: An International Journal*, 32, 8, 708–731.

Catalyst (2012) *Report on Women Leaders in Fortune 500 Corporations, and 2013 Report on Canadian Women Leaders*, http://www.catalyst.org/knowledge, accessed July 5, 2013.

A. Chan (2005) 'Authentic Leadership Measurement: Challenges and Suggestions', in W. L. Gardner, B. J. Avolio and F. O. Walumbwa (eds) *Authentic Leadership Theory and Practice: Origins, Effects and Developments* (Amsterdam: Elsevier), pp. 227–251.

J. B. Ciulla (2000) *The Working Life: The Promise and Betrayal of Modern Work* (New York and Toronto: Random House).

_____. (2008) 'Leadership Studies and the Fusion of Horizons', *The Leadership Quarterly*, 19, 393–395.

M. Cohen (2006) '"A Little Learning?" The Curriculum and the Construction of Gender Difference in the Long Eighteenth Century', *British Journal for Eighteenth-Century Studies*, 29, 321–335.

_____. (2007) 'To Think, to Compare, to Combine, to Methodize: Girls' Education in Enlightenment Britain', in S. Knott and B. Taylor (eds) *Women, Gender and the Enlightenment* (London: Palgrave Macmillan), pp. 224–241.

M. Coleman (2010) *Women at the Top: Challenges, Choices and Change* (London: Palgrave Macmillan).

L. Colley (2005) *Britons: Forging the Nation, 1707–1837* (Reading: Yale University Press).

R. W. Connell and J. W. Messerschmidt (2005) 'Hegemonic Masculinity: Rethinking the Concept', *Gender & Society*, 19, 6, 829–859.

C. D. Cooper, T. A. Scandura and C. A. Schriesheim (2005) 'Looking Forward but Learning from Our Past: Potential Challenges to Developing Authentic Leadership Theory and Authentic Leaders', *The Leadership Quarterly*, 16, 3, 475–493.

J. Crary (2013) *24/7: Late Capitalism and the Ends of Sleep* (London and New York: Verso).

K. Crenshaw (1991) 'Mapping the Margins: Intersectionality, Identity Politics and Violence against Women of Color', *Stanford Law Review*, 43, 6, 241–299.

O. de Gouges (1791) 'Declaration of the Rights of Woman and Woman as Citizen', Paris, https://www.scribd.com/doc/73806528/Olympe-de-Gouges-1791

D. R. Dean, S. J. Bracken and J. K. Allen (eds) (2010) *Women in Academic Leadership: Professional Strategies, Personal Choices* (Sterling, VA: Stylus Publishing).

D. Diderot (1966) *Rameau's Nephew/D'Alembert Dream*, L. Tancock (trans. and intro.) (London: Penguin).

L. J. Disch (1994a) 'Claire Loves Julie: Reading the Story of Women's Friendship in La Nouvelle Héloïse', *Hypatia*, 3, 19–45.

_____. (1994b) *Hannah Arendt and the Limits of Philosophy* (Ithaca and London: Cornell University Press).

Y. Due Billing and M. Alvesson (2000) 'Questioning the Notion of Feminine Leadership: A Critical Perspective on the Gender Labelling of Leadership', *Gender, Work and Organization*, 7, 3, 144–157.

A. H. Eagly (2005) 'Achieving Relational Authenticity in Leadership: Does Gender Matter?', *The Leadership Quarterly*, 16, 3, 459–474.

A. H. Eagly and L. Carli (2007) *Through the Labyrinth: The Truth about how Women become Leaders* (Boston: Harvard Business School Press).

A. H. Eagly and S. J. Karau (2002) 'Role Congruity Theory of Prejudice toward Female Leaders', *Psychological Review*, 109, 3, 573–598.

P. Eddy (2010) 'Leading Gracefully: Gendered Leadership at Community Colleges', in D. R. Dean, S. J. Bracken and J. K. Allen (eds) *Women in Academic Leadership: Professional Strategies, Personal Choices* (Sterling, VA: Stylus Publishing).

K. M. Elsesser and J. Lever (2011) 'Does Gender Bias against Female Leaders Persist? Quantitative and Qualitative Data from a Large-Scale Survey', *Human Relations*, 64, 12, 1555–1578.

N. Endrissat, W. R. Müller and S. Kaudela-Baum (2007) 'En Route to an Empirically-Based Understanding of Authentic Leadership', *European Management Journal*, 25, 3, 207–220.

P. England (2010) 'The Gender Revolution: Uneven and Stalled', *Gender and Society*, 24, 2, 149–166.

A. Ferrara (1998) *Reflective Authenticity: Rethinking the Project of Modernity* (London and New York: Routledge).

H. A. Fielding (2011) 'Multiple Moving Perceptions of the Real: Arendt, Merleau-Ponty and Truitt', *Hypatia*, 26, 3, 518–534.

L. Fisher (2009) 'Debating Phenomenological Research Methods', *Phenomenology and Practice*, 3, 1, 6–25.

_____. (2010) 'Feminist Phenomenological Voices', *Continental Philosophy Review*, 43, 83–95.

P. Fleming (2007) *Authenticity and the Cultural Politics of Work: New Forms of Informal Control* (Oxford: Oxford University Press).

J. Ford (2006) 'Discourses of Leadership: Gender Identity and Contradiction in a UK Public Service Industry', *Leadership*, 2, 1, 77–99.

J. Ford and N. Harding (2011) 'The Impossibility of the "True Self" of Authentic Leadership: A Critique through Objects Relations Theory', *Leadership*, 7, 4, 463–479.

M. Foucault (1995) *Discipline & Punish: The Birth of the* Prison, A. Sheridan (trans.) (New York: Vintage Books).

R. Gardiner (2013) 'Cameo: A Powerful Antidote: Hannah Arendt's Concept of Uniqueness and the Discourse of Authentic Leadership', in D. Ladkin and C. Spiller (eds) *Authentic Leadership: Clashes, Convergences and Coalescences* (Cheltenham: Edward Elgar), pp. 65–69.

W. L. Gardner and B. J. Avolio (2005) 'Authentic Leadership Development: Getting to the Root of Positive Forms of Leadership', *The Leadership Quarterly*, 16, 315–338.

W. L. Gardner, B. J. Avolio and F. O. Walumbwa (eds) (2005) *Authentic Leadership Theory and Practice: Origins, Effects and Developments* (Amsterdam: Elsevier).

W. L. Gardner, C. C. Cogliser, K. M. Davis and M. P. Dickens (2011) 'Authentic Leadership: A Review of the Literature and Research Agenda', *The Leadership Quarterly*, 22, 6, 1120–1145.

B. George (2003) *Authentic Leadership: Rediscovering the Secrets to Creating Lasting Value* (Cambridge: Harvard University Press).

B. George, D. Gergen and P. Sims (2007) *True North: Discover Your Authentic Leadership* (San Francisco: Jossey Bass).

A. Giorgio (2009) *The Descriptive Phenomenological Method in Psychology: A Modified Husserlian Approach* (Pittsburgh: Duquesne University Press).

D. Goodman (1994) *The Republic of Letters: A Cultural History of the French Enlightenment* (New York: Cornell University Press).

_____. (2007) 'L'Ortografe des Dames: Gender and Language in the Old Regime', in S. Knott and B. Taylor (eds) *Women, Gender and the Enlightenment* (London: Palgrave Macmillan), pp. 195–223.

J. Gosling and P. Villiers (eds) (2013) *Fictional Leaders: Heroes, Villains and Absent Friends* (London: Palgrave Macmillan).

R. K. Greenleaf (2002[1977]) *Servant Leadership: A Journey into the Nature of Legitimate Power and Greatness*, 25th Anniversary edn, L. Spears (ed.) (New York: Paulist Press).

K. Grint (2005) *Leadership: Limits and Possibilities* (New York: Palgrave Macmillan).

C. B. Guignon (2004) *On Being Authentic* (*Thinking in Action*) (New York and London: Routledge).

J. Habermas (1994) *The Structural Transformation of the Public Sphere: An Inquiry into a Category of Bourgeois Society*, Thomas Burger (trans.) (Cambridge: MIT Press).

S. Harding (1987) 'Introduction: Is There A Feminist Method', in S. Harding (ed.) *Feminism and Methodology* (Bloomington: Indiana University Press), pp. 1–14.

M. Heidegger (1962) *Being and Time*, J. Robinson and E. Macquarrie (trans.) (Oxford: Blackwell).

_____. (1977) 'Letter on Humanism', in D. Farell Krell (ed. and trans.) *Martin Heidegger: Basic Writings* (San Francisco: HarperSanFrancisco).

_____. (March 1985) 'The Self-Assertion of the German University and the Rectorate 1933–34: Facts and Thoughts', *Review of Metaphysics*, 38, 3, 467–502.

_____. (1994) 'What is Metaphysics?' in W. McNeil (ed.) *Pathmarks* (Cambridge: Cambridge University Press), pp. 82–97.

D. Heil (Spring 2010) 'Understanding and Leading Organizations: A Hermeneutic Phenomenological Investigation', *Philosophy Today*, 7–17.

D. Hertz (1988) *Jewish High Society in Old Regime Berlin* (West Hanover: Yale University Press).

M. Hill (1979) (ed.) *The Recovery of the Public World* (New York: St. Martin's Press), p. 314.

P. Hill Collins (1994) 'Shifting the Center: Race, Class, and Feminist Theorizing about Motherhood', in E. Nakano Glenn, G. Chang and L. Rennie Forcey (eds) *Mothering: Ideology, Experience and Agency* (London: Routledge), pp. 45–67.

J. Hodge (1995) *Heidegger and Ethics* (London and New York: Routledge).

O. Hufton (1995) *The Prospect before Her: A History of Women in Western Europe, Volume I, 1500–1800* (London: HarperCollins Publishers).

H. Ibarra, R. Ely and D. Kolb (Sept. 2013) 'Women Rising: The Unseen Barriers', *Harvard Business Review*, 61–66.

H. Ibarra and O. Obodaru (Jan 2009) 'Women and the Vision Thing', *Harvard Business Review*, 1–9.

B. J. Irby, G. Brown, J. A. Duffy and D. Trautman (2002) 'The Synergistic Leadership Theory', *Journal of Educational Administration*, 40, 4, 304–322.

I. Kant (1995) 'An Answer to the Question "What is Enlightenment?"', in J. Schmitt (ed.) *What is Enlightenment? Eighteenth-Century Answers and Twentieth-Century Questions* (Berkeley and Los Angeles: University of California Press), pp. 58–65.

K. Kay and C. Shipman (2014) *The Confidence Code: The Science and Art of Self-Assurance – What Women Should Know* (New York: HarperCollins).

B. Kellerman and D. L. Rhode (eds) (2007) *Women and Leadership: The State of Play and Strategies for Change* (San Francisco: John Wiley and Sons).

A. Kezar and J. Lester (2010) 'Breaking the Barriers of Essentialism: Positionality as a Promising Approach', *Feminist Formations*, 22, 1, 163–185.

A. Kinsella (May 2006) 'Hermeneutics and Critical Hermeneutics: Exploring Possibilities within the Art of Interpretation', *Forum: Qualitative Social Research*, 7, 3, 1–13.

K. Klenke (2007) 'Authentic Leadership: A Self, Leader, and Spiritual Identity Perspective', *International Journal of Leadership Studies*, 3, 1, 68–97.

J. M. Kouzes and B. K. Pozner (2007) *The Leadership Challenge: How to Make Extraordinary Things Happen*, 4th edn (San Francisco: John Wiley and Sons).

J. Kristeva (2001) *Hannah Arendt: Life is a Narrative*, F. Collins (trans.) (Toronto: University of Toronto Press).

D. Ladkin (2006) 'When Deontology and Utilitarianism Aren't Enough: How Heidegger's Notion of "Dwelling" Might Help Organizational Leaders resolve Ethical Issues', *Journal of Business Ethics*, 65, 87–98.

_____. (2010) *Rethinking Leadership: A New Look at Old Leadership Questions* (Cheltenham: Edward Elgar).

D. Ladkin and C. Spiller (eds) (2013) *Authentic Leadership: Clashes, Convergences and Coalescences* (Cheltenham: Edward Elgar).

D. Ladkin and S. Taylor (2010) 'Enacting the "True Self": Towards a Theory of Embodied Authentic Leadership', *The Leadership Quarterly*, 21, 1, 64–74.

L. Levy and M. Bentley (2007) *More 'Right' than 'Real': The Shape of Authentic Leadership in New Zealand* (Auckland: The University of Auckland).

C. Lindholm (2008) *Culture and Authenticity* (Oxford: Blackwell).

M. Lugones and E. Spelman (1983) 'Have We Got a Theory for You! Feminist Theory, Cultural Imperialism and the Demand for the Woman's Voice', *Women's Studies International Forum*, 6, 6, 573–581.

S. R. Madsen (2006) 'Developing Leadership: Exploring Childhoods of Women University Presidents', *Journal of Educational Administration*, 45, 1, 90–118.

A. Marturano (2008) 'Understanding Leadership: Is it Time for a Linguistic Turn?, in J. B. Ciulla (ed.) *Leadership at the Crossroads, Vol. 3, Leadership and the Humanities* (Westport, NJ: Praeger), pp. 117–131.

P. McDonald (2009) 'Neurological Correlates to Authentic Leadership, Victoria Management School Working Paper Series', 1–23.

Montesquieu (1973) *Persian Letters*, C.J. Betts (trans., intro. and notes) (London: Penguin Books).

_____. (2008) *Persian Letters*, M. Mauldon (trans. with editorial remarks by A. Kahn) (Oxford: Oxford University Press).

L. Morley (2013) 'The Rules of the Game: Women and the Leaderist Turn in Higher Education', *Gender and Education*, 25, 1, 116–131.

H. Nicholson and B. Carroll (2013) 'Essay: So You Want to be Authentic in Your Leadership: To whom and for What End?', in D. Ladkin and C. Spiller (eds) *Authentic Leadership: Clashes, Convergences and Coalescences* (Cheltenham: Edward Elgar), pp. 286–302

P. Northouse (2013) 'Authentic Leadership', *Leadership: Theory and Practice*, 6th edn (Thousand Oaks and London: Sage Publications), pp. 253–286.

M. M. Novicevic, M. G. Harvey, M. R. Buckley, J. A. Brown and R. Evans (2006) 'Authentic Leadership: A Historical Perspective', *Journal of Leadership and Organizational Studies*, 13, 1, 64–76.

T. L. Price (2003) 'The Ethics of Authentic Transformational Leadership', *Leadership Quarterly*, 14, 67–81.

C. Roulston (1998) *Virtue, Gender, and the Authentic Self in Eighteenth-Century Fiction: Richardson, Rousseau, and Laclos* (Gainesville: University Press of Florida).

K. Roulston (2010) *Reflective Interviewing: A Guide to Theory and Practice* (London: Sage).

J. J. Rousseau (1953) *The Confessions*, J. M. Cohen (trans.) (London: Penguin Books).

_____. (1960) *Politics and the Arts: A Letter to M. D'Alembert* (intro., trans. and note A. Bloom) (Ithaca: The Free Press).

_____. (1968) *The Social Contract* (trans. and intro. M. Cranston) (Aylesbury: Penguin Books).

_____. (1979) *Emile or On Education* (intro., trans. and note A. Bloom) (New York: Basic Books).

_____. (1997[1760]) *Julie, or the New Héloïse. Letters of Two Lovers Who Live in a Small Town at the Foot of the Alps* (trans. and annotated P. Stewart and J. Vache) (Hanover and London: University Press of New England).

S. Sandberg with Nell Scovell (2013) *Lean in: Women, Work, and the Will to Lead* (New York: Alfred A. Knopf).

C. E. Scott (2011) 'Care and Authenticity', in B. W. Davis (ed.) *Martin Heidegger: Key Concepts* (Durham: Acumen Press), pp. 57–69.

J. W. Scott (Dec. 1986) 'Gender: A Useful Category of Historical Analysis', *The American Historical Review*, 91, 5, 1053–1075.

_____. (1996) *Only Paradoxes to Offer: French Feminists and the Rights of Man* (Cambridge: Harvard University Press).

_____. (1999) *Gender and the Politics of History* (New York & Chichester, W. Sussex: Columbia University Press).

R. Sennett (1974) *The Fall of Public Man* (New York: Alfred A. Knopf).

B. Shamir and G. Eilam (2005) 'What's Your Story? A Life-Stories Approach to Authentic Leadership Development', *The Leadership Quarterly*, 16, 3, 395–417.

J. Shaw (2010) 'Papering the Cracks with Discourse: The Narrative Identity of the Authentic Leader', *Leadership*, 6, 1, 89–108.

A. Sinclair (2007) *Leadership for the Disillusioned: Moving beyond Myths and Heroes to Leading that Liberate* (Crow's Nest NSW: Allen and Unwin).

_____. (2013) 'Essay: Can I Really Be Me: The Challenges for Women Leaders Constructing Authenticity', in D. Ladkin and C. Spiller (eds) *Authentic Leadership: Clashes, Convergences and Coalescences* (Cheltenham: Edward Elgar).

D. E. Smith (1987) *The Everyday World as Problematic* (Toronto: University of Toronto Press).

_____. (1990) *The Conceptual Practices of Power: A Feminist Sociology of Knowledge* (Toronto: University of Toronto Press).

O. Smolović Jones and K. Grint (2013) 'Essay: Authentic Leadership and History', in D. Ladkin and C. Spiller (eds) *Authentic Leadership: Clashes, Convergences and Coalescences* (Cheltenham: Edward Elgar), pp. 21–39.

R. T. Sparrowe (2005) 'Authentic Leadership and the Narrative Self', *The Leadership Quarterly*, 16, 3, 419–439.

C. Taylor (1989) *Sources of the Self: The Making of the Modern Identity* (Cambridge: Harvard University Press).

_____. (1991) *The Ethics of Authenticity* (Cambridge: Harvard University Press).

_____. (2005) 'Authenticity', in H. L. Dreyfus and M. A. Wrathall (eds) *A Companion to Heidegger* (Oxford: Blackwell Publishing), pp. 285–296.

R. W. Terry (1993) *Authentic Leadership: Courage in Action* (New York: John Wiley and Sons).

The United Nations Global Gender Gap Report (2013).

S. P. Thomas and H. R. Pollio (2002) *Listening to Patients: A Phenomenological Approach to Nursing Research and Practice* (New York: Springer Publishing Co.).

L. Todres (2007) *Embodied Enquiry: Phenomenological Touchstones for Research, Psychotherapy and Spirituality* (London: Palgrave Macmillan).

L. Trilling (1972) *Sincerity and Authenticity* (Cambridge: Harvard University Press).

U N Women (2014) http://www.unwomen.org, accessed August 11, 2014.

US States Bureau of Labor Statistics (2013), http://www.bls.gov, accessed June 3, 2014.

M. Van Manen (1997) *Researching Lived Experiences: Human Science for an Action Sensitive Pedagogy* (London: The Althouse Press).

V. Vasterling (2007) 'Cognitive Theory and Phenomenology in Arendt's and Nussbaum's Work on Narrative', *Human Studies*, 30, 79–95.

H. Walpole (1795) *Letters of Horace Walpole*, http://www.gutenberg.org, accessed August 29, 2014.

S. Wilson (2013) 'Viewpoint: The Authentic Leader Reconsidered: Integrating the Marvellous, Mundane and Mendacious', in D. Ladkin and C. Spiller (eds)

Authentic Leadership: Clashes, Convergences and Coalescences (Cheltenham: Edward Elgar).

A. Wolf (2014) *The XX Factor: How Working Women are Creating a New Society* (London: Profile Books).

J. Wolfe (June 2014) 'Caught in the Trap of His Own Metaphysics', http://standpointmag.co.uk/node/5583, accessed August 15, 2014.

M. Wollstonecraft (1985) *Vindication of the Rights of Woman* (ed. and intro. M. Brody Kramnick) (London: Penguin Books).

F. J. Yammarino, S. D. Dionne, C. A. Schriesheim and F. Dansereau (2008) 'Authentic Leadership and Positive Organizational Behavior: A Meso, Multi-Level Perspective', *The Leadership Quarterly*, 19, 693–207.

I. M. Young (1990) *Throwing Like a Girl and Other Essays in Feminist Philosophy and Social Theory* (Indiana: Indiana University Press).

Index

CPI Antony Rowe
Eastbourne, UK
March 12, 2020